I0063647

LAW AND DIGITAL TECHNOLOGIES: THE WAY FORWARD ▶▶▶▶▶

Authors:

Elizaveta A. Gromova, Daniel Brantes Ferreira, Anna Carolina Pinho, Berg de Holanda Melo, Chaitra V., Cristiana Maia, David Gabriel Dutra Martins, Popova Elizaveta Igorevna, Golda Sahoo, Gorremutchu Mahith Vidyasagar, Luane Silva Nascimento, Nabanita Sen, Natalia Savenko, Rosa Maria Torraco, Rusman Galina Sergeevna, Sunitha Abhay Jain, Vladislav Dmitrievich Tuktamyshev, Ritu Paul, Seema Yadav

AMBRA
UNIVERSITY
press

Copyright 2023 © by
Ambra University Press, Daniel Brantes Ferreira, Elizaveta A. Gromova
All rights reserved.

Publisher: Ambra University Press
First edition: AUGUST 2023 (Revision 1.0a)

Author: Elizaveta A. Gromova, Daniel Brantes Ferreira; Berg de Holanda Melo; Cristiana C. M. Maia, Rosa Maria Torraco; Ritu Paul, Seema Yadav; Golda Sahoo; Vladislav D. Tuktamyshev; Gorremutchu Mahith Vidyasagar; Nabanita Sen; Galina Rusman, Popova Elizaveta Igorevna; David Gabriel Dutra Martins, Luane Silva Nascimento, Anna Carolina Pinho; Sunitha Abhay Jain, Chaitra. V.; Natalia Savenko;
Title: Law and Digital Technologies: The Way Forward
Cover design: Ambra University Press
Book design: Ambra University Press
Proofreading: Ambra University Press

E-book format: EPUB
Print format: Print format: Paperback- 6 x 9 inch

ISBN: 978-1-952514-48-7 (Print - Paperback)
ISBN: 978-1-952514-47-0 (e-book – EPUB)
Library of Congress Control Number: 2023942649

Ambra is a trademark of Ambra Education, Inc. registered in the U.S. Patent and Trademark Office.
Ambra University Press is a division of Ambra Education, Inc.
Orlando, FL, USA
https://press.ambra.education/ • https://www.ambra.education/

Copyright 2023 © por
Ambra University Press, Daniel Brantes Ferreira, Elizaveta A. Gromova
Todos os direitos reservados.

Editora: Ambra University Press
Primeira edição: agosto 2023 (Revisão 1.01)

Autores: Elizaveta A. Gromova, Daniel Brantes Ferreira; Berg de Holanda Melo; Cristiana C. M. Maia, Rosa Maria Torraco; Ritu Paul, Seema Yadav; Golda Sahoo; Vladislav D. Tuktamyshev; Gorremutchu Mahith Vidyasagar; Nabanita Sen; Galina Rusman, Popova Elizaveta Igorevna; David Gabriel Dutra Martins, Luane Silva Nascimento, Anna Carolina Pinho; Sunitha Abhay Jain, Chaitra. V.; Natalia Savenko;
Título: Law and Digital Technologies: The Way Forward
Design da capa: Ambra University Press
Projeto gráfico: Ambra University Press
Revisão: Ambra University Press

Formato e-book: EPUB
Formato impresso: Capa mole - 6 x 9 polegadas

ISBN: 978-1-952514-48-7 (Impresso – capa mole)
ISBN: 978-1-952514-47-0 (e-book – EPUB)
Library of Congress Control Number: 2023942649

Ambra é uma marca da Ambra Education, Inc. registrada no U.S. Patent and Trademark Office.
Ambra University Press é uma divisão da Ambra Education, Inc.
Orlando, FL, EUA
https://press.ambra.education/ • https://www.ambra.education/

INDEX

AUTHORS

ELIZAVETA A. GROMOVA

Lawyer in Russia and researcher; more than 15 years of legal and educational experience; coordinator of the master's degree program "Law and Digital Technologies" offered in English at the Institute of Law at the South Ural State University (SUSU) in Russia; Deputy Director for International Cooperation of the Institute of Law, South Ural State University; Ph.D. from the Ural State Law University, Diploma in Jurisprudence by SUSU.

DANIEL BRANTES FERREIRA

CEO do Centro Brasileiro de Mediação e Arbitragem (CBMA); mais de 15 anos de experiência em advocacia, ensino jurídico e arbitragem; Fellow no Chartered Institute of Arbitrators (CIArb); Editor chefe da Revista Brasileira de Alternative Dispute Resolution; Pesquisador visitante na Law School da State University of New York at Buffalo; Pós-doutorado em direito pela Universidade do Estado do Rio de Janeiro (UERJ), doutorado em direito pela PUC-Rio, mestrado em direito pela PUC-Rio, bacharelado em direito pela PUC-Rio.

ANNA CAROLINA PINHO

Doutoranda em Direito Internacional Econômico e Estudos Europeus e Mestre em Direito Internacional pela Faculdade de Direito da Universidade de Lisboa, Portugal. Pós Graduada em Direito Administrativo e Tributário pela Faculdade de Direito da Universidade Federal Fluminense. Bacharel pela Faculdade de Direito da Universidade Candido Mendes, Rio de Janeiro, Brasil. Advogada no Brasil e em Portugal. http://lattes.cnpq.br/9033123127251504. Email: annapinholaw@gmail.com

BERG DE HOLANDA MELO

Lawyer. Business law specialist candidate (Fundação Getúlio Vargas). Bachelor of Law (Federal University of Pernambuco).

CHAITRA V.

Phd in law, LLM in Business Law, Assistant Professor at School Law, Christ (Deemed to be University) Bengaluru, India 560029. Area of Interest/expertise- Law of Torts, Law of Insurance, Interpretation of Statutes, Legal Language and Legal Writing.

CRISTIANA MAIA

Privacy and Compliance Specialist; Privacy Manager at Stone/Linx; Master in Law - Candido Mendes University; IT Forensic Expert Ibituruna University; Public Law Expert - EMERJ; Regulation Law Expert

- FGV/RJ; Member of the Legal Research Group ADR and Technology of the University Candido Mendes and CDTII - Brazilian Bar Association's Committee on Information Law and Technology and Innovation ; Brazilian Lawyers Institute's Digital Law Committee and the Governance and Compliance Committee ; National Association of Personal Data Protection Professionals – ANPPD.. E-mail: cristianamaia@gmail.com

DAVID GABRIEL DUTRA MARTINS

Advogado formado pela Faculdade Evangélica Raízes. Capacitado em Direito Empresarial: Empresário e Sociedade Empresária pela Faculdade.

POPOVA ELIZAVETA IGOREVNA

In 2021 she graduated from the Law Institute of the South Ural State University in the specialty "Forensic examination". Today she is PhD student of the department of Criminal Procedures, Criminal Science and Forensic Enquiry, South Ural State University, Chelyabinsk, Russian Federation. In addition, she works as a laboratory assistant in my department's forensic laboratory.

GOLDA SAHOO

Ms.Golda Sahoo,working as an Assistant Professor of Law(Senior Scale),Tamil Nadu National Law University Trichy.since 7 years.In her more than a decade teaching experience, she served many reputed Law Schools such as, Christ University Bangalore and KIIT University Bhubaneswar. Her interest area is Criminal Law. She has tought various subjects in that area such as,Criminal Procedure Code,IPC,Criminology Penology Victimology,Socio-Economic Offences. She has published number of research papers including UGC CARE listed Journals, contributed book chapters (international & national publishers) and presented papers in various national and international conferences. She is Coordinator for Centre of Study on Victimology and started a Minor Project on "Victim Compensation Schemes For Women Victims Of Sexual Abuse Under District Legal Service Authority, Tiruchirapalli ,TNNLU,Trichy".Apart from her teaching and research activities, she is in charge of various administrative responsibilities of the University such as Dean of UG Academics, Covenor of Mentorship Committee, Chairperson of ICC.

GORREMUTCHU MAHITH VIDYASAGAR

Ph.D. Research Scholar in Damodaram Sanjivayya National Law University, working on Investor-State Dispute Settlement (ISDS). Studied Master of Laws (LL.M.) in Commercial Laws from Damodaram Sanjivayya National Law University, Visakhapatnam and graduated from Smt. V. D. Siddhartha Law College, Vijayawada. Qualified UGC-NET in 2020 and Junior Research Fellowship Awardee (JRF) under NFSC scheme. Published articles in referred law journals on various topics relating to arbitration, insolvency laws, data localization, ISDS. Areas of research interest international law, investor-state arbitration, alternative dispute resolution and insolvency laws.

LUANE SILVA NASCIMENTO

Attorney and professor, has mastering course at Constitucional Law from College of Law in Coimbra's University. Has management executive program course from College of Business in Ohio University and experience in Law, acting on the following subjects: business law, civil law, digital law and public law. Researcher and speaker.

NABANITA SEN

Ms. Nabanita Sen, is presently pursuing her doctorate programme in law from Bankura University, a public state University, West Bengal, India. With schooling from St. Agnes Convent, Kharagpur, West Bengal she was awarded University Gold Medal for being University topper in BA.LLB (Hons.) as well as in MBA (Human Resource) from Vidyasagar University, public state University, West Bengal, India. She is a master degree holder (LLM) in Human Rights with interest in Women Studies, Gender Justice, Child Rights, Intellectual Property Rights (IPR) and Cyber Law. She pursued Cyber Law course from Indian Law Institute (ILI), Delhi. Prior to the doctorate studies, she was a full-time Lecturer at Pailan College of Management and Technology, Kolkata. She was associated faculty at Sikkim Manipal University and Punjab Technical University in her initial professional career. She holds academic experience as well corporate exposure. She published research articles in reputed national and international journals published by esteemed publishers including Wiley-Blackwell, Sage Publications. She holds credit of publications in Scopus and Web of Science Indexed Journals. She has presented papers at various National and International seminars, workshop and conferences organized by institutions of repute.

NATALIA SAVENKO

Savenko (Amelina) Natalia Evgenievna was born in 1981 in Chelyabinsk, Russian Federation. She graduated from the higher education at the South Ural State University in 2004 with a degree in Law, defended her

PhD thesis in 2007. Currently, he is an associate Professor of the Department of Civil Law and Civil Procedure at the Law Institute of the South Ural State University (National Research University), Chelyabinsk, Russia. Subjects taught: civil law, state regulation in the field of consumer protection, Contracts in the field of professional and entrepreneurial activity. Research interests: digitalization in civil circulation, smart contracts, entrepreneurial and economic activities of citizens and other legal entities.

ROSA MARIA TORRACO

Rosa Maria is currently attending a Single Cycle Master's Degree in Law at the University of Bologna (Italy), and she spent an Erasmus+ study semester at Leiden University (Netherlands). She is also a Managing Editor at the University of Bologna Law Review and an International Editor at the Cambridge Law Review. Previously, she worked as a legal intern at the leading Italian law firm Portolano Cavallo.

RUSMAN GALINA SERGEEVNA

Candidate of Law, Associate Professor, Head of the Department of Criminal Procedure, Criminalistics and Forensic Examination of the Law Institute of South Ural State University (National Research University), Chelyabinsk, Russia. ORCID: 0000-0001-7776-2538

SUNITHA ABHAY JAIN

Professor, School of Law, CHRIST (Deemed to be University), Bengaluru, holds a Doctoral Degree in Law from NLSIU, Bengaluru. She is the coordinator for the

LLM Program at Christ (Deemed to be University), Bengaluru. She holds an LL.B. and LL.M degree from Bangalore University and has specialized in Corporate and Commercial Laws and had secured Second Rank in the University for her BA LLB (Hons.) program. She also completed her Master of Human Rights from Pondicherry University and a Post Graduate Diploma in Cyber Laws from NALSAR, Hyderabad and has also completed the UGC NET examination. She has been a full time faculty in law and has a teaching experience of over two decades. She has been a part of the Experts Consultation Workshop on Karnataka Municipalities Bill, 2019 organised by NLSIU in association with Directorate of Municipal Administration, Government of Karnataka. Has taught many courses ranging from International Trade Law, Centre-State Relations & Constitutional Governance, Media law, Administrative law, Law of Contracts, Human rights, Property law amongst others. She has numerous publications to her credit in the form of chapters and research articles in reputed Journals and books. She has been invited as a resource person for various Faculty Development programs at the National level.

VLADISLAV DMITRIEVICH TUKTAMYSHEV

In 2018 graduated from the Institute of Procuracy of the Ural State Law University. In 2020 obtained LLM on Civil Procedure in the Ural State Law University. Since 2021 I've been working as an assistant of the Civil Procedure Department in the Ural State Law University named after V.F. Yakovlev and as a Head of the Legal Clinic of the Ural State Law University named after V.F. Yakovlev.

RITU PAUL

Assistant Professor, IPEM Law Academy, Ghaziabad
Uttar Pradesh, India

SEEMA YADAV

Professor, School of Law Galgotias University

PREFACE

The rapid development of digitalization has led to the spread of digital technologies. Artificial intelligence, cryptocurrencies, smart contracts, distributed ledger technologies, self-driving cars, virtual and augmented reality, and others are not the future anymore. They became our reality. They conquered almost all spheres of our everyday life. Moreover, modern states primarily focus on developing competitive technologies. Meanwhile its creation, application and turnover require suitable regulation for them.

This, in its turn, represents a massive challenge to the law and lawmakers. Innovative essence of the digital technologies doesn't allow defining proper regulation at once. Different legal barriers, such as "lag" of law from rapidly developing relations or absence of the regulation for emerging technologies are the obstacles that not only hinder development of technologies but also can lead to violations of the human rights. Moreover, the regulation, being designed today, will influence our future and further progress of digital technologies.

Therefore, it is crucial to discuss state-of-the-art issues and define future steps in regulation of the digital technologies across the world. It requires cross-cultural international cooperation between scholars. To make our contribution we created The Research Group "Law, Digital Technologies & ADR" to establish an international virtual hub for the research and cross-cultural collaboration in the sphere of Law and Digital Technologies from the international and comparative perspective.

The Group unites experienced and young researchers from 7 countries (Brazil, USA, Russia, Italy, India, Portugal, and Uganda), 15 universities (South Ural State University, Universidade Candido Mendes, AMBRA University, University of Bologna, Caruso School of Law (Pepperdine University), Amity Law School, Universidade Portucalense Infante D. Henrique, Goenka

University and others). It was registered in CNPq Brazil and co-hosted by Ambra University (USA), Universidade Candido Mendes (Brazil) and South Ural State University (Russia).

To give to Research Group members the opportunity to share their ideas we held the International conference "Law and Digital Technologies: The Way Forward" with the support of AMBRA University, Candido Mendes University and National Research South Ural State University to create a discussion between the experts across the world on the topics related to law and governance in the sphere of the creation, implementation, and usage of digital technologies. It was a unique opportunity for students, researchers, and professors to discuss law and digital technologies from a comparative perspective and do international networking.

Participants from USA, Brazil, Russia, India, Italy, Romania, and Poland discussed different issues in the sphere of national and international regulation of the digital technologies.

The Book "Law and Digital Technologies: the Way Forward" contains the chosen papers of the participants of the Conference. The book is truly international because it unites authors from different countries such as Poland, Brazil, Italy, India, Russia, and Romania. Moreover, collection of the articles represents cutting-edge research in the sphere of international and national regulation of digital technologies from international and comparative perspective.

The Book consists of 5 chapters. For readers' convenience we subdivided papers due to crucial issues in the sphere of law and digital technologies it cover. First chapter "Searching for Proper Regulation of Digital Technologies: Difficulties and Solutions" devoted to the general aspects of the regulations of different digital technologies. Second Chapter "Digital Technologies and the Future of Dispute Resolution" aimed at showing modern trends and prospects of using digital technologies in civil and criminal proceedings. Chapter 3 "Digital Technologies and Data: Regulatory Issues" covers highly-relevant issues in the sphere of intellectual property and data protection. Chapter 4

"Digital Technologies and Cyber Crimes". And, last but not least, chapter 5 "Using Digital Technologies In Different Spheres: Challenges and Perspectives" show perspectives and issues of applications of the digital technologies in such areas as financial transactions and unmanned vehicles.

We cordially thank all Research Group members for the inspiration and authors, who gave us the honor to publish their articles in this Book. We also are sincerely grateful to Francisco Netto and Alfredo Freitas from AMBRA University, Elena V. Titova, Director of the Institute of Law at South Ural State University, Andreya Navarro, rector of the Candido Mendes University for their constant support and their faith in us and our project.

Elizaveta A. Gromova and Daniel Brantes Ferreira

DIGITAL STATE SURVEILLANCE AND THE NEED FOR PROPER REGULATION: AN ANALYSIS THROUGH HUMAN RIGHTS FROM THE BRAZILIAN PERSPECTIVE

Author:

Berg de Holanda Melo

The proper regulation and limitation of state digital surveillance are one of the biggest challenges humanity is facing in the 21st century. The digital revolution brought great changes to life in society, such as the need for dealing with a data-driven economy and the internet as one of the main tools of political manifestation and human coexistence. However, these innovations did not take place only among civil society. States have modernized themselves, embraced technologies, and seen the potential of using digital surveillance techniques and accessing the population's data to prevent crime, conduct investigations, and maintain control over what and who may confront them. Taking into consideration the role the internet nowadays has on people's lives, including social interactions and ideas expression, and the aptitude of the combination of Big Data and Artificial Intelligence providing deep and broad information about almost every single aspect of a person, the risk of significant damages to human rights and Democracy rises. In light of that issue, this article seeks to analyze, through literature and review of the Brazilian Federal Constitution and statutes in effects as of November 2021, whether really there are risks towards state digital surveillance that justify the mentioned concerns, and based on the Brazilian legal system, to identify the normative constraints already in force and whether they are strong enough. Moreover, this article argues, based on the human rights doctrine and recognition of data protection as a fundamental right, a new and comprehensive regulatory framework is needed, mainly in view of the perception that unfettered digital state surveillance could result in inhibiting people's self-determination and self-development rights and eroding grounds of democracy regime. Finally, by investigating what the literature advocates worldwide and with a deeper look at the Human Rights Council of the United Nations reports and suggestions, this article proposes some standards that should be theoretical guidelines for   digital state surveillance regulation, which, even though they are formulated with a specific focus on Brazil, could be universalized to other countries's realities.

Keywords: digital surveillance, human rights, data protection

INTRODUCTION

There is no denying that the Internet is now one of the main means of human interaction, it has become a prominent instrument for freedom of expression, political manifestation, right of assembly, and association of people with common interests. The Internet is today an utterance of the human as a social being, who interconnects, interchanges, and lives with his peers.

Going further, the way digital technology is currently present in almost every part of people's routine makes the digital environment develop a reflexive relationship with the physical environment, there is no longer a clear division between what is done in "real life" and what is on the Internet. Everything is going to be connected in view of the imminent reality of the Internet of Things.

This digital socioeconomic structure is subsidized by massive processing of data, personal or not, that comes from the most diverse sources, many of which individuals are not aware of. Consequently, people are more exposed to misuse of their personal data and violation of fundamental rights, such as privacy. In order to combat the illegal use of data and establish a regulatory framework for the regular processing of data, especially by the private sector, legislation for the protection of personal data has been enacted worldwide, including the European General Data Protection Regulation (GDPR) and the General Data Protection Law in Brazil ("LGPD").

However, these regulations did not cover comprehensively the use of personal data by state surveillance for the purpose of crime prevention, investigation, public security, and criminal prosecution.

We believe that state digital surveillance is one of the biggest challenges the democratic regimes are ought to face. It is true that state surveillance is not a novelty and in various situations it is necessary to carry out legitimate purposes of rule of law. The issue may become problematic in our digital society due to the ubiquitous and unceasing reach of the internet and digital technology, allowing the State to have access to and control all aspects of human life, with individuals being much more vulnerable to excesses and harms to their fundamental rights, and the damage can take place on a colossal scale only after a few clicks.

Therefore, state surveillance, if it does not become subject to well-established checks and balances, may result in corrosion of fundamental rights and pillars of democracy. Even though businesses and corporate surveillance is also a matter of major importance, this article, for methodologic reasons, focuses only on surveillance from public entities because it holds a peculiar position towards the inhibition of fundamental rights: the allegation of the existence of a legitimate power of surveillance.

That said, this article aims to assess what are the risks of digital surveillance and whether, from a brazilian perspective, there are already control mechanisms in place. Secondly, what elements of human rights, with emphasis on the right to data protection, should be taken into consideration over the digital state surveillance limitation discussion, and, ultimately, if a new regulatory framework is needed to address the risks eventually identified.

More than investigating whether new legislation is necessary – in Brazil, there is a ripe discussion around the development of a criminal data protection law[1] -, this article seeks to analyze whether there are grounds for a specific framework that shall underlie state digital surveillance, and, consequently, the legislation towards it. For doing so, we will employ a theoretical approach and will have as the main resource scholars' papers, the Brazilian Constitution, statutory law, and some Brazilian and European court's rulings.

THE RISKS OF DIGITAL SURVEILLANCE AND THE CURRENT BRAZILIAN REGULATION LANDSCAPE

As a first step, it is necessary to clarify how state digital surveillance occurs and what its risks may be, as well as the rules in force in Brazil that concern such surveillance.

---

1   As per the discussion over Brazilian bill drafting for a data protection law for criminal investigation and public security: BIONI, Bruno; EILBERG, Daniela Dora; CUNHA, Brenda; SALIBA, Pedro; VERGILI, Gabriela. Proteção de dados no campo penal e de segurança pública: nota técnica sobre o Anteprojeto de Lei de Proteção de Dados para segurança pública e investigação criminal. São Paulo: Associação Data Privacy Brasil de Pesquisa,

2020.

In general, digital surveillance takes place on two levels. The first one is broader and has a generic, constant, and preventive approach to surveillance. There is no delimitation of the people SWAYED by this kind of surveillance and a massive volume of data (the "massive surveillance") is collected. We can point out as an example the installation of cameras with artificial intelligence of facial recognition and the extensive monitoring of navigation in the world web. In this first modality, an issue that arouses is that the whole society has its life monitored in an unrestricted way, which is, at the very least, worthy of a profound pondering.

The other surveillance format is the targeted surveillance, whose object is a specific person or a group, usually for investigation purposes within also a specific and determined case. In this scenario is highlighted the possibility of misuse of technologies, for example, to embarrass people who are politically opposed to governments.

It may be alleged that surveillance is only a problem for those who want to hide illicit or shameful conduct, but this is not true. Mass surveillance has repercussions not only on the maintenance of information as a secret, but it also affects individuals' predisposition to free expression, association, and engagement in political activities, in addition to weakening the civil society in the individual-state relationship because of potential secondary use of data collected by the State.[2]

But why does digital surveillance cause deeper concerns? The current state of the art of surveillance technologies allows everything to be done quietly so that those affected do not even become aware of state meddling. This prevents

---

2   SOLOVE, Daniel J. I've got nothing to hide and other misunderstandings of privacy. San Diego Law Review. 44, 2007, p. 765-767.

the state from being subject to pressure and control of society and allows it to have a carte blanche to monitor individuals.[3]

In addition, there is a symbiosis between states and the private surveillance industry, which involves large private actors who make available to states colossal databases and cutting-edge technology. The phenomenon of state digital surveillance currently combines the interests of public agents and obscure tools provided by companies.[4]

Further to that, the use of artificial intelligence substantially reduces the costs of surveillance, while considerably expanding the universe of data over which the state can have control. Therefore, without the need for human interference, it eliminates scalability restrictions, overcoming factors that were once a disincentive to the implementation of large surveillance structures.[5]

Another factor is the rapid development of technologies that enable decision-making based on predictive models of human behavior employing computer reading and data mining to understand and anticipate people's emotions[6] and an array of new sensors able to infer and dictate people's judgment and beliefs.[7]

---

3   PILLAY, Navi. The right to privacy in the digital age (A/HRC/27/37). The Office of the United Nations High Commissioner for Human Rights, 2014.

4   RICHARDS, Neil M. The dangers of surveillance. Harvard Law Review, n° 126, 2012, p. 1940-1941.

5   FELDSTEIN, Steven. The global expansion of AI surveillance. Washington, DC: Carnegie Endowment for International Peace, 2019, p. 13.

6   DWOSKIN, Elizabeth; RUSLI, Evelyn M. The technology that unmasks your hidden emotions. Wall Street Journal (January 28), v. 1, p. 2017, 2015.

7   LANGHEINRICH, Marc. Personal privacy in ubiquitous computing: Tools and system support. Doctoral Dissertation, ETH Zurich, 2005, p. 40.

Finally, as already said in advance, we are moving forward to the ubiquity of digital technology and this, added to Big Data, will provide States with means to collect, process, and aggregate data on the most diverse branches of life in society, for many purposes. Consequently, the capillarity and scope of State surveillance become extremely vast and remarkably worrying,[8] even though it is important to stress that those technologies are not necessarily bad, how they may be used, however, is where the problem lies.

The aforementioned, in brief, is enough to demonstrate the potential damages of unloosed digital state surveillance. On the other hand, is such surveillance indeed unfettered? This article aims to answer this question, at the first moment, by contemplating Brazilian law and some international treaties.

There is already a set of norms that somehow limit or govern the action of State and companies surveillance. Internationally, there are the Universal Declaration of Human Rights, the American Convention on Human Rights, and the International Covenant on Civil and Political Rights (the "ICCPR"). All these diplomas deal with the limits of state intervention in private life and human freedom and must, undoubtedly, serve as boundaries for state action, nevertheless, its lack of specificity reduces enforcement capability.

The ICCPR, especially, has some provisions which should be outlined herein. In light of this diploma, integrated into the Brazilian legal system by Decree No. 592/92, any interference with privacy and freedom of expression must cumulatively be predicated on i) legality, there must be an abstract and public provision that in advance makes the fundamental right restriction possible; ii) necessity and proportionality, supported by the exceptionality nature of rights restrictions, being the States the ones who bear the burden of demonstrating the adequacy and inevitability of the measure; iii) legitimacy, given colliding interest must have normative support, such as national security, public order, health or morality, all pursuant to the article 19 of the Covenant.

---

8   LYON, David. Surveillance, Snowden, and big data: Capacities, consequences, critique. Big data & society, v. 1, n. 2, p. 2053951714541861, 2014, p. 4.

Bringing it closer to the Brazilian context, the Constitution of the Federative Republic provided an important normative framework for the protection of individuals against unlawful surveillance through the promotion of human rights prevalence (art. 4°, II), fundamental rights such as the dignity of the human person (art. 1°, III), privacy as a fundamental right (art. 5°, X) and the inviolability of communications (art. 5°, XII), provided an important normative framework for the protection of individuals before unlawful surveillance.

Within the infra-constitutional scope, the Internet Bill of Rights (Law No. 12.963/13), which certainly constrains internet surveillance,[9] authorizes access to registration data by authorities provided there is an explicit legal basis that allows such access, per articles 10, §3 of the Bill and article 11 of the decree that regulates it (Decree No. 8.711/16). Concerning internet connection records and access to applications, the Internet Bill of Rights requires the existence of a court decision (art. 10, §2), which is a necessary measure to preserve the separation of the figures of the investigator and the judge.[10]

Law 12.963 also has an inviolability of communications rule that can be overcome only in the event of a court deciding otherwise, and goes beyond the inviolability established in the Federal Constitution since it guarantees the protection of stored communications (art. 7, II and III), which is consistent with what is proposed below.

There is also the aforementioned General Data Protection Law (Law No. 13.709/18), that, despite bringing very important limitations to uncontrolled use of data and ensuring the right to data protection, excludes from its sphere the processing of data for public security, national defense, state security and activities of investigation and repression of criminal offenses (article 4).

---

9 ANTONIALLI, Dennis; ABREU, Jacqueline SOUZA. Vigilância das comunicações pelo Estado brasileiro e a proteção a direitos fundamentais. São Francisco, CA: EFF, 2015, P. 20.

10 SOUZA, Carlos Affonso, LEMOS, Ronaldo. Marco Civil da Internet: construção e aplicação. Juiz de Fora: Editar, 2016, p.139.

It is also worth mentioning the law establishing the Brazilian Intelligence System (Law No. 9,883/99), whose content establishes that intelligence activities must be carried out with unrestricted observance of individual rights and guarantees (art. 3, single paragraph) and that binds the Brazilian Intelligence Agency to all the legal limitations listed above.[11]

While there is this normative landscape, the empirical experience reveals that there is in Brazil a culture of interceptions that disregards fundamental rights of individuals and there is a predisposition of investigative authorities to use techniques for obtaining data while ignoring legal requirements.[12]

Due to the risks mentioned above, it is possible to conclude the current legal framework faces a scarcity of tools to address the problems of state digital surveillance as a whole, and because of that, it is necessary to strengthen the human rights perspective and establish related mechanisms.

DIGITAL STATE SURVEILLANCE FROM THE PERSPECTIVE OF HUMAN RIGHTS

The first point to be addressed is the scrutiny of the interests colliding when the matter is digital state surveillance. As pointed out, every act internet-based and what is done in the physical world that is somehow reflected in data on the Internet are subject to the request (legitimate or not) of authorities.

---

11   FRANCISCO, Pedro Augusto P, VENTURINI, Jamila. Privacidade, Vigilância e Inteligência no Brasil: O marco legal e suas lacunas. . In: Horizonte presente: tecnologia e sociedade em debate. Coord. SILVA, Alberto... [et al.]; org. REIA, Jhessica... [et al.]. - Belo Horizonte : Casa do Direito ; FGV – Fundação Getúlio Vargas, 2019, p. 304.

12   ANTONIALLI, Dennis; ABREU, Jacqueline SOUZA. Op. cit., p. 26-27.

Limits to data processing are usually associated with the fundamental right to privacy. From this perspective, the information not publicly disclosed concerns the private life of the individual, who would have the power to restrict it from people's knowledge, including the State. It is a reformulation of the traditional right to be left alone[13] to adapt it to the digital society. Privacy finds constitutional protection as a fundamental right in article n° 5, X of brazilian Constitution.[14]

A second perspective is to justify this limitation on a broad understanding of human freedom and Internet usage as an instrument for the exercise of personality rights, with roots in the dignity of the human person, under article 1, III of the Brazilian Constitution.[15]

Finally, starting from a similar principle, but with the development of a specific concept, protection against unauthorized use of data should be based on informational self-determination, meaning determining one-self extension as a person depends substantially on the control over the data towards such individual,[16] which also affects the capacity of exercising inherent rights to citizenship. In other words, informational self-determination refers to a precondition for someone to live an existence that may be said self-determined,

---

13   WARREN, Samuel; BRANDEIS, Louis. The right to privacy. Harvard Law Review, Vol. 4, No. 5 (Dec. 15, 1890), p. 193-220

14   X - healthy inviolable the intimacy, private life, honor and image of the people, ensured the right to indemnification for material or moral damage arising from their violation.

15   DONEDA, Danilo. Da privacidade à proteção de dados pessoais. Rio de Janeiro: Renovar, 2006, p. 91.

16   BIONI, Bruno Ricardo. Proteção de dados pessoais. A função e os limites do consentimento. Rio de Janeiro: Forense - 2° ed., 2019, p. 103-104.

and that is not viable if an individual is unable to control the data produced about him.[17]

All in all, the informational self-determination is the foundation for an autonomous fundamental right to the protection of personal data, which, despite the lack of normative provision expressed in this sense in most systems,[18] should be implicitly absorbed by the Brazilian Constitution through the combination and adaptation of the various normative guidelines that indicate the importance of preserving the data that regards the data subject.[19]

The right to data protection unfolds not only to hedge privacy but also to serve as a limit to the abuse of state power, as an instrument for the exercise of innate rights to democracy, personality rights and to reduce informational asymmetry.[20]

A global milestone of this theory of informational self-determination is the decision on the Census Act case (BVerfGE 65, 1) of the German Federal

---

17   ROUVROY, Antoinette, POULLET, Yves. The right to informational self-determination and the value of self-development: Reassessing the importance of privacy for democracy. In Reinventing data protection? Springer, Dordrecht, 2009, p. 51.

18   At the time this article has been written, the Brazilian Senate approved the amendment n° 17/2021 that incorporates into the Federal Constitution the autonomous right to data protection, but it wasn't promulgated yet. It is a much-celebrated change that corroborates the premises of this article.

19   SARLET, Ingo Wolfgang. Proteção de Dados Pessoais como Direito Fundamental na Constituição Federal Brasileira de 1988: Contributo para a construção de uma dogmática constitucionalmente adequada. Revista Brasileira de Direitos Fundamentais & Justiça. v. 14, n. 42, 2020, p. 185-188.

20   LYNSKEY, Waterfront. Deconstructing data protection: the 'added-value' of a right to data protection in the Eu legal order. International and Comparative Law Quarterly, 63 (3). p. 592- 597

Constitutional Court in 1983, which deemed provisions of the German census act unconstitutional and thus overturned it, on the grounds that individuals, based on their freedom to determine how their personality may develop (self-determination),[21] have the authority to define how their personal data is disclosed, communicated and used by others.

In Brazil, the ruling in preliminary relief Adin No. 6.387/DF is noteworthy. In this case, it was asserted by the Federal Supreme Court the existence of the right to privacy and informational self-determination, in accordance with the LGPD, as a reverberation of personality rights and specific foundations of the right to data protection.

We understand none of the previous perspectives for data protection are conceptually misguided, actually, they complement, support, and foster each other.[22]

However, it is notable that the first (focused on privacy) provides limited protection regarding state digital surveillance since it is a safeguard only towards what happens in the intimate life of an individual or the limited bubble of his private life.

The second one composes a solid framework for the protection of the individual against illegitimate state intrusions, still, when observed only from the perspective of individual rights, it may be voided when counterbalanced with public interest.

On the other hand, the later and broader approach of data protection explained previously, with emphasis on the relation between data protection

---

21   ROUVROY, Antoinette, POULLET, Yves. The Right to Informational Self-Determination and the Value of Self-Development: Reassessing the Importance of Privacy for Democracy. In: Reinventing data protection? Springer, Dordrecht. 2009, p. 48.

22   SARLET, Wolfgang Ingo. Op. cit., p. 184.

and citizenship exercise nowadays, recalibrates such balance, as illustrated in the following pages.

This apprehension of data protection and the recognition of it as a fundamental right echo in concrete terms on how digital state surveillance should be controlled, being much of this article's focus the inviolability of individuals' information.

To begin with, when it comes to state surveillance, the status quo should arguably be the secrecy of individuals' data, except for duly reasoned and previously established hypotheses. Therefore, since the primary foundation of data protection is not privacy, but self-determination and the very status of a citizen in a digital society, a dogma must be thrown off: digital surveillance permission is not about personal privacy versus the public interest inserted in criminal prosecution efficiency or public security, it is crucial to go beyond.

Strictly, to outweigh individuals' right to oppose their data disclosure to the State should only be justified when the state investigative interest prevails over privacy[23] and democracy-related rights. That said, the decision that privileges surveillance has a greater burden to be valid, it is not a question of countering an individual interest which the data subject is being deprived of and the public interest, the equation includes the ability to justify derogation of not only private but also prerogatives necessary to the democratic State.

We need to stress this assumption is not a hermetic argument from a legal perspective. This higher argumentative effort is also based on practical perceptions about what unbridled surveillance can result in. The chilling effect it is how is named the phenomenon of people finding themselves inhibited from expressing and having contact with controversial or deviant ideas,

---

23   which remains a fundamental element, under penalty of annihilation of the individual. QUEIROZ, Rafael Mafei Rabelo, PONCE, Paula Pedigoni. Tércio Sampaio Ferraz Júnior e Sigilo de dados: o direito à privacidade e os limites à função fiscalizadora do Estado: o que permanece e o que deve ser reconsiderado. Revista Internet & Sociedade. n.1, v.1, fevereiro, 2020, p. 75-76.

movements, and spaces, or simply widely exercising their fundamental rights, for fear of state repression.[24] Empirical evidence demonstrates consistent correlations between state surveillance environments and high perception of chilling effects in society.[25]

The second argument is that the recognition of data protection as a fundamental right imposes an approach from an objective point of view. This means there is a pulverized duty of recognition of this right in and by the society – the horizontal effectiveness - and a general duty of the State to realize it, whose consequence is the necessary compliance with the fundamental right in the context of the relationship between individuals and non-public entities in general.[26]

Robert Alexy elucidates the existence of completed fundamental rights, the composition of which involves a bundle of definitive and prima facie positions, related to each other.[27] As defended by the author, this link between different legal positions may arise from three types of relationships, and it should be noted that at least two of them are present to justify a complex of duties that sustain the fundamental right to data protection.

The first is the means-ends relationships, established by the need for instrumental duties to perform a larger and generic command, revealing itself

24   RICHARDS, Neil M. Op. cit., p. 1935.

25   PENNEY, Jonathon W. Internet surveillance, regulation, and chilling effects online: a comparative case study. Internet Policy Review 6.2 (2017). Web. 14 Aug. 2021.

26   SARLET, Ingo. A Eficácia dos Direitos Fundamentais: uma teoria geral dos direitos fundamentais na perspectiva constitucional. 11° ed., Porto Alegre: Livraria do Advogado Editora, 2012, p. 125-128.

27   ALEXY, Robert. Teoria dos Direitos Fundamentais. Translated by SILVA, Virgílio Afonso Da. 2° Edição, 4° Tiragem, 1986, p. 253.

mainly by norms of organization and procedure.[28] The other is the weighing technique, materialized by collision norms to conciliate a conflict between a fundamental right and other legitimate interest.[29]

In this regard, the deep and undeniable relationship between data protection and the emerging complexity of a society intimately digital shows the combination of negative and positive duties of performance and of regulation is a must.[30]

Those premises are the basis for arguing that the fundamental right to data protection, as contemporaneously understood, imposes and backs up the implementation of new mechanisms, normative or not, for its realization. Ergo, it is already possible to answer the main question raised herein, the sum of unprecedented challenges towards state surveillance in a digital society and expanded configuration of data protection yields a social and legal urgency of a new regulatory framework for digital state surveillance.

A FEW PROPOSED STANDARDS

Laid down the reasons that invoke a particular regime for digital state surveillance regulation, we intend to formulate some standards that should govern such a regulatory structure. Notwithstanding, the goal of doing so is to provide examples of how a new approach is important, without the intention to suggest a comprehensive regulation framework

---

28   Ibidem, p. 251.

29   Ibidem, p. 252.

30   SALGADO, Eneida Desiree, SAITO, Vitória Hiromi. Privacidade e proteção de dados: por uma compreensão ampla do direito fundamental em face da sua multifuncionalidade. International Journal of Digital Law, Belo Horizonte, ano 1, n. 3, set./dez. 2020, p. 121-122.

At first, in the sphere of criminal investigation and discovery, it is necessary to approximate the protection of data not generally available to the constitutional inviolability of communications provided for in article 5°, XII of the Brazilian Federal Constitution, which requires a specific legal statute and/or duly reasoned court order for a lawful disclosure.[31]

Actually, we propose the scope of protection goes even further, to cover interception of data communication in the digital environment as a whole. Traditionally, when the matter is the inviolability of communications from brazilian legal perspective, the admission of interception – therefore, a right restriction - only finds a legal basis in the case of telephone communications due to its instantaneity, because insuperable inadmissibility could lead to stifling state investigation and crime prevention capability, but this conclusion would not apply to stored data, since it may be accessed through other equally effective measures.[32]

The problem is that this distinction is outdated when it comes to digital data and hence should be put into ostracism.[33] Although at a first glance the use of the internet reveals ephemeral and fleeting interactions, the data is not lost or vanished. On the contrary, being on the internet means leaving

---

31   defending this equivalent protection SARLET, Ingo Wolfgang. Proteção de Dados Pessoais como Direito Fundamental na Constituição Federal Brasileira de 1988: Contributo para a construção de uma dogmática constitucionalmente adequada. Op. cit., p. 211

32   FERRAZ JÚNIOR, Tércio Sampaio. Sigilo de dados: o direito à privacidade e os limites à função fiscalizadora do Estado. Revista da Faculdade de Direito, Universidade de São Paulo, v. 88, 1993. p. 447.

33   QUEIROZ, Rafael Mafei Rabelo, PONCE, Paula Pedigoni. Op. cit., p. 80.

your fingerprint in all over it.[34] Going further, data storage towards what an individual has done or failed to do has reached an unprecedented volume which will achieve an even higher level with the dissemination of the Internet of Things. There is, thus, no justification for interceptions, and any intrusions should be made post factum.

Concerning judicial determinations, the controversy over access to digital data for the purpose of criminal investigation by the State is always limited to a conflict of legitimate interests abstractly accepted by the law, the resolution of which must be based on a balancing of the interests at stake, whose tool is a judgment of proportionality.[35]

Historically Brazil Supreme Federal Court has, generally, taken into consideration when doing such balancing the right to privacy against other public interests, such as public security, law enforcement, and criminal prosecution,[36] but, as mentioned above, this is not enough. The court order must go into the merits of state meddling impacts (or lack thereof) in the right to self-development and the exercise of political rights.

On top of that, we argue that there should be a pre-defined balancing rule in favor of the protection of sensitive data,[37] prevailing public interest

---

34   BLAKEMORE, Christine; REDOL, Joao; CORREIA, Miguel. Fingerprinting for web applications: From devices to related groups. In: 2016 IEEE Trustcom/BigDataSE/ISPA. IEEE, 2016. p. 144-151.

35   ALEXY, Robert. Op. cit., p. 116-118.

36   AVILA, Ana Paula Oliveira, WOLOSZYN, André Louis. A tutela jurídica da privacidade e do sigilo na era digital: doutrina, legislação e jurisprudência. Revista de Investigações Constitucionais, 4, Curitiba, vol. 4, no. 3. p. 167-200, Sep./Dec. 2017.

37   In accordance with the LGPD article 5, II, and similarly to GDPR sensitive data means: personal data on racial or ethnic origin, religious conviction, political opinion, membership of a trade union or religious, philosophical or political organization, data

related arguments only when necessary to safeguard, in a concrete situation, other vital human rights, such as life and freedom, otherwise the core[38] of the fundamental right to data protection would be harmed and would leave leeway to discriminatory acts harmful to the right to equality.[39]

Moreover, for the sake of combating public administration arbitrary decisions and preventing fundamental rights from being tossed by a simple discretionary act, it is proposed the implementation of preventive, continuous and mass surveillance mechanisms must be made by law, because it is essential – and mandatory in a democratic regime - that society participates in the control, even indirectly, of the technologies by which it is monitored.

It is non-negotiable that in cases where access to data is allowed, there is a strict bond to the purpose for which the collection of data was authorized, which may not transit internally between bodies of the State. Informational separation of powers[40] is a nowadays issue.

Finally, since fundamental rights are not only realized by State's actions, it is also imperative the recognition that individuals' adoption of technologies to safeguard their own data is legitimate. The most enigmatic and prominent example of this is the use of cryptography techniques, especially encryption,

---

related to health or sexual life, genetic or biometric data, when related to a natural person.

38   MENDES, Gilmar Ferreira. Direitos Fundamentais e Controle de Constitucionalidade. 4° ed., 2012, p. 28

39   about the relationship between data protection and the right to equality: MENDES, Laura Schertel. Transparência e privacidade: violação e proteção da informação pessoal na sociedade de consumo. Dissertação de Mestrado, Universidade de Brasília, p. 57-58.

40   BIONI, Bruno; EILBERG, Daniela Dora; CUNHA, Brenda; SALIBA, Pedro; VERGILI, Gabriela. Op. cit., 2020, p. 11.

which should be seen as a lawful instrument for guaranteeing human rights, such as data protection, freedom of expression, and privacy,[41] highlighting that the status quo should be its admissibility, not its prohibition. Despite that, we recognize the cryptography debate is very complex and full of peculiarities that transcends this article.

Converging this that idea, the Brazilian Superior Court of Justice once ruled that companies, by employing end-to-end encryption, arelegitimately seeking mechanisms to protect freedom of expression and private communication, and ergo, are protecting fundamental rights.[42]

Besides the foregoing, the United Nations Human Rights Council report on the adverse effects of the surveillance industry on freedom of expression published in 2019 can also furnish some minimum standards that should guide digital state surveillance regulation and, because of that, we will reproduce part of them to complement the above propositions, mostly due to the fact that an international approach to internet regulation through the prism of human rights is of paramount importance for broad and uniform protection of fundamental rights in the digital environment.[43]

This hidden surveillance industry numerous technologies to silently subjugate data protection of individuals to State interests, sometimes having

---

41   SARAIVA, Raquel Lima. COSTA, André Barbosa Ramiro. A vigilância estatal e o uso de criptografia como ferramenta de efetivação dos direitos humanos. in: Tecnologias e Transformações no Direito, organização: SALDANHA, Paloma Mendes, PIMENTEL, Alexandre Freire, SALDANHA, Alexandre. - Recife: Fasa, 2017, p. 307-308.

42   Ordinary Appeal in the writ of mandamus n° 60.531.

43   BENEDEK, Wolfgang, KETTEMANN, Matthias C., SENGES, Max. The Humanization of Internet Governance: A Roadmap Towards a Comprehensive Global (Human) Rights Architecture for the Internet. GigaNet: Global Internet Governance Academic Network, Annual Symposium 2008, p. 4-7.

in the background a legitimate goal, in other situations for undoubtedly totalitarian purposes.[44]

Before suggesting new regulation, it is claimed by the Council the need to rescue and ensure the effectiveness of what is already in force, such as the above-mentioned International Covenant on Civil and Political Rights. It should be highlighted the committee's understanding that national security only serves as a reason to restrict fundamental rights when it deals with protecting the interest of the entire nation.[45]

Accordingly, not only states are encumbered with data protection duties. Companies should follow guidelines for good data protection practices and relationships with States, beyond being liable for human rights violations.[46]

Moving on to what is proposed by the Committee as a new specific regulation to curb unmeasured surveillance and protect individuals and human rights, a set of obligations involving a variety of agents is needed, some of which are mentioned below.

The Committee alleges sale and license of surveillance technologies to governments should be acceptable in very restricted situations until satisfactory standards of public disclosure of the operation, consequences, and purpose of the technology in question are met.[47]

State surveillance can only be justified in the event of serious criminal offenses, and legislation on surveillance must be imposed widely with well-delimited content, in accordance with Article 19 of the International Covenant

---

44   United Nations Human Rights Council. Report on the adverse effect of the surveillance industry on freedom of expression, 2019. p. 4-7.

45   Ibidem., p. 9.

46   Ibidem., p. 10.

47   Ibidem., p. 14.

on Civil and Political Rights. Also, intrusion into an individual's protected sphere presupposes judicial authorization.[48]

Also, on the surveillance directed against a specific subject, all existing procedural guarantees should be observed for other procedural steps, such as the search and seizure warrant, for example, and there should be all formalization and registration of all acts performed and science of the person who had his data protection mitigated.[49]

Although the judicial reserve rule reduces the risk of arbitrary activities, it is necessary to democratize control over state surveillance, and the purchase and development of surveillance technologies should be subject to supervision, consultation, control of the population, and accountability in regards to the surveillance technology.[50]

Getting back to companies, among the various suggestions, we highlight the duty of the creation of due diligence processes of Human Rights, such as evaluations of the impacts of technology on these rights, the implementation of policies and contractual clauses that have obligations following the protection of human rights, to provide transparency about the use of its technology by government entities for surveillance purposes, among others.[51]

These recommendations of the Council are of great relevance and seem to have a relationship of complementarity and convergence with the dogmatic reasons exposed in the previous chapter. Furthermore, the main conclusion corroborated by the combination of these ideas is that, to preserve data

---

48   Ibidem., p. 15.

49   Ibidem., p. 15.

50   Ibidem., p. 16.

51   Ibidem., p. 18.

protection and equalize state surveillance to the rule of law, it is urgent to develop a proper normative set for these issues.

CONCLUSION

This article's purpose was to assess what are the relevant risks of digital state surveillance and whether specific regulation is needed, and if so, on what grounds it should be developed, and what is the role of human and fundamental rights in this discussion. Further to that, based on the affirmative response to the question about the need for a new normative framework, we aimed at proposing some standards that should underlie these new rules.

We were able to identify major risks that may arise if digital state surveillance goes out of control, whose impacts could damage democracy founding elements. Furthermore, despite already existing some constitutional boundaries to surveillance and statutory law regulation, they do not address the found risks.

For example, Brazilian Federal Constitution lays down relevant protection, but lacks concrete rules. The Brazilian Internet Bill of Rights has a positive effect but a very limited scope. The Brazilian Data Protection Law does not cover data processing for criminal purposes.

It is in this context that the fundamental rights, particularly the data protection right, relevancy unfolds. The recognition of data protection as an autonomous fundamental right based on informational self-determination results in a much broader area of what is it protected by data protection - it is no longer a matter of an individual privacy; it is about civil and political rights. Beyond that, the nature of fundamental right imposes positive and negative duties and responsibilities.

That said, a proper regulation must take into consideration this elaborate aspect of data protection, leading to new premises for the regulation, which needs to address more relevant interests at stake. Consequently, more severe standards must sustain those new rules.

In terms of what some of those standards should be, we assessed the literature and international bodies are developing good mechanisms to limit digital state surveillance, namely, for example, a heavier court reasoning burden to mitigate data inviolability, law enactment as a mandatory requirement for the adoption of massive surveillance technologies and the concept of Informational separation of powers.

Even though is desirable that technological innovation yields an improvement for the state's investigative activity and crime prevention ability, but it cannot be achieved at any cost. Conciliating it with the human rights and democracy protections is an urgent matter of this century.

REFERENCES

ANTONIALLI, Dennis; ABREU, Jacqueline SOUZA. Vigilância das comunicações pelo Estado brasileiro e a proteção a direitos fundamentais. São Francisco, CA: EFF, 2015.

AVILA, Ana Paula Oliveira, WOLOSZYN, André Louis. A tutela jurídica da privacidade e do sigilo na era digital: doutrina, legislação e jurisprudência. Revista de Investigações Constitucionais, 4, Curitiba, vol. 4, no. 3. p. 167-200, Sep./Dec. 2017.

BENEDEK, Wolfgang, KETTEMANN, Matthias C., SENGES, Max. The Humanization of Internet Governance: A Roadmap Towards a Comprehensive Global (Human) Rights Architecture for the Internet. GigaNet: Global Internet Governance Academic Network, Annual Symposium 2008.

BLAKEMORE, Christine, REDOL, Joao; CORREIA, Miguel. Fingerprinting for web applications: From devices to related groups. In: 2016 IEEE Trustcom/BigDataSE/ISPA. IEEE, 2016.

BIONI, Bruno Ricardo. Proteção de dados pessoais. A função e os limites do consentimento. Rio de Janeiro: Forense - 2° ed., 2019.

BIONI, Bruno; EILBERG, Daniela Dora; CUNHA, Brenda; SALIBA, Pedro; VERGILI, Gabriela. Proteção de dados no campo penal e de segurança pública: nota técnica sobre o Anteprojeto de Lei de Proteção de Dados para segurança pública e investigação criminal. São Paulo: Associação Data Privacy Brasil de Pesquisa, 2020.

DONEDA, Danilo. Da privacidade à proteção de dados pessoais. Rio de Janeiro: Renovar, 2006.

DWOSKIN, Elizabeth; RUSLI, Evelyn M. The technology that unmasks your hidden emotions. Wall Street Journal (January 28), v. 1, 2015. Accessed on October 14, 2021: < https://www.wsj.com/articles/startups-see-your-face-unmask-your-emotions-1422472398>

FELDSTEIN, Steven. The global expansion of AI surveillance. Washington, DC: Carnegie Endowment for International Peace, 2019.

FERRAZ JÚNIOR, Tércio Sampaio. Sigilo de dados: o direito à privacidade e os limites à função fiscalizadora do Estado. Revista da Faculdade de Direito, Universidade de São Paulo, v. 88, 1993

FRANCISCO, Pedro Augusto P, VENTURINI, Jamila. Privacidade, Vigilância e Inteligência no Brasil: O marco legal e suas lacunas. In: Horizonte presente: tecnologia e sociedade em debate. Coord. SILVA, Alberto... [et al.]; org. REIA, Jhessica... [et al.]. - Belo Horizonte : Casa do Direito ; FGV – Fundação Getúlio Vargas, 2019.

LANGHEINRICH, Marc. Personal privacy in ubiquitous computing: Tools and system support. Doctoral Dissertation, ETH Zurich, 2005.

LYNSKEY, Waterfront. Deconstructing data protection: the 'added-value' of a right to data protection in the Eu legal order. International and Comparative Law Quarterly, 63 (3).

LYON, David. Surveillance, Snowden, and big data: Capacities, consequences, critique. Big data & society, v. 1, n. 2, p. 2053951714541861, 2014.

MENDES, Gilmar Ferreira. Direitos Fundamentais e Controle de Constitucionalidade. 4° ed., rev., e ampl. 2012.

MENDES, Laura Schertel. Transparência e privacidade: violação e proteção da informação pessoal na sociedade de consumo. Dissertação de Mestrado, Universidade de Brasília

PENNEY, Jonathon W. Internet surveillance, regulation, and chilling effects online: a comparative case study. Internet Policy Review. 6.2, 2017.

PILLAY, Navi. The right to privacy in the digital age (A/HRC/27/37). The Office of the United Nations High Commissioner for Human Rights, 2014.

QUEIROZ, Rafael Mafei Rabelo, PONCE, Paula Pedigoni. Tércio Sampaio Ferraz Júnior e Sigilo de dados: o direito à privacidade e os limites à função fiscalizadora do Estado: o que permanece e o que deve ser reconsiderado. Revista Internet & Sociedade. n.1, v.1, fevereiro, 2020.

RICHARDS, Neil M. The dangers of surveillance. Harvard Law Review, n° 126, 2012, p. 1940-1941.

ROUVROY, Antoinette, POULLET, Yves. The right to informational self-determination and the value of self-development: Reassessing the importance of privacy for democracy. In: Reinventing data protection? pp. 45-76. Springer, Dordrecht, 2009.

SALGADO, Eneida Desiree, SAITO, Vitória Hiromi. Privacidade e proteção de dados: por uma compreensão ampla do direito fundamental em face da sua multifuncionalidade. International Journal of Digital Law, Belo Horizonte, ano 1, n. 3, set./dez. 2020

SARLET, Ingo. A Eficácia dos Direitos Fundamentais: uma teoria geral dos direitos fundamentais na perspectiva constitucional. 11° ed., rev. e ampl. Porto Alegre: Livraria do Advogado Editora, 2012.

SARAIVA, Raquel Lima. COSTA, André Barbosa Ramiro. A vigilância estatal e o uso de criptografia como ferramenta de efetivação dos direitos humanos. in: Tecnologias e Transformações no Direito, organização:

SALDANHA, Paloma Mendes, PIMENTEL, Alexandre Freire, SALDANHA, Alexandre. - Recife: Fasa, 2017

SARLET, Ingo Wolfgang. Proteção de Dados Pessoais como Direito Fundamental na Constituição Federal Brasileira de 1988: Contributo para a construção de uma dogmática constitucionalmente adequada. Revista Brasileira de Direitos Fundamentais & Justiça. v. 14, n. 42, 2020.

SOLOVE, Daniel J. I've got nothing to hide and other misunderstandings of privacy. San Diego Law Review. 44, 2007, p. 765-767.

SOUZA, Carlos Affonso, LEMOS, Ronaldo. Marco Civil da Internet: construção e aplicação. Juiz de Fora: Editar, 2016.

United Nations Human Rights Council. Report on the adverse effect of the surveillance industry on freedom of expression, 2019.

WARREN, Samuel; BRANDEIS, Louis. The right to privacy. Harvard Law Review, Vol. 4, No. 5 (Dec. 15, 1890), p. 193-220.

HOW A REVOLUTION EVOLVES: A COMPARATIVE ANALYSIS OF ITALIAN, BRAZILIAN AND UK REGULATORY SANDBOXES

Authors:

Cristiana Maia

Rosa Maria Torraco

RESUME

After the first Regulatory Sandbox was launched in the UK in 2016, many other countries decided to follow its example, and a long path has been walked since then. Recently, Brazil and Italy have finally approved a regulation that will allow it to be equipped with a regulatory sandbox. Thus, based on this new global scenario and on comparative law studies, this article aims to compare the Italian, Brazilian and UK Fintech Regulatory Sandboxes, underlying their similarities and differences in order to understand the path that these sperimentations have followed during these years. We will focus on the activities that can be tested, the requirements of admissibility to the experimentation and the level of protection of the customers, in order to demonstrate the importance of equalizing privacy and information protection requirements with the necessary incentive to technological development and innovation.

KEY-WORDS: Sandbox. Regulation. Privacy. Innovation. Comparative Law

INTRODUCTION

The COVID-19 pandemic resulted in the acceleration of the digital transformation process of various sectors, thus reinforcing the need for approximation between the public power of the private sector and facilitating the emergence of new technologies and systems without the obstacles that the lack of regulation can provide.

In this context, we can see the practical application of the "Moore's law[1]", for which the exponential growth of technological solutions drive the digital transformation of society, forcing the State and the Right to rethink ways to monitor the speed of economic and social transformations caused by technology, and the emergence of new business dynamics, as can be seen by

---

1   Moore's law calls for a 100% increase in hardware power every short time, it is a rule that although it has not been foreseen in the world legal system, will increasingly impact the legal system. See in: <https://www.tecmundo.com.br/curiosidade/701-o-que-e-a-lei-de-moore-.htm> Acess 17 September 2021.

the increase in global legislation related to the regulatory sandbox[2], which a fifth percent were linked to fintechs[3] and emerged in the first semester of 2020.

These "safe spaces" for experimentation "are especially relevant in the fintech world, where there is a growing need to develop regulatory frameworks for emerging business models[4]". It is a framework set up by a financial sector regulator to allow small-scale, live testing of innovations by private firms in a controlled environment (operating under a special exemption, allowance, or other limited, time-bound exception) under the regulator's supervision.

These are being called "sandbox regulation" in all parts of the world and had the purpose of adopting "compliance with strict financial regulations to the growth and pace of the most innovative companies, in a way that doesn't smother the fintech sector with rules, but also doesn't diminish consumer protection[5]".

The term sandbox[6] is a closed testing environment designed for experimenting safely with web or software projects. It's very similar to the

---

2   With a total of 73 regulatory frameworks in 57 different jurisdictions, according to information available in: <https://www.worldbank.org/en/topic/fintech/brief/key-data-from-regulatory-sandboxes-across-the-globe> Access on 17 Sep. 2021.

3   The origin of the word Fintech is the contraction of the English words 'finance' and 'technology', which encompass the services of financial sector companies that use new technologies to create innovative financial products.

4   See WHAT IS A REGULATORY SANDBOX?, BBVA (Apr. 26 2018) Available in: <https://www.bbva.com/en/what-is-regulatory-sandbox/> Acess on 19 ago. 2022.

5   See WHAT IS A REGULATORY SANDBOX?, BBVA (Apr. 26 2018) Available in: <https://www.bbva.com/en/what-is-regulatory-sandbox/> Acess on 19 ago. 2022.

6   It is an isolated environment for testing new codes and applications to avoid programming errors. See: < https://realprotect.net/definicoes-de-seguranca-o-que-e-

virtualization technique, by which - roughly so - a virtual machine is created that allows to test any prototypes, often called MVP - Minimum viable product, preventing any failures from affecting the system that is already in operation, since sandbox applications allow all records and damage that may be caused by the system under test run within this isolated environment to be erased as soon as the computer is restarted, thus protecting the operating system of the machine to which it is inserted.

These programs do not require a second system to start, allowing the machine on which they are installed to be used typically and without performance loss[7]. Thus, transporting this idea to regulation law, this concept started to be used in the digital economy arena, to refer to regulatory sandboxes: testing grounds for new business models that are not protected by current regulation, or supervised by regulatory institutions. So, we can say that the "Regulation Sandbox" was born to allow the construction of experimental environments capable of assisting regulatory agents in anticipating any future contingencies that are necessary in the face of social and technological innovations.

Recently, Brazil and Italy have finally approved a regulation that will allow it to be equipped with a regulatory sandbox. Thus, based on this new global scenario and comparative law studies, this article aims to compare the Italian, Brazilian and UK Fintech Regulatory Sandboxes, underlying their similarities and differences, to understand the path these experimentations have followed through years.

The reason for this comparison lies not only in the fact that these are all Fintech Sandboxes, but also in our willingness to show the evolution of the Sandbox Revolution throughout time and to juxtapose two different

---

sandbox/> Access on 17 Sep. 2021.

7   See article in:<https://www.tecmundo.com.br/spyware/1172-o-que-e-sandbox-.htm> Access on 17 Sep. 2021.

approaches in the regulation of Regulatory Sandboxes: the UK one, which is typical of a Common Law Country, and the Italian and Brazilian one, which is that of Civil Law Countries.

A BRIEF HISTORY OF ITALIAN, BRAZILIAN AND UK REGULATORY SANDBOXES

The advent of these experimental environments in several countries of the world has enabled the approximation of law with technology, and the collaboration of private and public bodies, thus facilitating the development of innovative businesses and the construction of a regulatory framework more appropriate for innovation.

It should be noted, however, that even though there are general characteristics shared among the regimes of the countries, there is no single procedure for regulatory sandboxing. In this act, it is possible to identify at least two regulatory sandbox models: The first, more linked to economic freedom, has as characteristic the setting of a direct agreement made between the regulator and innovative companies, being possible to predict specific parameters of the testing period. The latter, typical of civil law countries, is characterized by the establishment of legislation that constitutes the pillar for sandbox experimentation and that regulates the relationship between the innovator and the supervising authorities.

The Pioneering Country for Regulatory Sandboxes is the UK. The first regulatory sandbox in the UK was launched by the Financial Conduct Authority (FCA) as part of Project Innovate. This programme commenced in October 2014, aiming to remove unnecessary barriers to innovation for businesses involved in banking and finance in the United Kingdom[8].

At the end of 2015, the FCA "published a report as part of its Project Innovate, where it explained why a regulatory sandbox was needed. The project was implemented in mid-2016. Fintech companies from around the world presented applications to continue growing and complying with the strict financial regulations, working alongside the FCA. Meanwhile, the FCA aims is to create incentives for competition so that consumers have more and better alternatives to manage their money[9]". So the first edition of the British regulatory sandbox began in early 2017. Since then, 89 firms have been chosen to test their product in the FCA Regulatory Sandbox.

In Brazil, since 2020, several regulators[10] have been operating their experimental environments, however only with the advent of the civil framework of startups – Complementary Law 182, of June 1, 2021 – that the concept of regulatory sandbox came to be reinforced before Brazilian society.

---

8   JDSUPRA.World-First Regulatory Sandbox Open for Play in the UK, May, 9, 2016. Available in: <World-First Regulatory Sandbox Open for Play in the UK | Latham & Watkins LLP - JDSupra> Access on 19 ago. 2022.

9   BBVA. WHAT IS A REGULATORY SANDBOX?. Apr. 26, 2018. Available in: <https://www.bbva.com/en/what-is-regulatory-sandbox/> Acess on 19 ago. 2022.

10   This is the case of the Central Bank itself (BACEN), which disciplined last year its first Sandbox (BCB Resolution No. 50/2020); the Brazilian Securities and Exchange Commission (CVM), regulated by CVM Instruction 626/2020; and the Superintendence of Private Insurance (SUSEP), which was the first to officially institute a Regulatory Sandbox program in Brazil.

It should be noted that the model adopted by the FCA[11] could be compared to the initial Brazilian purpose of regulation, special at article 3, VII of Provisional Measure n. 881[12], of April 30, 2019 - vetoed at the time of the conversion of the aforementioned MP in Law No. 13,874 of September 20, 2019. This provision allowed legal interpretation to implement a less restrictive model of the experimental regulatory environment, however it was vetoed on the grounds that the deletion of an originating section in which this article was exceptionalised to the national, public, health and public health security made it impossible to apply such a provision.

The second model would be the one in which the regulatory authority defines the general criteria and participation in the experimental database, being possible for those agents who meet such previously defined requirements, with a prior selection of possible participants. This is the model adopted in Brazil, as can be seen from the wording applied to BCB Resolution No. 50/2020 and CVM Instruction 626/2020, in which the experimental regime is only open temporarily to some previously authorized companies. This is a more reactive and cautious stance of regulators in the face of technological developments and the experimental innovative conducts of the regulated.[13]

---

11   FINANCIAL CONDUCT AUTHORITY. The regulatory sandbox allows businesses to test innovative propositions in the market with real consumers. FCA, May 10, 2015. Available in: <https://www.fca.org.uk/firms/regulatory-sandbox> Access on 17 Sep. 2021.

12   BRAZIL. Provisional Measure No. 881 of April 30, 2019. Declaration of Economic Freedom Rights. Official Gazette, 30 Apr. 2019. Available from: < http://www.planalto.gov.br/ccivil_03/_ato2019-2022/2019/Mpv/mpv881.htm> Access on 17 Sep. 2021.

13   COUTINHO Filho, Augustus. Regulation 'Sandbox' as a regulatory instrument in the capital market: main characteristics and international practice. Digital Journal of Administrative Law. University of São Paulo. Vol. 5, no. 2, 2018.

Although the regulatory sandbox was born by the innovations of the banking sector, these have been extending to several regulated sectors, such as the Brazilian energy sector, as it's shown by the recent ANEEL's Public Consultation No. 049/2021[14], to collect subsidies and additional information for the improvement of the proposal to regulate the application of Pilot Tariff Projects (Tariff Sandboxes). This project has the goal to adapt the Brazilian tariff model applied to the vast majority of low voltage consumers (Group B) not only to technological innovations - through which distributors evolve from simple network operators to distribution system managers (DNO-DSO), but also to the consequent change in consumer behaviour in relation to the way in which they consume electricity, with the active choice of the time of use of the network.

The Regulatory Sandboxes have been introduced in Italy through the law decree n. 34[15] of the 30th of April 2019, which has been converted into the law n.58[16] on the 28th of June 2019. The law decree is also known as the "Growth decree" because, as the press release of the Council of Ministers says,

---

14   ANEL. Public Consultation 049/2021. Available in: <https://www.aneel.gov.br/consultas-publicas?p_auth=7uNy6XzL&p_p_id=participacaopublica_WAR_participacaopublicaportlet&p_p_lifecycle=1&p_p_state=normal&p_p_mode=view&p_p_col_id=column-2&p_p_col_pos=1&p_p_col_count=2&_participacaopublica_WAR_participacaopublicaportlet_ideParticipacaoPublica=3580&_participacaopublica_WAR_participacaopublicaportlet_javax.portlet.action=visualizarParticipacaoPublica> Access on 17 Sep. 2021.

15   Law decree n. 34 of April 30, 2019. «Urgent measures of economic growth and for the resolution of specifical crisis situations». Official Gazette, 30 Apr. 2019. Available from: <https://www.gazzettaufficiale.it/eli/id/2019/06/29/19A04303/sg>. Access 5 Aug. 2021.

16   Law n. 58 of June 28, 2019. Conversion in law, with adaptations, of the law decree 30 April 2019, n. 34, bearing urgent measures of economic growth and for the

it introduces urgent measures for economic growth and for the industrial sectors which are experiencing a period of crisis.

According to paragraph 2-bis of the "Growth Decree ", the Ministry of Economics and Finances has to define the conditions and the ways to pursue such experimentations through the adoption of regulations. So, the Ministry of Economics and Finances (MEF) proposed a Regulation Scheme, which was subjected to a public consultation, which came to an end on March 31st. The final regulation was adopted with a decree of the Ministry of Economics and Finances n.100[17] of the 30th April 2021, published in the Official Gazette of July 2nd 2021 and entered into force on July 17th 2021.

On September 30th 2021, the Bank of Italy, the IVASS and CONSOB, which are the three authorities that were designed as supervising authorities for the FinTech Experimentation, through a Press Release[18] have established that the first time window for the presentation of the requests of admissibility to the Regulatory Sandbox will be opened from November 15 to January 15.

---

resolution of specific crisis situations. Official Gazette, 30 Apr. 2019. Available from: <https://www.gazzettaufficiale.it/eli/id/2019/06/29/19G00066/sg>. Access 5 Aug. 2021.

17   Decree of the Ministry of Finances n. 100 of April 30 2021. Regulation bearing implementation of art. 36, para. 2-bis and following, of the law-decree 30 April 2019, n.34, converted, with adaptations, from the law June 28 2019, n.58, on the discipline of the Committee and the FinTech experimentation. Available from: <https://www. gazzettaufficiale.it/eli/id/2021/07/02/21G00109/sg>. Access 5 Aug. 2021.

18   Press release of Bank of Italy, CONSOB, and IVASS of 30 September 2021. Available here: <https://www.bancaditalia.it/media/comunicati/documenti/2021-02/ cs-SANDBOX.pdf >. Accessed 2 Oct. 2021

THE FINTECH SERVICES AND TECHNOLOGIES CAN BE TESTED

Article 36, paragraph 2-bis of the Italian "Growth Decree", states that the experimentation concerns the FinTech activities aimed at pursuing, through new technologies which AI and Distributed Ledgers, of innovation of services and products in the financial, credit and regulated markets sectors.

However, a more specific definition of which services and technologies can be tested is given in article 5 of the Decree on the discipline of the Committee and the Fintech Experimentation, which specifies that the experimentation can be asked for a technological innovation activity that relates to the banking, financial and insurance sectors.

Otherwise, can be admitted to the experimentation an activity which: is subjected to the registration in a register kept by at least one supervisory authority which takes part in the experimentation, even if it is subjected to the authorization or registration in a register of one supervisory authority, it re-enters in an exclusion case foresaw by the law, consists in a service or an activity that affects outlines which are the object of regulation in the banking, financial, insurance sectors to be performed in favor of a subject vigilated by at least one surveillance authority which has in Italy his registered office or a secondary office or that operated in Italy in the EU regime of freedom to provide services.

In Brazil, the regulatory sandbox is established by specific law that authorizes the regulatory body of the sector to issue selection. The selection procedure is open for a specific time lap with restrictive criteria that must be complied with by the companies which are interested. There is no restriction on the theme that can be treated in the regulatory sandboxes. Besides, it began with banking issues, such as the PIX instant payment system that has recently become popular in the country and is currently the so-called open bank. However, only recently -in 2021- began some initiatives related to insurance and electricity.

In the FCA Regulatory Sandboxes, the regulatory sandbox is open to all types of propositions and applications from all sectors of the financial services market are welcome. So it seems that the Italian approach, even if it comes after many years of Regulatory Sandboxes experimentations, is in a sense still more shy than the UK and the Brazilian ones, which allows all kinds of financial services to be experimented.

REQUIREMENTS OF ADMISSIBILITY

The art. 36 of the so-called "Growth Decree", states that the regulations must decide the conditions of admission to the experimentationSo, the Regulamentation n.100 of 2021 contains an overview of the conditions for the admission to the experimentation.

As for the UK case, the conditions for eligibility are directly established by the FCA. So, the first evidence which appears is that both in Italy and in the UK, the innovation should be intended for the national market. Otherwise, the second requisite common to both countries to be admitted to the experimentation is innovativeness. According to the Italian regulation, the activity must be significantly innovative, or it must contribute, through the use of new technologies to offer services, products or processes in the banking, insurance or financial sectors that are truly new and different compared to those already existing in the national market.

As to the FCA requisites, the innovation has to have a significantly different offering in the marketplace. Indeed, as for the Italian case, if numerous examples of similar offerings are already established on the market, the activity is not eligible for sandbox experimentation.

In innovation promotion, the Brazilian Central Bank has two regulatory projects: the Laboratory of Financial and Technological Innovations (LIFT) and Sandbox regulatory. The distinction between LIFT and Sandbox is that the first serves to monitor the development of the application of technology or the business model of maturing projects. In contrast, the second serves to accompany innovative projects already matured, but there is the need to validate the business model through its effective implementation. Also, the sandbox model enables participants to provide products and services to real customers. At the same time, LIFT does not allow participants to provide products or services to real customers in the lab environment. Finally, the regulatory Sandbox in Brazil only allows the participation of companies, while LIFT allows the participation of individuals.

As to the benefits, in the UK case, the innovation has to offer a good prospect of identifiable benefit to consumers. The criteria are met if the innovation is likely to lead to a better deal for consumers directly or indirectly, for instance, through higher quality services or lower price due to enhanced efficiency, the business has identified any possible consumer risks, and proposed mitigation or the innovation will promote effective competition[19]. The Italian regulation makes instead a concrete analysis of how the experimentation can bring added value. In fact, it can bring benefits for the final users in terms of quality of service, promotion of the competition, access conditions, protection of the end-user or costs, contribute to the efficiency of the banking, financial, insurance system or of the operators that take part to it or make cheaper or more effective the application of the regulation in the banking, insurance or finance sector, allow an improvement of the systems, the procedures or the internal processes of the banking, insurance or financial sector regarding the risk management.

Another criterion to be met to participate in the FCA experimentation is that the business must be ready to test the innovation in a live environment. Also, here there are some positive indicators that allow us to understand whether the criteria are met. Firstly, testing plans must be well developed with clear objectives, parameters and success criteria. Then, some testing has been conducted to date, and the firm has the tools and resources required to enable testing in the sandbox. Finally, the firm has sufficient safeguards in place to protect customers and is able to provide appropriate redress if required.

---

19   See FCA. Sandbox Eligibility Criteria. . Available in: https://www.fca.org.uk/publication/documents/sandbox-eligibility-criteria.pdf Acess on 19 ago. 2022.

In the same way, in Brazil, during the regulatory Sandbox testing period, companies are subject to differentiated regulatory requirements. They can receive personalized guidance from regulators on how to interpret and enforce appropriate regulations. That means if the regulatory authority understands that the project is dangerous to customers or for a company, it may establish more restrictive rules or finalize the project at its discretion.

As to the readiness of the business to take part in the sandbox, the Italian regulation n.100 of 2021 says that the business must be in a state advanced enough for experimentation. However, it seems to be lacking any relevant information. Indeed, how should be assessed the fact that the business is in a state advanced enough for experimentation?

This issue emerged also after the public consultation which followed the Regulation Scheme in 2020. For instance, during the consultation, Hogan Lovells indicated as an example to be followed by the Joint Report of the European Supervisory Authorities "FinTech: Regulatory sandboxes and innovation hubs[20]". The Report identifies a number of criteria through which could be evaluated the "readiness" of the activity to take part in the experimentation. For example, it can be requested that: the sufficiently advanced state is parameterized to the idoneity of the activity to be conducted in a realistic context, that the needed software licenses have been obtained or that the customers or potential customers for the purpose of the experimentation have been identified.At this point, it seems that the UK, Brazil and Italy, follow two different paths. In fact, one of the eligibility criteria for the FCA Sandbox is that the business must have a genuine need to test the innovation on real customers and in the FCA Sandbox. Here again, there are hints that the requisites are met: the innovation does not easily fit the existing regulatory framework, thus making it difficult or costly to get the innovation to market, there is a clear need for a sandbox tool in order to test this product in a live

---

20   See ITALY. Consultazione Pubblica. Available in: <http://www.dt.mef.gov.it/it/dipartimento/consultazioni_pubbliche/consultazione_regolamento.html> Acess. 19 ago. 2022

environment, the business has no alternative means of engaging with the FCA or achieving the testing objective or the full authorization process would be too costly or burdensome for the purposes of a short test of the viability of a particular innovation.

We believe that it is very significant that while the FCA cares about the effective need of a sandbox, the Italian regulation among the conditions for eligibility states that the activity subjected to the experimentation must be economically and financially sustainable or has to have an adequate financial covering. Also, in Brazil, energetic markets are using the sandbox regulation to test new technologies, as we can see from the ANEEL regulation.

THE SUPERVISORY AUTHORITIES

According to the "Growth Decree", the competent authority monitors the trend of the experimentation, on which it reports to the Fintech Committee at least every six months. In the Italian Regulatory Sandbox there are three authorities that monitor the trend of the experimentation, each for its own competence: Bank of Italy[21], CONSOB and IVASS. As a supervising Authority, the Bank of Italy is tasked to maintain the financial stability according to the supervising powers and responsibilities on each intermediary and on the overall financial system that derives from the national legal system. As to the CONSOB[22], its task is to supervise the Italian securities market, promoting its efficient and transparent development and protecting the investors and

---

21   See BANCA D'ITALIA. Available in: <https://www.bancaditalia.it/chi-siamo/index.html> Acessed on 19 ago. 2022

22   See CONSOB. Available in: < https://www.consob.it/web/consob-and-its-activities/activities> Accessed on 19 ago. 2022

savers that ask for protection. And, finally, the IVASS[23] grants protection to the policyholders, pursuing the healthy and prudent management of the insurance and reinsurance, and their transparency towards the users.

In the UK, the Regulatory Sandboxes Supervising Authority is only the FCA, which aims at the well-functioning of markets for individuals, firms and the economy as a whole.

And in Brazil, there are two authorities: Brazilian Central Bank and ANEEL. Also, the selection and classification of projects submitted to the regulatory Sandbox of the Central Bank of Brazil are made by the Strategic Management Committee (CESB), which will decide executively on issues related to the matter. The transparency towards the users occurs through the official journal or on the official regulatory institution's website.

CONCLUSION

Therefore, that the usefulness, application and risks assessed of regulatory sandboxes will depend on several factors, such as the legislative structure to which they are inserted and whether or not the regulatory or legislative authority will have the discretion to waive or customize the regulatory requirements applicable in experimental environments to establish and mitigate the potential risks of the applications of new technologies.

This comparative analysis has underlined some general features common to all kinds of Regulatory Sandboxes, such as the definition of several admissibility requirements and the establishment of supervisory authorities. However, Civil Law and Common Law Countries have different approaches in regulating FinTech Regulatory Sandboxes. The former is characterized by the establishment of legislation that regulates the relationship between the

---

23   See IVASS. Acailabre in: <https://www.ivass.it/chi-siamo/index.html > Accessed 19 ago. 2022.

innovator and the supervising authorities and, as we have seen in this paper, sets tighter rules for the experimentation. Following an economic freedom approach, the latter lies more on the direct relationship between the innovator and the supervising authority.

It must also be noted that the Italian Regulatory Sandbox, even if it comes after many years of Sandboxes experimentation in several countries of the world, has a more cautious approach than the Brazilian and the UK ones, dictated by the willingness to try to assure the highest level of protection of the customers.

This time, it can be concluded that the adoption of regulatory sandbox models brings several benefits besides allowing the approximation of law and technology, accelerating the evolution of the former in the face of the exponential evolution of the second, especially in the field of service offerings and disruptive products linked to so-called grey areas, in which the use of new technologies and the provision of innovative services cannot be easily framed in the typical services and regulations[24].

REFERENCES

ALVIM, Teresa Arruda. A look at modulation from Law 13.655/2018. Conjur, May 2. 2018. Available at: <https://www.conjur.com.br/2018-mai-02/teresa-arruda -alvim-modulacao-olhar-partir-lei-13655> Access on September 17, 2021.

AMURIM, Vitor. NEW LEGAL FRAMEWORK OF STARTUPS AND THE IMPULSE TO THE "REGULATORY SANDBOX" IN BRAZIL. Portal connect Smartcities. June 15, 2021. Available in: <https://portal.connectedsmartcities.

---

24   COUTINHO Filho, Augustus. Regulation 'Sandbox' as a regulatory instrument in the capital market: main characteristics and international practice. Digital Journal of Administrative Law. University of São Paulo. Vol. 5, n. 2, 2018, p. 270.

com.br/2021/06/15/   novo-marco-legal-das-startups-e-o-impulso-ao-sandbox-regulatorio-no-brasil/>. Accessed on 17 Sep. 2021.

ANEL. Public Consultation 049/2021. Available in: <https://www.aneel.gov.br/consultas-publicas?p_auth=7uNy6XzL&p_p_id=participacaopublica_WAR_participacaopublicaportlet&p_p_lifecycle=1&p_p_state=normal&p_p_mode=view&p_p_col_id=column-2&p_p_col_pos=1&p_p_col_count=2&_participacaopublica_WAR_participacaopublicaportlet_ideParticipacaoPublica=3580&_participacaopublica_WAR_participacaopublicaportlet_javax.portlet.action=visualizarParticipacaoPublica> Accessed on 17 Sep. 2021.

BAUMAN, Zygmunt. Liquid Modernity. Rio de Janeiro: Jorge Zahar, 2001.

BORGES, João Paulo Resende. Law 13.655/18 and the regulatory sandbox of the central bank of Brazil: legal certainty for a differentiated regulatory regime. Revista Caderno Virtual, v.1, n.46 Available in: https://www.portaldeperiodicos.idp.edu.br/cadernovirtual/article/view/4167 Accessed on 17 Sep. 2021.

BRAZIL. Complementary Law No. 182 of June 1, 2021. Marco Legal of Startups. Official Gazette, June 2. 2021. Available in: < http://www.planalto.gov.br/ccivil_03/leis/lcp/Lcp182.htm>. Accessed 17 Sep. 2021.

BRAZIL. Provisional Measure No. 881 of April 30, 2019. Declaration of Economic Freedom Rights. Official Gazette, 30 Apr. 2019. Available from: < http://www.planalto.gov.br/ccivil_03/_ato2019-2022/2019/Mpv/mpv881.htm> Accesseed on 17 Sep. 2021.

BRAZIL. Veto message 438 of September 20, 2019. Veto item VII of Art. 3 for contrary to the public interest and unconstitutionality, the Conversion Bill No. 21, 2019 (MP No. 881/19), which "Institutes the Declaration of Rights of Economic Freedom. Available in: < http://www.planalto.gov.br/ccivil_03/_ato2019-2022/2019/Msg/VEP/VEP-438.htm> Accessed on 17 Sep. 2021.

BRAZILIAN SECURITIES COMMISSION (CVM). Normative Instruction 626 of May 15, 2020. It provides for the rules for the constitution and operation of an experimental regulatory environment (regulatory sandbox). Available in: <http://conteudo.cvm.gov.br/export/sites/cvm/legislacao/instrucoes/anexos/600/inst626.pdf> Accessed on 17 Sep. 2021.

CENTRAL BANK OF BRAZIL. Collegiate Board. Resolution 50 of 16 December 2020. It provides for the requirements for the establishment and execution by the Central Bank of Brazil of the Controlled Environment of Tests for Financial innovations and Payment (Regulatory Sandbox). Official Gazette: section 1, Brasília, DF, ed. 241, p. 101, 17 December 2020. Available in: < https://www.in.gov.br/web/dou/-/resolucao-bcb-n-50-de-16-de-dezembro-de-2020-294621288>. Accessed on 17 Sep. 2021.

COUTINHO Filho, Augustus. Regulation 'Sandbox' as a regulatory instrument in the capital market: main characteristics and international practice. Digital Journal of Administrative Law. University of São Paulo. Vol. 5, no. 2, 2018.

FEIGELSON, Bruno. Sandbox: The future of regulation. AB2L, January 28, 2018. Available in: < https://ab2l.org.br/sandbox-o-futuro-da-regulacao/> Accessed on 17 Sep. 2021.

FINANCIAL CONDUCT AUTHORITY. The regulatory sandbox allows businesses to test innovative propositions in the market with real consumers. FCA, May 10, 2015. Available in: <https://www.fca.org.uk/firms/regulatory-sandbox> Accessed on 17 Sep. 2021.

IDA IBDR. Global Experiences From Regulatory Sandboxes, The World Bank, November 1, 2018. Available in: <https://www.worldbank.org/en/topic/fintech/brief/key-data-from-regulatory-sandboxes-across-the-globe> Accessed on 17 Sep. 2021.

ITALY. Law decree n. 34 of April 30, 2019. «Urgent measures of economic growth and for the resolution of specifical crisis situations». Official Gazette, 30 Apr. 2019. Available from: <https://www.gazzettaufficiale.it/eli/id/2019/06/29/19A04303/sg>. Accessed on 5 Aug. 2021.

ITALY. Law n. 58 of June 28, 2019. Conversion in law, with adaptations, of the law decree 30 April 2019, n. 34, bearing urgent measures of economic growth and for the resolution of specific crisis situations. Official Gazette, 30 Apr. 2019. Available from: <https://www.gazzettaufficiale.it/eli/id/2019/06/29/19G00066/sg>. Accessed on 5 Aug. 2021.

ITALY. Decree of the Ministry of Finances n. 100 of April 30 2021. Regulation bearing implementation of art. 36, para. 2-bis and following, of the law-decree 30 April 2019, n.34, converted, with adaptations, from the law June 28 2019, n.58, on the discipline of the Committee and the FinTech experimentation. Available from: <https://www.gazzettaufficiale.it/eli/id/2021/07/02/21G00109/sg>. Accessed on 5 Aug. 2021.

SIMON, Alexander Herbet. Rational choice and the structure of the environment. Psychological Review, 63 (2), 1956.

HOW A REVOLUTION EVOLVES: A COMPARATIVE ANALYSIS OF ITALIAN, BRAZILIAN AND UK REGULATORY SANDBOXES

Authors:

Ritu Paul

Seema Yadav

INTRODUCTION

Online Dispute Resolution or ODR is a branch of dispute resolution which resolves disputes between the parties using the information technology. ODR is a process to settle disputes with the means of technology and acts as a counterpart to the alternate dispute resolution (ADR) mechanisms such as, mediation, negotiation, arbitration, or as a combination of them. Initially, the mechanism of arbitration came into effect as an alternative to court for a certain kind of disputes and also to make the procedure simple and cost-effective but rather eventually it has changed into a complex and expensive method to settle disputes.

On introduction of ODR, the disputed parties have got the freedom to select the way of handling their disputes and the use of technology facilitates the whole process making it faster, convenient, efficient and cost-efficient. Also, the best way to deliver justice in this COVID-19 pandemic from the corners of our home shifts our focus to the modern counterpart of ADR is ODR. From filing to the appointment of arbitrators, under ODR everything is carried out online.

Throughout the world, ODR witnessed a boom with the e-commerce sector in settling disputes online. Separate platforms have been constituted in Brazil, USA, etc. to resolve disputes by Online Dispute Resolution mechanism. On the other hand, in India the ODR mechanism is at its infancy stage. The application of ODR in India has reached to limited sectors such as to resolve disputes related to online transactions, online shopping and the like. This online dorm of dispute resolution mechanism has enable novel happenings which were earlier not available like, to ensure presence of parties in the proceedings were needed in earlier times but by the use of Online Dispute Resolution mechanism the parties can attend the proceedings from their comfortable corners of home.

Apart from the above, there can be many kinds of ODR which are ordered or annexed by certain types of platforms such as, government – operated platforms, court – ordered ODR providers and private ODR service providers, that have been discussed later in the paper.

Talking about India, here people are habitual with the traditional legal system and believe in the face-to-face interaction procedure. So, considering the current situation it will be easier to opt for a court – annexed ODR procedure, for which following three fundamentals must be fulfilled:-

1. This court – annexed ODR must be conducted online majorly through video – conferencing and the documents must be submitted through the e – filing option, whereby the concept of digital signature should be incorporated for the purpose of authenticating the documents submitted.

2. A litigant pro system must be developed in order to assist them in attending the procedure without any technological obstacles.

3. Unlike ADR, this court – annexed ODR works as a discipline under the judiciary and should be applied to an extent whereby not only petty offences would be resolved but should be diversified into a great number of matters.[1]

The Online Dispute Resolution (ODR) mechanism not only makes a favourable and safe condition for the parties and for the quick disposal of the cases but also provides a platform for employment of advocates and arbitrators.

OBJECTIVE AND FUNCTIONING OF ODR

OBJECTIVES:

The principal objective of Online Dispute Resolution is to authorize the parties/litigants to resolve their disputes by using technology. The process of ODR mainly prevents face to face meetings to mediate or negotiate in order to resolve disputes and as an outcome it makes the process more convenient and cost efficient.

In the case of online negotiation and mediation, the concerned parties to the agreement get the leverage upon the terms of the agreement to broaden them or restrict them as much as they desire. Where an international dispute comes before an ODR platform, the rules and jurisdiction of the ODR provider has the capacity to enforce the settlement agreement.

---

1   Online Dispute Resolution (ODR) | India https://disputeresolution.online/ (last visited on October 2, 2021)

Following are the points which determine ODR as an appropriate mechanism to resolve disputes, these are[2]:-

a. ODR is considered as the most desirable kind of mechanism in order to deal with only handful of cases. It is also proficient in dealing with the issues where stake is at a particular amount of money rather on any issues related to liability.

UNCITRAL ON ONLINE DISPUTE RESOLUTION
(as per UNCITRAL Technical Notes on ODR)

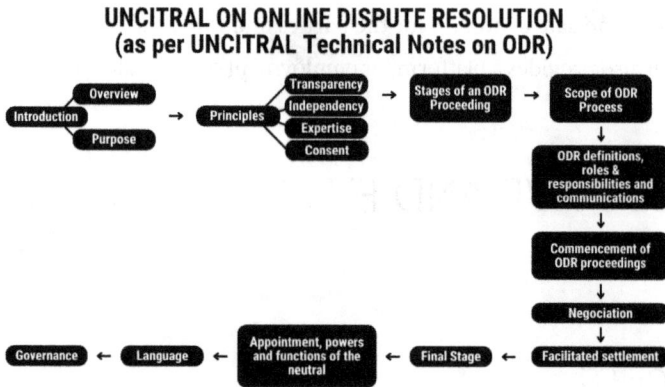

b. ODR works at its finest when the parties concerned are less in number.

c. The issues can be clearly stated by the parties as ODR includes electron.

d. ODR works the best when the factual matters/issues are not dependent upon their credibility.

e. Certain ODR platforms specifically deal with mediation or negotiation stage of a dispute and may not permit to testify the witnesses or where the parties concerned hope for an unrealistic outcome.

f. Most recently with the emergence of the Covid-19 pandemic, issues of law are also being settled.

---

2   Online Dispute Resolution - Dispute Resolution Reference Guide (justice. gc.ca) https://www.justice.gc.ca/eng/rp-pr/csj-sjc/dprs-sprd/res/drrg-mrrc/10.html#ii (last visited on October 27, 2021)

FUNCTIONING:

One can observe that there are both assisted and automated modes to resolve offline as well as online disputes.

A. Assisted Online Dispute Resolution:-

Under Assisted ODR, the mediator coordinates with the concerned parties in the conflict or dispute and then tries to resolve the same. Using ODR certainly leads to the use of technology and under assisted ODR; the mediator makes communication with the parties through email which enables all the concerned parties to see each other's statements.

B. Automated Online Dispute Resolution:-

The Automated ODR is mainly used in the matters where the dispute originated since the terms of the agreement were not properly negotiated or agreed upon[3]. The automated systems help in negotiating the terms of agreement and the disputants generally arrive at a win-win situation.

BENEFITS OF ODR:

- The major advantage of this mechanism is to provide speedy resolution of disputes and conflicts and it is economical as well.

- It is simple and accessible.

- It diminishes the cost of hiring an attorney

- Parties settle their claims from their respective residences or offices

- Paperless proceedings are conducted which in consequence protects our ecosystem.

---

3   Hammond A-MG. How do you write "yes"? A study on the effectiveness of online dispute resolution. Conflict Resolution Quarterly. March 2003;20(3):261-286. DOI: 10.1002/crq.25

DRAWBACKS OF ODR:

- Requirement of availability of adequate technology to the concerned parties

- Appointed arbitrator/mediator may not be proficient in using technology

- Lack of confidentiality and safety

- Parties can become subject to hackers attack

- Shortfall of security and loss of information

UNCITRAL ON ODR

The UNCITRAL Model Law has made an attempt towards explaining the concept and procedure of ODR through its "Technical Notes on ODR". It has defined the principles which together form the bedrock for this mechanism and also, the stages that should be necessarily involved in the process (i.e., Negotiation, Facilitated Settlement, Final Stage). Apart from these, the other significant matters like, Appointment, Powers and Functions of the Neutral, Language and Governance have been explained briefly.

VIABILITY OF ODR AT INTERNATIONAL LEVELS DURING COVID-19

The ODR systems can be categorised into three forms:-

1. GOVERNMENT-OPERATED ODR PLATFORMS

The Government-operated ODR platforms are established and regulated by government departments. The process of ODR under this category is very quick and cost-effective, especially in labour and consumer disputes.

a. ODR services offered in Hong Kong: with the emergence of COVID-19 pandemic a scheme has been introduced to ensure the ecosystem of dispute resolution is not affected. COVID-19 Online Dispute Resolution (ODR) Scheme has been introduced to resolve disputes that are emerging because of COVID-19 pandemic or where at least one of the parties belongs to Hong Kong as a resident or where the amount claimed is HKD (Hong Kong Dollar) 500,000 or less.[4] The ODR Provider that is appointed in Hong Kong to conduct the online process is eBRAM.

b. ODR services offered in the United States: In the United States, the major ODR platform that offers its services is the Technology Assisted Group Solutions (TAGS) by Federal Mediation and Conciliation Service (FMCS). The nature of dispute that are handled by this platform are labour disputes. The mechanism used for dispute resolution by FMCS is mediation, whereby FMCS has engaged TAGS to assist mediators in resolving labour – management disputes effectively. Technology tools such as, eRoom, FacilitatePro, minimo and NetMeeting in order to conduct online caucuses and meetings and offer an efficient online dispute resolution system.

2. COURT-ANNEXED ODR PLATFORMS

The court-annexed ODR has two major benefits, first and foremost is that ODR reduces the case burden on the courts and additionally, it supplements the efforts of the Judiciary. These benefits can be exercised only if technology tools are integrated with the ADR procedure and by constructing ODR's capacity.

a. ODR services offered in UAE: The Dubai International Finance Centre Courts (DIFC) is based on the UNCITRAL Model, which uses arbitration as an ODR mechanism for dispute resolution. Filing of documents such as wills, etc. and commercial disputes are mainly resolved by DIFC Arbitration law.

---

4   Matthew Love, 'Hong Kong Announces Its New Online Dispute Resolution Scheme' (Hugill and Ip, 22 April 2020) https://www.hugillandip.com/2020/04/hong-kong-announces-its-new-online-dispute-resolution-scheme/

The process that is exercised by this court-annexed ODR platform requires the Government to appoint the judges for DIFC Courts. The DIFC Courts function as courts of first appeal and supervisory courts. It must be noted that in the first-half of the year 2020, the DIFC Courts experienced a 96% increase in number of cases as compared to the previous year.

b. ODR services offered in Singapore: Singapore State Courts have opted e – mediation and e – negotiation platforms for providing ODR services. Establishments like, Community Disputes Claims Tribunal (CDCT), Small Claims Tribunal (SCT) and Employment Claims Tribunal (ECT) have opted for providing ODR services to resolve disputes of the public. Singapore State Courts utilizes two ODR mechanisms for dispute redressal, these are:-

I. E-Mediation: A court mediator is appointed to resolve the disputes between the disputants. The tribunal orders for a mediation session between the disputed parties and the appointed mediator only if the parties agree.

II. E-Negotiation: Under the negotiation process, each party gets numerous opportunities to make offers such as, three rounds in matters of small value claims and five in matters of employment related claims. However, if no settlement is reached through the negotiation process then, court-ordered consultation is suggested whereby the disputed parties are required to attend the consultation meeting on the given date and time.

3. PRIVATE ODR PLATFORMS

The Private ODR platforms are established by private enterprises in the private realm.

a. ODR services offered in Canada: The private ODR service provider established in Canada is the Platform to Assist in the Resolution of Litigation Electronically (PARLe) which explicitly deals with consumer disputes.[5] The procedure followed by PARLe requires the consumer and the trader/merchant

---

5   About The Office (PARLe) https://www.opc.gouv.qc.ca/en/opc/parle/ description/

to resolve the dispute by negotiation process on the platform. If no settlement is reached within 20 days then, a mediator is automatically appointed by the platform for resolution.

b. ODR services offered in Europe: In Europe, YOUSTICE is the ODR service provider which also earlier dealt with only consumer disputes but now it has expanded its sphere and has incorporated gambling, travel and car-rental disputes.[6] YOUSTICE follows a two-stage ODR procedure:-

I. On the platform consumers and traders can do direct negotiations.

II. If the disputants fail to resolve the dispute through negotiation process then, they can approach the ADR platform for assigning of a neutral/third party in order to resolve the conflict.

Therefore, it can be concluded that with the evolution of Internet and development in technology, not only the private enterprises but the governments and courts of different states and nations have also contributed in encouraging the utilization of ODR mechanism into the system.

VIABILITY OF ODR IN INDIA DURING COVID-19

Indian courts today are leading the way in adapting and adopting leading practices in an extremely sustainable and forward thinking manner. The pandemic has actually forced a shift towards solutions that minimize contact and can be activated through technology including the resolution of disputes. The unfortunate circumstances have iterated the crucial role of technology in allowing remote, contactless support to daily work roles by flagging its importance to a flat and affordable form of access to justice.

---

6   Homepage (Youstice) https://www.youstice.com/en/

Now if we want to realize the full utility of Online Dispute Resolution, then we must try and explore a much wider spectrum of where it can be used. There are three principles with which the researcher has tried to analyse if that can be achieved:-

(1). Can we make things faster?

In real life about twenty – five percent of the lifecycle of any case is spent just notifying the other parties dispatching documents to the other parties. In a civil trial in a civil court which is about five or six years on an average, roughly one and a half years are spent on just communicating with the other party and sending the other party documents. Now this is one very crucial element where technology can play a huge role.

I. Firstly is on notification of the parties by using technological means of notification by using email or SMS or WhatsApp.

II. In addition to this, we can also use our physical means of delivery but we don't have to use physical means of delivery with the same limitations that are there presently, like using courier with an automated tracking system which automatically stores the records of thing dispatched or delivered on a system can make the process of notifying the other person faster even if in reality it is a physical parcel that is moving from place A to place B.

Therefore, this is one way by which ODR can benefit all.[7]

(2). Can we make things more fair?

Online Dispute Resolution is a process which resolves disputes outside of the court system by combining technology with the mechanisms of Alternative Dispute Resolution. Hence, redressal of disputes through ODR is done online in the cyberspace. Initially, arbitration was held as a substitute to avoid the tiring court system however, with time the process of arbitration itself has

---

7   Vikas Mahendra & Vignesh Raj, Online Dispute Resolution: Potential challenges and the path forward LawSikho https://www.youtube.com/ watch?v=DcjiqYAd4xE

become a complex procedure and it cannot be considered as a cost-efficient mechanism.

With the emergence and practice of Online Dispute Resolution (ODR) the process of arbitration, mediation and negotiation has become faster, as explained above, and transparent. The accessibility of ODR has increased as most of the companies with the emergence of COVID-19 pandemic have added dispute resolution option on their respective websites for high – value to low – value cases. In the past five years, India has seen valuable development within the number of matters related to online transactions, which has made ODR a convenient option for resolution of disputes as an effective mechanism and therefore, execute faster and more fair dispute redressal system.[8]

(3). Can we make things more effective?

ODR has the capacity to build a strong link between the litigants and their way to access justice, however, it also comes with certain limitations and complications which questions its effectiveness and efficiency. Following is the non-exhaustive list of such instances[9]:-

1. In today's world Internet has a greater accessibility; however, people face connectivity issue sometimes because of weather or even his/her geography which obstructs a person from getting online.

2. Most of us use our smartphones primarily to access internet with limited data plans. Certain apps require special applications which are not mobile-

---

8   Online Dispute Resolution (ODR): A Positive Contrivance To Justice Post Covid- 19 - Litigation, Mediation & Arbitration - India (mondaq.com) https://www.mondaq.com/india/arbitration-dispute-resolution/935022/online-dispute-resolution-odr-a-positive-contrivance-to-justice-post-covid-19

9   Katsh, Ethan, and Wing, Leah, Ten Years of Online Dispute Resolution: Looking at the Past and Constructing the Future, 38 University of Toledo Law Review 101 (2006). http://www.ombuds.org/articles/toledo.pdf

friendly and so acts as an obstacle from the perspective of their data usage and design.

3. Confidentiality is the key feature of ODR mechanism. It is somehow difficult to share or submit sensitive information or documents online into the cyberspace as it leaves traces which can lead to breach of trust of the disputed parties. Therefore, an automatic log-off feature must be incorporated in the system or by the ODR service providers on their platforms to maintain confidentiality.

4. Language should not be a barrier to communication at least in the district courts where regional language is allowed for communication. So, the ODR service providers should provide a language selection tab upon their platforms.

5. With our tiring and burdensome court system, emergence of Online Dispute Resolution mechanism has come as a boon to make the system hassle-free. The disputants or litigants who rely and work on hourly or daily wages used to suffer a lot in order to present themselves before the court and lose their day's wage. But with the practice of ODR with the emergence of COVID-19 pandemic, now people can attend hearings in their regular business hours without losing their wages.

6. ODR acts as an effective and efficient mechanism for the disabled individuals and makes them part of the system to resolve their claims and disputes online without facing any inconvenience.

7. The ODR service providers should consider integrating resources such as links and guides to legal aid on their platforms to assist the consumers or disputants in filing cases and resolving their disputes online.

8. Some individuals face problem in navigating technology without assistance and for such users backup systems should be created.[10]

---

10   Resolution Systems Institute (RSI) https://www.aboutrsi.org/special-topics/online-dispute-resolution

The implications of the COVID-19 Pandemic have crawled into every aspect of life together with the justice delivery system. There have been certain instances where the need for ODR mechanism was identified and discussed by the courts. For instance, the current Chief Justice, Justice N.V. Ramana stated that "ODR can be used to successfully resolve consumer, family, business and commercial disputes". He even discussed the need to cut-down on paper and precede with the paper-less methods to save our environment, such as e-filing the documents for the proceedings.

Even the former Chief Justice, Justice S.A. Bobde has noted the need for virtual court hearings in order to avoid the shutdown of the top courts amid coronavirus threat. He also accentuated upon the need of artificial intelligence (AI) and international arbitration as a leading alternative to the current status quo.

Therefore, the intervention of technology in resolving disputes across courts has come under a larger scheme such as, the institution of 'SUVAS' (Supreme Court Vidhik Anuvaad Software) whereby an artificial intelligence translation engine translates judgments from English to Indian languages.

As a matter of fact, in 2019 the divulgence of establishment of formal ODR platform was initiated by the Nilekani panel suggesting the setting up of online dispute resolution platforms to handle complaints arising out of digital payments. The committee recommended that such ODR system should have two levels/stages – one human and one automated, along with a provision related to appeal.

Though India completely awakened after the appearance of COVID-19 crisis to identify the need of paper-less proceedings and the significance of ODR for all times but certain key initiatives were taken before this current situation of pandemic. Also, after the occurrence of COVID-19 pandemic in India the Online Dispute Resolution mechanism took over as a major mode of dispute resolution system and an effective justice delivery system. Recently, in the year 2020 NITI Aayog took an initiative in association with Omidyar Network India and Agami and organised a meeting on "Catalyzing

Online Dispute Resolution in India" where the key stakeholders were brought together to work collaboratively to ensure efforts that shall be taken to scale Online Dispute Resolution (ODR) in India. The handbook for the same was launched on 10th April, 2021 in order to enhance access to justice and mitigate of doing business, as efficient dispute resolution shall be key in reviving the economy from the challenges posed by the COVI-19 pandemic[11].

JUDICIAL APPROACH – The Supreme Court of India has played a crucial role in establishing the foundation of ODR in to the nation. The validity of video-conferencing as a medium of accepting evidence and testimony of witnesses was upheld in the case of State of Maharashtra v. Praful Desai[12] and went on to call "virtual reality the actual reality". In another case of Grid Corporation of Orissa Ltd. v. AES Corporation[13], the court held that if consultation could be attained by remote conferencing and electronic media, it was not needed for people to sit with each other in the same physical space. In another case of Balram Prasad v. Kunal Saha and Ors.[14], the Apex Court upheld the use of video conferencing as a mode to gain the expert opinion of a foreign doctor.

---

11   Deepika Kinhal, Tarika Jain, Vaideshi Misra, Aditya Ranjan, ODR: The Future of Dispute Resolution in India, VIDHI CENTRE FOR LEGAL POLICY, (May11, 2021, 10:09 AM), https://vidhilegalpolicy.in/research/the-future-of-dispute-resolution-in-india/

12   State of Maharashtra v. Praful Desai, (2003) 4 SCC 601

13   Grid Corporation of Orissa Ltd. v. AES Corporation, (2002) 7 SCC 736

14   Balram Prasad v. Kunal Saha and Ors., (2014) 1 SCC (Civ) 327

In another case of Central Electricity Regulatory Commission v. National Hydroelectric Power Corporation Ltd[15], the apex court held that service of summons can be done via email along with various other means. Further, in the case of Kross Television India Pvt Ltd v. Vikhyat Chitra Production[16], the Bombay High Court has permitted the use of WhatsApp for the purpose of serving summons.

Furthermore, the Supreme Court of India in the case of M/S Meters and Instruments Pvt. Ltd. v. Kanchan Mehta[17], recognized that complete reliance could be surfaced upon technology for the purpose of resolving disputes. It was also noted that certain cases can be settled 'online' by utilizing electronic mechanisms which consequently makes the process hassle free.

With the absence of legislative framework for the practice of mediation, so for the first time the Supreme Court of India in the landmark case of Salem Advocate Bar Association v. Union of India[18], took a stand for mediation which consequently made the courts to recognize this specific means of ADR mechanism which made "court – annexed mediation" a thing which can generally be seen in the Indian Courts. This was upheld in the famous case of Afcons Infrastructure Ltd. v. Cherian Varkey Construction Co. (P)

---

15   Central Electricity Regulatory Commission v. National Hydroelectric Power Corporation Ltd., (2010) 10 SCC 280

16   Kross Television India Pvt Ltd v. Vikhyat Chitra Production, 2017 SCC OnLine Bom 1433

17   M/S Meters and Instruments Pvt Ltd v. Kanchan Mehta, 2017 (4) RCR (Criminal) 476

18   ODR: The Future of Dispute Resolution in India (vidhilegalpolicy.in) https://vidhilegalpolicy.in/research/the-future-of-dispute-resolution-in-india/

Salem Advocate Bar Association v. Union of India, AIR 2005 SC 3353

Ltd.[19], whereby it was held that equal recognition must be given to the ADR mechanisms as given to the traditional legal procedure, to which the Supreme Court of India determined certain kinds of matters whereby ADR can be utilized in resolving disputes, these are:-

- Matters in relation to contracts

- Matters in relation to trade and commerce

- Matters in relation to matrimonial disputes

- Matters in relation to petty cases such as, traffic challan, etc.

- Matters in relation to consumer disputes

LEGISLATIVE APPROACH – In the case of Shakti Bhog v. Kola Shipping[20], it was held that an online arbitration agreement is valid until it is in compliance with Sections 4 and 5 of the Information Technology Act, 2008 read with Section 65B of the Indian Evidence Act, 1872[21].

The above case shows that the present legislative framework of India can be utilized and followed to implement the practice of online dispute resolution mechanism. Apart from the Indian legislative provisions such as Section 65B of the Indian Evidence Act, 1872 and Sections 4, 5 10-A & 11-15 of the Information Technology Act[22] which grants recognition to digital signatures

---

19   ODR: The Future of Dispute Resolution in India (vidhilegalpolicy.in) https://vidhilegalpolicy.in/research/the-future-of-dispute-resolution-in-india/

Afcons Infrastructure Ltd. v. Cherian Varkey Construction Co. (P) Ltd., (2010) 8 SCC 24

20   Shakti Bhog v. Kola Shipping, (2009) 2 SCC 134

21   Indian Evidence Act, 1872, No. 1, Acts of Parliament, 1872 (India)

22   Information Technology Act, 2000, No. 21, Acts of Parliament, 2000 (India)

to enable the validity of online contracts, the UNCITRAL Model Law on Electronic Commerce in 1996 and the Model Law on Electronic Signatures in 2001 granted certain provisions which enhances the applicability of ODR mechanism into Indian legislature framework by making India adopt these Model Laws[23].

Further, in the case of M.R. Krishna Murthi v. The New India Assurance Co. Ltd.[24], the Apex Court noted that there is a requirement of legislation in relation to mediation for the purpose of strengthening its process in the nation.

SCOPE OF ODR IN INDIA'S FUTURE

The implications of the COVID-19 crisis have already extended to plague the justice delivery system. One of the greatly admired answers in this regard ODR. ODR is considered as the future of the traditional ADR. In the course of COVID-19 pandemic, courts as well as arbitral tribunals have been taking up cases through video conferencing[25].

ODR is already pervasive in the sphere of International Commercial Arbitration, which is applicable when the concerned parties reside in different nations. Even the testimony of witnesses and the recording of evidences are

---

23   Deepika Kinhal, Tarika Jain, Vaideshi Misra, Aditya Ranjan, ODR: The Future of Dispute Resolution in India, VIDHI CENTRE FOR LEGAL POLICY, (October11, 2021, 10:09 AM), https://vidhilegalpolicy.in/research/the-future-of-dispute-resolution-in-india/

24   M.R. Krishna Murthi v. The New India Assurance Co. Ltd., Civil Appeal No. 2476-2477 of 2019

25   WHITE CODE VIA MEDIATION AND ARBITRATION CENTRE, https://viamediationcentre.org/readnews/OTEy/Scope-of-ODR-In-India, (last visited July 12, 2021)

also done through the use of digital media by doing video conferencing in the case of international commercial arbitration. Thus, implementation of ODR with the occurrence of COVID-19 crisis has grown widely.

Therefore, ODR's viability in India can be seen blooming after the appearance of this COVID-19 Pandemic. This is the correct time to upgrade the already existing laws so that a uniform procedure can be laid down for the purpose of virtual hearing[26].

There is a necessity of a detailed handbook or guideline for the application of the ODR mechanism by widening its region. This will eradicate the difficulties that are faced by lawyers while opting for online dispute resolution. As it is seen that under arbitration mainly document based process is followed, whereby opting for ODR will definitely relieve the stress upon the parties as well as the arbitrator to travel all the way to talk out the things.

There is no ambiguity in that all these mechanisms of traditional ADR require recourse to technology advancement and further technological updates and upgrades shall be done. Although people have become habitual of the offline and physical process of getting justice, this may take some time to embrace the pros of ODR mechanism and using ODR platforms to resolve disputes at cost-effective and convenient manner.

---

26   Nilava Bandhopadhyay, India: Future of Litigation And ADR in India-Post COVID-19, MONDAQ CONNECTING KNOWLEDGE & PEOPLE, (October 12, 2021, 10:07 PM), https://www.mondaq.com/india/arbitration-dispute-resolution/1046078/future-of-litigation-and-adr-in-india-post-covid-19-

CONCLUSION & SUGGESTIONS

CONCLUSION:

ODR has now become the "new normal" which also seems to be the future and its usage has been encouraged majorly with the emergence of the COVID-19 pandemic around the globe which would palpably leave a huge impact upon the legal health of the court system post pandemic. It is a human tendency to resist change as they think that if they will allow the occurring changes then they might lose something valuable, in the same way people have faced difficulty in adapting the change of opting for Online Dispute Resolution mechanism instead of reaching courts physically and experience personal touch with face-to-face interaction. However, in the last two years some crucial alterations have been seen and experienced by the public at large because of the pandemic, that is, there has been a greater use of Internet across the globe, in order to follow the social – distancing norms, to resolve disputes which seem to be par for the course.

Till now people are not aware of ADR and ODR mechanisms and what advantages they come with. If these mechanisms can be properly encouraged, it would certainly allay the burden of the judicial system. Therefore, the Online Dispute Resolution mechanism can assuredly be utilized as a popular means for dispute resolution[27].

Therefore, it can be concluded from the above discussion that the objective of alternative dispute resolution mechanisms is not only to reduce the stress of the courts but to make a healthier legal system where disputed parties can resolve their disputes with quick and cost – efficient process. Albeit, the

---

27   Online Dispute Resolution System- A way toward hassle free dispute resolution and a road into the future - iPleaders https://blog.ipleaders.in/odr/#Procedures_adopted_for_ODR

development in the utilization of Online Dispute Resolution has taken place with the emergence of the COVID-19 pandemic across the world, when the world is following social – distancing norms and is under lockdown, but people require to resolve their claims and conflicts anyway, this is where the Online Dispute Resolution mechanism comes into the picture. This mechanism not only makes the process hassle free but also effective and efficient. At the same time it has certain limitations but if they are cured and tackle then, this could be the best mode for resolving disputes and making the legal system healthier.[28]

SUGGESTIONS:

In the light of the above study and conclusion drawn from it and there could be certain steps for the improvement in the structural issues as well as on how the implementation of certain provisions should be incorporated. Therefore, following are certain suggestions which have been made to make the law regarding Online Dispute Resolution more effective:-

1. The first and the foremost step which should be taken by the government of any nation or state is to entail a definition to the term "Online Dispute Resolution (ODR)" according to one's legislative structure. The definition must be so strong that no one can in the future be able to question upon it by filing suits in the courts. Ambiguity in such a definition will affect the whole process and thus, it must be interpreted the same by each and every person. In a nation like India where from lower courts to the apex court in aggregate 3.5 crores cases are pending, the acceptance of Online Dispute Resolution mechanism will only lessen the burden of the judicial system and will additionally assist them in resolving the disputes at a faster pace.[29]

---

28   Concept of Online Dispute Resolution and its scope (legaldesire.com) https:// legaldesire.com/concept-of-online-dispute-resolution-and-its-scope/

29   nline Dispute Resolution and Arbitration: Is India ready for change? (thearbitrationworkshop.com) https://www.thearbitrationworkshop.com/post/online-

2. In addition to the above – mentioned suggestion, making ODR an efficient, effective and lucrative process would require a focal or national governing authority whose primary objective would be promotion of ODR to a great extent. The qualities that must be possessed by such governing body are:-

(a). The authority should act as an official certification body which will recognize the organizations to serve as an Online Dispute Resolution Service Provider. This kind accreditation will assist the governing or focal authority in recognizing the bodies which are legitimate from those which are not recognized by such authority.

(b). A uniform set of rules should be framed by the governing authority related to substantial and procedural laws in a particular country.

For the above – mentioned purpose one can look into the Technical Notes adopted by the UNCITRAL Model which contours suggestions related to the governing of Online Dispute Resolution at global level.

(c). The question related to the credibility of awards given by such Online Dispute Resolution Service Providers lingers on. However, with the establishment of focal or governing authority will provide the users with such credibility of awards which will build trust amongst its users. This will make the award legally binding upon the disputed parties.

(d). With the establishment of a focal authority on ODR, a bridge or a linkage can be formed between the judicial system and the alternative dispute resolution mechanisms or platforms which will regulate all the proceedings by keeping track of the same.

3. Furthermore, a suggestion which should be considered is that after the passing of awards by the ODR Service Providers they must be considered for their enforcement by developing proper enforcement mechanisms or bodies. This scenario can be explained by WIPO's UDRP Process which is one of the most popular existing Online Dispute Resolution mechanisms, whereby the

---

dispute-resolution-and-arbitration-is-india-ready-for-change

disputed parties are not only consider such awards as legally binding but also consider those for enforcement. Therefore, a central legislation should be formed in every country to regulate Online Dispute Resolution mechanisms properly.

4. Apart from the formulation of central legislation in countries, an international treaty must also be considered for formulation in order to regulate the Online Dispute Resolution mechanisms across the globe, especially in international arbitration cases. The signatory or member countries of such international treaty would require them to follow the guidelines issued under such treaty and implement the same. Such treaty must not only allow the disputants to file fresh matters but should also offer appellate powers so that the parties could have recourse to such appellate forum. Moreover, the decisions made under such treaty should be considered as final and binding in nature.[30]

5. In order to have a viable ODR mechanism it must fulfil two pre-requisites – fair play and due process. There should not be any kind of favouritism be done any participating user or party. Prevention of bias must be done. Also, the Neutrals must be well qualified and trained to commence the meetings online.[31]

6. Confidentiality is the key concern in the proceedings which are conducted online. This requires a stringent standard of security and surveillance rules to keep track of the sensitive documents, information or data uploaded on the online platforms. In regard to this, digital signatures play a crucial role by serving majorly two purposes, these are:-

---

30   Microsoft Word - Dispute Resolution Bulletin - Issue V.doc (psalegal.com) https://psalegal.com/wp-content/uploads/2017/01/Dispute-Resolution-Bulletin-Issue-V01072010113348AM.pdf

31   ibid

(a). Primarily, the digital signatures provide security by encrypting sensitive data or document or information uploaded on such platforms during their transmission.

(b). The authenticity of such data or document or information received by the receiver on the other end which can be maintained through digital signatures.[32]

Therefore, the traditional legal system has formed its mainstay which has been taken over by ADR mechanisms to some extent only till now. However, ODR had not achieved the same until the emergence of COVID-19 pandemic across the world, especially in India. Most of the countries have initiated to adopt ODR into their legal procedure the notion of ODR through video-conferencing and online chats. If ADR and ODR are compared for instance then, ODR might win the battle as it is less time consuming since it cut downs the travel time completely. In addition to this, it is cost – efficient to a greater extent which makes the process more effective and considered as one of the best economical means of dispute resolution.

BIBLIOGRAPHY

BARE ACTS:

- The Arbitration and Conciliation Act, 1996
- The Arbitration and Conciliation (Amendment) Act, 2019
- The UNCITRAL Arbitration Rules, 1976
- The UNICITRAL Notes on Arbitral Proceedings, 2016

---

32   Udaan - B2B Buying for Retailers https://udaan.com/

Books

- Katsh, E.E., Katsh, M.E. and Rifkin, J., 2001. Online dispute resolution: Resolving conflicts in cyberspace. John Wiley & Sons, Inc..

- Dr. Venkateshwarlu N., Law Relating to Online Dispute Resolution in India (Theory And Practice), SCJ Publications.

Miscellaneous Sources:

- UNCITRAL Technical Notes on ODR

- WIPO's online case administration tools (WIPO eADR)

- NITI Aayog's draft report "Designing the Future of Dispute Resolution: The ODR Policy Plan for India"

Web Sources:

- https://www.aboutrsi.org/special-topics/online-dispute-resolution

- https://blog.ipleaders.in/odr/#Procedures_adopted_for_ODR

- https://lk-k.com/wp-content/uploads/Online-Dispute-Resolution-and-Its-Significance-for-International-Commercial-Arbitration.pdf

- https://www.intechopen.com/chapters/61440

- http://egyankosh.ac.in/bitstream/123456789/7639/1/Unit-12.pdf

- https://www.niti.gov.in/

- https://legaldesire.com/concept-of-online-dispute-resolution-and-its-scope/

THE ROLE OF ARTIFICIAL INTELLIGENT AS A RISK ASSESSMENT TOOL: THE CHALLENGES AND SOLUTION

Author:

Golda Sahoo

ABSTRACT

Artificial intelligence has proven capable of fixing many of the world's most urgent concerns and enhancing our daily lives during the last few decades. One of the most well-known applications of AI is in the criminal justice system, which now can assess a defendant's risk and assist judges in formulating sentencing judgments. COMPAS and PSA are the most widely used risk/needs assessment tools today. Compustat can forecast an offender's recidivism rate, risk of violent recidivism, and failure to appear in court based on a variety of data factors.

Unlike COMPAS, PSA makes decisions without taking into account factors like socio-economic status or self-efficacy. According to a study undertaken by Stanford University and the University of California at Berkeley, risk assessment technologies are far superior to people at clarifying the complexities of the criminal justice system and making more accurate judgements. In certain tests, they were approximately 90 percent accurate, whereas in humans, they were only about 60 percent correct. The big question, however, is whether AI tools can assist judges in making decisions that are nearly 100 percent accurate and free of human bias.Furthermore, whether AI should be held to a greater degree of transparency than human decision-making must be determined. Judges who use the technology are unable to adequately assess its benefits and downsides since algorithms are cloaked in secret and it is impossible to explain their thinking. Understandably, concerns regarding AI's inherent bias have arisen as a result of its usage in criminal justice. Many sentencing choices can be biassed or influenced by unrelated circumstances due to human biases, variability, and differences in opinion, resulting in inadvertently unjust consequences. Furthermore, each judge has their own favoured style of sentencing; some favour parole, while others prefer to give prisoners extra time in prison for specific crimes. Indeed, a variety of "irrelevant" factors can influence judges' choices, resulting in less-than-just outcomes. This is related to their own beliefs about the efficacy of various punishment and rehabilitation methods. Artificially intelligent algorithms to help judges in determining sentencing judgments could be one answer to this bias. The higher the risk rating, the more likely it is that the offender will commit the same offence again. Indeed, a variety of "irrelevant" factors can influence judges' choices, resulting in less-than-just outcomes. This is related to their own beliefs about the efficacy of various punishment and rehabilitation methods. Artificially intelligent algorithms to help judges in determining sentencing judgments could be one answer to this bias. The higher the risk rating, the more likely it is that the offender will commit the same offence again.

The paper begins by highlighting how AI is used in the criminal justice system, as well as where and how AI tools might make a difference. It then goes on to examine the challenges of transparency and bias associated with AI applications. Finally, the author proposed a number of solutions for dealing with the issues.

INTRODUCTION

Artificial intelligence has proven capable of fixing many of the world's most urgent concerns and enhancing our daily lives during the last few decades. One of the most well-known applications of AI is in the criminal justice system, which now can assess a defendant's risk and assist judges in formulating sentencing judgments. AI has a positive impact on public safety and criminal justice. AI is also assisting in determining the likelihood of a person under criminal justice supervision reoffending.1 NIJ-funded research is paving the path for AI to be used in criminal justice applications, such as recognising people and their behaviours in recordings involving criminal activity or public safety, DNA analysis, gunshot detection, and crime prediction.

Artificial intelligence (AI) is one of the fast developing areas of computer science. During the mid-1950s, John McCarthy, who is known as the "Father of AI," defined AI as "the science and engineering of constructing intelligent machines." [1] At its core, AI is a machine's capacity to independently study and react to its environment, as well as perform activities that would usually require human intelligence for decision-making processes, but at the same time, without any direct human involvement. There is a possibility of human error due to exhaustion and various other factors. But unlike human beings, machines never get tired. Through some research projects like the Intelligence Advanced Research Projects Activity's Janus computer-vision project, analysts are able to test algorithms that can learn to recognise one human being from another using facial features in the same manner that a human analyst can.[2]

---

1   http://facebookhinthelp.blogspot.com/2018/10/what-is-artificial-intelligence-ai-what.html

2   https://www.networkworld.com/article/2225788/us-intelligence-wants-to-radically-advance-facial-recognition-software.html

APPLICATIONS FOR CRIMINAL JUSTICE AND PUBLIC SAFETY

On a daily basis, we interact with algorithms that forecast and inform our activities throughout time. Algorithms and predictive models in criminal justice, on the other hand, have the potential to change someone's life. When an algorithm introduces prejudice into the criminal justice system, it might result in unjust arrests and convictions. As a public safety resource, AI is being researched in a variety of ways. In a typical law enforcement application, a photo of an individual of interest would be run by a facial recognition system, which is capable of searching massive databases in a few seconds. In recent years, the excellence of facial recognition technologies has skyrocketed. In government tests, facial recognition algorithms were compared to a database of 1.6 million mug pictures. The algorithm usually proceeds to a score indicating how much similarity the image displayed is to one or more of the database images. Investigators were looking for people who were unable to identify themselves, such as Alzheimer's patients and murder victims. The technology is highly effective in helping to recognise witnesses.

BACKGROUND OF RISK/NEEDS ASSESSMENT TOOLS

WHAT IS RISK ASSESSMENT AND WHY IS IT SO IMPORTANT IN THE CRIMINAL JUSTICE SYSTEM?

One of the most essential principles in criminal justice is recidivism. It is a convicted criminal's proclivity to reoffend.[3] Pretrial risk assessments, according to a recent quasi-experimental study, can help maximise pretrial release while decreasing misconduct. [4]Courts and review boards (such as parole boards) seeking an answer to this topic frequently seek the advice of criminal justice or mental health specialists, whose choices influence both individual liberty and public safety. On the other hand, unstructured professional risk judgments that are based purely on a professional's competence are usually incorrect. In reality, a 1981 study found that psychiatrists' projections about the danger of future violent behaviour by mentally ill offenders released into the community were only true in around one out of every three cases.[5] Research found that many sentencing choices can be biassed or influenced by unrelated circumstances due to human biases, variabilities, and differences in

---

3   https://nij.ojp.gov/topics/corrections/recidivism#:~:text=It%20 refers%20to%20a%20person's,intervention%20for%20a%20previous%20 crime.&text=Recidivism%20is%20an%20important%20feature,incapacitation%2C%20specific%20deterrence%20and%20rehabilitation.

4   https://tnjconsulting.net.au/a-historical-overview-of-the-risk-assessment-tools-utilised-in-the-criminal-justice-system/

5   https://www.ncbi.nlm.nih.gov/pmc/articles/PMC2686644/

opinion, resulting in inadvertently unjust consequences.[6] One study found that judges were giving fewer sentences and forgiving the sentence choices early in the morning and shortly after lunchtime. But in the last part of the day and shortly before their breaks, they were considerably more likely to issue heavier sentences. This is only one example of how an absolutely arbitrary aspect can influence a judge's sentencing decision (the time of day of the trial). Indeed, a variety of "irrelevant" factors can influence judges' choices, resulting in less-than-just outcomes. For example, because judges can have drastically different viewpoints, a sentence that appears fair and impartial to one judge may appear ludicrous to another. Furthermore, each judge has their own preferred style of sentencing: some may favour parole, while others prefer to give prisoners additional time in prison for specific crimes. This is related to their own beliefs about the efficacy of various forms of punishment as well as rehabilitation methods. As a result, a sentence can differ dramatically depending on which judge is sentencing them. As a result, academics have focused their efforts on building and upgrading structured risk assessment techniques in order to improve risk prediction accuracy. Artificially intelligent as an effective tool to help the judge in determining sentencing judgments could be one answer to this bias. One of the most common applications of AI in the profession is in risk and needs assessment tools, which are algorithms that use the data about an offender to determine their likelihood of recidivism. [7]If the risk is higher than the rating, the more likely it is that the offender will commit the same offence again.

---

6   https://link.springer.com/article/10.1007/s11896-020-09425-8

7   https://www.eff.org/files/2018/12/21/ai_policy_issues_handout.pdf

WHAT RISK ASSESSMENT TOOL WORKS?

An algorithm is used to make a choice or to deliver information to a human decision-maker. It is possible for an algorithmic tool to be as simple as "Complete a questionnaire." Count how many "Yes" responses there are. If the value exceeds a certain threshold, perform X. Otherwise, carry out Y. "These forecasts help judges make high-stakes choices like whether or not to imprison someone before their trial. The Public Safety Assessment (PSA),[8] for example, evaluates an individual's age and history of misconduct, as well as other characteristics, to generate three risk scores:The possibility of being convicted of a new crime,The possibility of being convicted of a new brutal crime, and The possibility of failing to appear in court.The abovementioned risk scores are translated into conditions for release recommended by a supervisory framework, with higher scores for risk equating to tougher release criteria. If these guidelines appear to be excessively stringent or too lax, judges can dismiss them. Other RAIs have an impact on a large range of judicial decisions, including sentencing, parole, and probation.

For about a century, risk assessment tools have been used to minimise the number of offenders confined with a low risk of recidivism, which enables the judicial system to aid and sentence offenders as effectively as possible. AI, on the other hand, was not enlisted until 1998. The application of AI for this purpose represents a considerable advancement over earlier risk/needs assessment methods, which are typically comprised of questionnaires and interviews. But unfortunately, they were less trustworthy since the data they generated couldn't be examined as effectively or objectively as the AI-enabled, fourth-generation tools could.

Risk assessment instruments, which are known as "RAIs," are a type of computational tool that is used to forecast a defendant's future

---

8   https://pixelplex.io/blog/artificial-intelligence-criminal-justice-system/

criminalization.[9] These forecasts help judges make high-stakes choices like whether or not to imprison someone before trial. For instance, the public safety assessment evaluates the individual's history of misconduct, age, as well as various other grounds, to generate 3 risk scores, such as the risk of being convicted of any new crime, the risk of being convicted of a new violent crime, and the risk of failing to appear in court. These risk scores are translated into release-condition recommendations by the decision-making body, with higher scores for risk equating to tougher release criteria. If these guidelines appear to be excessively stringent or too lax, judges can dismiss them.

THE RAI COMPANY

RAIs have grown in popularity as they spread across the country, but they have also sparked controversy. RAIs have been criticised for four key reasons: lack of personalization, lack of openness on the issue relating to trade-secret claims, potential bias, and issues about their genuine impact. Many of these issues were addressed in the 2016 Wisconsin case Loomis v. Wisconsin.[10] The petitioner, Eric Loomis, raised various points in his sentencing decision against the use of a RAI. It is called "Correctional Offender Management Profiling for Alternative Sanctions" (COMPAS).

The first claim of Loomis was that sentencing was not tailored to him. In addition, he also claimed it was influenced by COMPAS' assessment of prior group misbehaviour patterns.But the court did not agree, claiming that the judgement delivered was not exclusively based on COMPAS, thereby circumventing Loomis' worries about personalization. Despite the court's merit, it's important to remember that algorithms and humans both learn from past conduct. As a result, whether from a judge or a RAI, a risk estimate for a

---

9   https://core.ac.uk/download/pdf/159571612.pdf

10   https://harvardlawreview.org/2017/03/state-v-loomis/

specific individual is based on the prior behaviour of comparable individuals. Second, Loomis claimed that the COMPAS creators refused to provide enough information about how the particular algorithm determined the score relating to risk and thus preclude him from analysing the correctness of all of the material provided at the time of his sentencing.[11] Various RAIs can describe how they make decisions, giving them an advantage over humans. On the other hand, commercial RAI providers frequently hide all this information behind their claim of trade-secret. Although the court did not totally agree with Loomis, deciding that simply watching COMPAS'[12] inputs and outputs was sufficient. Despite the fact that Loomis was uninformed of the model's full structure, he was aware that it included factors such as gender, which he argued was discriminatory. Impending discrimination in RAI

A risk assessment tool AIs have also been accused of discrimination, with critics claiming that they can worsen and perpetuate existing biases in the criminal justice system. As we've seen, prejudice is the most important ethical problem when employing AI as a risk/needs assessment tool in criminal justice. In AI, bias can be introduced in a variety of ways. The AI must be fed training data if it is a neural network. If an AI intends to discriminate, As we've seen, prejudice is the most important ethical problem when employing AI as a risk/needs assessment tool in criminal justice. The most famous accusation was made in a 2016 ProPublica report about the usage of COMPAS in Broward County, Florida, in conjunction with pretrial detention decisions. COMPAS was shown to be biassed since it performed worse for black people on one measure of performance, which is false positive cases when compared to white people. [13]Other academics, on the other hand, have pointed out a

---

11   https://www.lexisnexis.com/community/casebrief/p/casebrief-state-v-loomis

12   https://pixelplex.io/blog/artificial-intelligence-criminal-justice-system/

13   https://epic.org/issues/ai/ai-in-the-criminal-justice-system/

significant statistical problem in ProPublica's findings.[14] Through AI it is also possible to identify the criminogenic requirements of criminals who may be helped to reform through specific therapy. An innovative practise found in Finnish prisons is that AI training algorithms are used in the inmate training programme. Inmates are required to respond to simple questions or analyse content acquired from social media and the internet at large. These activities send information to Vainu, a corporation that carries out prison work and provides inmates with new employable skills that can assist them reintegrate into society once their terms are completed.Risk assessment systems outperform people at clarifying the complexities of the criminal justice system and making more correct judgements, according to a study done by Stanford University and the University of California at Berkeley.[15] When a larger number of factors are involved, however, algorithms usually outperform people. In other tests, they were nearly 90% accurate in predicting which offenders were likely to be arrested again. Humans, on the other hand, achieved only a 60% accuracy rate.[16] Despite the controversy that surrounds algorithm-based tools, research studies have proven that risk assessment methods produce more accurate and precise outcomes than human judgement in circumstances matching genuine criminal justice settings.[17]

---

14   https://arxiv.org/abs/1906.04711

15   https://news.berkeley.edu/2020/02/14/algorithms-are-better-than-people-in-predicting-recidivism-study-says/

16   https://www.ncbi.nlm.nih.gov/pmc/articles/PMC7041896/

17   https://journals.sagepub.com/doi/full/10.1177/1477370819876762

TRANSPARENCY CONSIDERATIONS

Individuals' rights to know how artificial intelligence and algorithms perform must be resolved with corporations' rights to secure both the data and material in order for AI to be used in an effective manner in the criminal justice system. Furthermore, whether AI should be held to a greater degree of transparency than human decision-making must be determined. Neural networks, a type of advanced AI, operate as a "black-box system," which implies that the AI's creators do not fully comprehend how it makes judgments.[18] No one knows exactly what happens inside the box.[19] It's a complicated system that learns from data, but we have no idea how it evaluates the data to make decisions.At the same time, judges who use this technology are unable to adequately appraise its benefits and downsides since algorithms are cloaked in secret and it is impossible to explain their thinking. If judges depend too much on these algorithms without understanding their functioning, they may end up making far more biased conclusions than they would if they worked in a more traditional manner. Bail is established, penalties are determined, and even guilt or innocence determinations are aided by these frequently patented processes. The underlying functioning of these technologies, however, is mostly hidden from view, which means two people charged with the same crime may obtain drastically different bail or sentencing outcomes depending on factors outside their control, and they have no method of evaluating or disputing the decisions.

Criminal justice algorithms have come under increased attention as they have become more widely used at the federal and state levels. "Risk assessment" tools have been criticised by several criminal justice specialists as being opaque, unreliable, and unconstitutional.Because they are unable to

---

18   https://www.technologyreview.com/2017/11/07/67713/new-research-aims-to-solve-the-problem-of-ai-bias-in-black-box-algorithms/

19   https://epic.org/issues/ai/ai-in-the-criminal-justice-system/

question the legitimacy of the results at sentencing hearings, defence activists are advocating for more transparent techniques. Professor Danielle Citron says that the public cannot complain to government authorities because it has no way of identifying problems with dysfunctional systems. As a result, government actors are powerless to sway policy.[20] In the last few years, notable organisations like the Pretrial Justice Institute (PJI) have pushed for the use of these risk assessment tools, as well as the Public Safety Assessment, among other risk assessments. In February 2020, however, the Pretrial Justice Institute changed its mind, claiming that "pretrial risk assessment technologies,[21] aimed to forecast an individual's arrival in court without a new arrest, can no longer be a component of our strategy for constructing equitable pretrial justice systems." After a week, the Laura and John Arnold Foundation's Public Safety Assessment, a commonly used risk assessment, issued a statement clarifying that "implementing an assessment cannot and will not result in the pretrial justice goals we aspire to achieve."[22] With pre-trial risk evaluations, transparency is rarely required. One of the most common critiques levelled at these risk assessment tools is that they are proprietary, produced by technology firms that refuse to reveal the inner workings of the "black box."[23] Demands for the underlying logic of the systems have been met with trade secret and other IP protection responses. Idaho was the first state to pass legislation emphasising more accountability, explainability, and transparency in pre-trial

---

20   https://parliament.vic.gov.au/images/EMC/35.b_Attachment_1_-_Kofi_ Annan_Commission_Issues_Paper_-_Democracy_and_the_Internet_Redacted.pdf

21   https://thecrimereport.org/2020/02/18/are-pretrial-risk-assessments- biased-the-debate-sharpens/

22   https://craftmediabucket.s3.amazonaws.com/uploads/PDFs/3-Predictive- Utility-Study.pdf

23   https://www.technologyreview.com/2017/11/07/67713/new-research-aims- to-solve-the-problem-of-ai-bias-in-black-box-algorithms/

risk assessment tools in March 2019. The law prohibits defendants from using trade secrets or intellectual property as a defence and requires public access to "all documents, data, records, and information used by the builder to build or validate the pretrial risk assessment tool."

THE DIRECTIVES OF ARTIFICIAL INTELLIGENCE

The European Union and supranational organisations such as IEEE, OECD, and others are establishing AI legislative and policy frameworks. In between 2016 and 2019, a slew of AI Ethics Guidelines were released in an effort to maintain social control over the technology. The three main concerns addressed by AI legislation and regulations and safety issues are: governance of autonomous intelligence systems, responsibility and accountability for the systems, and privacy. [24]The Universal Guidelines for Artificial Intelligence are a set of twelve human-rights-based principles aimed at influencing AI design, development, and deployment, as well as regulatory and legal frameworks.

The guidelines cover the following rights and responsibilities, such as 1. Transparency is a legal requirement. Everyone has the right to know why every AI decision that impacts them was made. This entails knowing the factors, rationale, and techniques that led to the outcome. 2. Human Beings' Right to Self-Determination. Every person has the right to a person's final decision. Requirement for Identification No. 3 The true operator of an AI system must be known to the general audience. 4. Obligation to Accountability Institutions must be held responsible for AI-based decisions. 5. It is a legal requirement to be fair. Institutions must ensure that judgments are accurate, dependable, legitimate, and repeatable. For data input into algorithms, institutions must assure data provenance, quality, and relevance. Data collected for AI

---

24   https://www.europarl.europa.eu/RegData/etudes/STUD/2020/634452/ EPRS_STU(2020)634452_EN.pdf

processing must not be used for purposes other than those for which it was originally collected. obligation to protect the public. Institutions must evaluate the threats to public safety posed by AI systems that direct or control physical equipment. Cybersecurity is a legal requirement. Institutions must safeguard AI systems against cyberattacks. The use of secret profiling is prohibited. No institution is allowed to create or keep a hidden profile on a person. National scoring is prohibited. No national authority has the authority to assign a score to its citizens or to keep track of where they live. Termination obligation.If an institution that has built an AI system loses control of the system, it has an affirmative commitment to terminate the system. These principles can also be applied to the employment of algorithms in the area of pre-trial risk. RAIs are just one of the algorithmic tools being considered right now. The usage of different algorithms poses its own set of problems. Specifically, in their use of facial recognition, public DNA databases, and other modern forms of surveillance, criminal justice authorities must explain how they propose to respect individual privacy and liberty.However, if utilised correctly and cautiously, algorithms can significantly improve the impact of decisions, making them more consistent and transparent to all stakeholders. These initiatives, like any new policy or practise, must include ongoing review and improvement to ensure that their implementation results in effective and equitable outcomes over time.

A WAY FORWARD

In 1976, Joseph Weizenbaum [25]suggested that AI should not be used to replace people in jobs that demand respect and care, such as Judge, police officer,soldier,Therapist customer service representatives (AI technology is already used today for telephone-based interactive voice response systems).

---

25   Weizenbaum, Joseph (1976). Computer Power and Human Reason. San Francisco: W.H. Freeman & Company. ISBN 978-0-7167-0464-5.

Weizenbaum adds that people in these positions must have genuine feelings of empathy. We will be alienated, devalued, and disappointed if machines replace us, because an artificially intelligent system will be unable to replicate empathy. Artificial intelligence poses a threat to human dignity if exploited in this manner. Weizenbaum claims that the fact that we are considering machines in these roles indicates that we have suffered an "atrophy of the human soul" as a result of thinking of ourselves as computers. [26]Pamela McCorduck replies that, speaking for women and minorities, "I'd rather take my chances with an unbiased computer," noting that there are times when we would prefer to have automated judges and police officers with no personal agenda.[27] On the other hand, Kaplan and Haenlein emphasise that "AI systems are just as smart as the data used to train them, as they are essentially fancy curve-fitting machines. Using AI to support a court ruling can be extremely problematic if previous rulings have shown bias toward certain groups, as those biases become formalised and engrained, making them even more difficult to spot and combat.[28]" The moralising tone of Weizenbaum's assessment irritates AI inventor John McCarthy. He argues, "When moralising is both vehement and ambiguous, it encourages authoritarian misuse." "Human dignity implies that we seek to erase our ignorance about the nature of life, and AI is crucial for that quest," asserts Bill Hibbard.[29]

Humans and machines can both be skewed in the end. Two people can have completely different interpretations and view points of the law and different

---

26   Joseph Weizenbaum, quoted in McCorduck 2004, pp. 356, 374–376

27   supra

28   https://www.nytimes.com/2019/04/14/technology/china-surveillance-artificial-intelligence-racial-profiling.html

29   Hibbard, Bill (17 November 2015). "Ethical Artificial Intelligence". arXiv:1411.1373

viewpoints on how a crime should be punished. Because of the data they are given and how they perceive it, algorithms are biassed. Fundamentally, these two types of biases are not the same. AI bias is a computational inaccuracy caused by a component of the very human bias that they are supposed to eliminate.

Human bias can be defined as various people applying diverse interpretations of the law to accomplish justice in the way they deem fit. However, when we examine the facts, we can discover that what appears to be a healthy judicial system is actually made up of individuals who fail to be consistent in their choices or who fail to distinguish their personal beliefs from the impartiality and reason necessary for a successful judge. It's vital to realise that human decision-making isn't going to get much better any time soon, whereas AI is constantly improving. We're figuring out how to remove bias from our algorithms in a way that's impossible to achieve in our heads.Anyone who is taking into consideration the effective application of algorithms in criminal justice should keep these problems in mind while developing policies that rely on algorithms, especially those that guide the decision-making process.

Firstly, governments must defend human control and exercise prudence when using machine learning algorithms. Unexpected circumstances could always alter an individual's likelihood of misbehaviour in the context of RAIs. As a result, a judge ought to have the authority to override a RAI's suggestions, even if this may compromise accuracy and consistency. One way to reconcile these competing aims when a judge deviates from a RAI recommendation is to require a long explanation. This would urge judges to make decisions based on conscious motivations and would make arbitrary violations of RAI principles illegal. In broad-spectrum, humans must make the final judgment, with any differences require a reason and some attempt on the judge's behalf.

Secondly, any algorithm used in a high-stakes policy situation, such as criminal sentencing, should be transparent. This has a particular advantage over human decision-making procedures in that everyone involved can see how a risk assessment is made. Transparency may aid in the development of confidence in this way, and it recognises the relevance of these instruments in making critical judgement.

Thirdly, the algorithms and the data which are to be used to predic future criminality should be extensively scrutinised for the danger of injuring any specific group unfairly. The prosecutors, Judges, and data scientists ought to examine every piece of the data fitted to an algorithm, mostly the expected consequences, to discover if the data is biassed against any one group. In addition, model predictions should be put to the test to make certain that people with identical risk ratings reoffend at comparable rates. Finally, interpretable models also can be used to show that each model's evaluations are fair and mainly conform to domain knowledge about what characterises risk.[30]

Fourthly, data scientists must focus their efforts on building next-generation risk algorithms which can foresee how supportive activities would lower risk. For instance, existing RAIs only infer the danger of delinquency when a person is freed without monitoring. Even if supporting measures, such as text-message reminders of court dates, may have a significant effect on an person's risk of crime, they are not taken into account. Consider someone who, according to a normal RAI, has a small chance of appearing in court if released without help. If a judge only received this rating, he or she would very certainly imprison the individual to ensure that they appeared in court. A judge employing next-generation RAIs, on the other hand, would note that text-message reminders boost the likelihood of an individual's appearance dramatically.[31] Based on this new information, the court may decide to release the person and put them on a reminder system.

Finally, and perhaps most significantly, when algorithms are implemented, they should be evaluated. In any complicated system, it's possible that players

30   file:///C:/Users/Lenovo/Downloads/entropy-23-00018-v2.pdf

31   https://www.povertyactionlab.org/evaluation/text-message-reminders-decreased-failure-appear-court-new-york-city

will react to a new policy in unexpected ways (e.g., by selectively using RAI predictions to penalise communities of color). [32]Given the hazard, authorities should rigorously review behaviour and outcomes when each new algorithm is adopted, and they should continue routine monitoring once a programme is established to determine long-term ramifications. These studies will be critical in determining whether algorithmic innovations have the expected outcomes.

THE PRESUMPTION OF INNOCENCE

When algorithmic tools are used in criminal proceedings, they can sometimes lead to violations of the right to a fair trial, particularly when it comes to the right to a judge chosen at random, the right to an independent and impartial tribunal, and the presumption of innocence.[33] The presumption of innocence is considered a cornerstone of common law. It means that everyone should be presumed innocent until proven guilty after a fair trial. Naturally, some people are concerned that AI technology could lead to skewed and inaccurate forecasts. The assumption of innocence and the purpose of reducing the number of people imprisoned before trial are being taken into account as AI decision-making systems are improved to assist courts in uncovering grounds to release inmates rather than merely focusing on particular risks. [34]A document titled "Rules for Human-AI Interaction," issued by a group of

---

32   https://www.brookings.edu/research/understanding-risk-assessment-instruments-in-criminal-justice/

33   https://www.mckinsey.com/~/media/mckinsey/industries/advanced%20electronics/our%20insights/how%20artificial%20intelligence%20can%20deliver%20real%20value%20to%20companies/mgi-artificial-intelligence-discussion-paper.ashx

34   https://www.brookings.edu/research/a-better-path-forward-for-criminal-justice-reimagining-pretrial-and-sentencing/

Microsoft researchers,[35] lays forth a set of rules for practitioners designing AI-powered products and features. The principles were culled from over 150 AI-related design concepts and put to the test in three rounds.[36]

CONCLUDING REMARKS

In order for AI to be used as efficiently as possible in the legal system, we must address these social and ethical considerations. We should also think about how important it is for the algorithm to be entirely transparent, because perfect openness in AI and human decision-making is not always possible. Humans and AI both have biases, but human biases in AI's training data cause a lot more algorithmic bias. When employing artificially intelligent risk/needs assessment tools, it's critical to make sure the training data is accurate. With this in mind, it's vital to recruit the assistance of a team of highly qualified professionals who will examine all areas of the legal system and do everything possible to properly and correctly implement AI.

---

35   https://dig.watch/updates/russian-president-calls-moral-rules-human-ai-interaction

36   https://www.mckinsey.com/~/media/mckinsey/industries/advanced%20electronics/our%20insights/how%20artificial%20intelligence%20can%20deliver%20real%20value%20to%20companies/mgi-artificial-intelligence-discussion-paper.ashx

BLOCKCHAIN ARBITRATION: PROBLEMS AND PROSPECTS

Author:

Vladislav Dmitrievich Tuktamyshev

ABSTRACT

The article is devoted to a specific method of dispute resolution called blockchain arbitration. In the paper the author considers the essence of blockchain technology, critically analyzes the blockchain-arbitration models offered in the legal science and describe a blockchain-arbitration model based on artificial intelligence. The author also analyzes the problems arising from the application of blockchain arbitration and ways to solve them.

Keywords: blockchain arbitration, arbitration, blockchain, smart contracts, online dispute resolution, artificial intelligence

> *"People don't understand the amazing possibilities for smart use of technology."*
>
> *Jacques Fresco*

INTRODUCTION

The 21st century is characterized by rapid development of digital technologies, which affects all spheres of social life and generates new ways of people interaction on markets by using certain technologies. One of them is blockchain.

Blockchain is a distributed database containing information about all transactions conducted by the system participants. Originally created for the cryptocurrency circulation, blockchain is used for authentication and verification, distributed data storage, financial transactions, etc.

IT has invaded the legal profession, because very few are those who, today, do not work on a daily basis with electronic communication technologies[1].

Despite clarity over digital relationships, disputes between parties are inevitable. It's also clear that nowadays state judicial systems aren't prepared to solve these disputes due to the low judges' technic qualifications.

Trends on the differentiation of bodies depending on the category of dispute lead to the conclusion that a specialized jurisdictional body may be an effective tool for resolving disputes that may arise from blockchain-enabled platforms.

One of the publications substantiated the position that traditional arbitration cannot function fully within the digital space and that "the existing procedural, organizational and technological infrastructure of traditional arbitration" should be replaced by a decentralized arbitration"[2].

---

1 G. Kaufmann-Kohler, T. Schultz. The Use of Information Technology in Arbitration (Oct. 28, 2021, 3:31 PM), https://lk-k.com/wp-content/uploads/The-Use-of-Information-Technology-in-Arbitration.pdf .

2 Theory of Future Decentralized Arbitration System (Oct. 28, 2021, 10:12 AM), https://geektimes.ru/company/jincor/blog/292033/ .

Other authors mention that the blockchain platform not only allows stakeholders to enter into a smart contract but also to resolve a dispute arising from that contract by submitting it to a panel of independent arbitrators who reach a decision by majority vote[3].[4]

V. Buterin also commented on this issue, arguing that "blockchain can be used to create a tiered system with randomly selected judges (jurors) sitting in a decentralized judicial system"[5].

It should be noted that, whether blockchain is considered promising by researchers[6] as well as international organizations, particularly the World Trade Organization, it's currently terra incognita of international arbitration[7] needs to be further explored.

---

3   Blockchain-based justice system (Nov. 5, 2021, 11:28 AM), https://hightech. fm/2017/10/31/blockchain-smart-contracts .

4   Notably, the term "blockchain arbitration" is also often used to refer to conciliation procedures. S. Raval, describing OpenBazaar arbitration, writes: "Anyone can become an arbitrator simply by checking a box in the profile settings... An arbitrator is charged with the responsibility of settling disputes and remitting funds to the right side. Arbitrators can charge conflict resolution fees" (Raval S. Decentralized Applications. Blockchain technology in action 139 (2017)).

5   Buterin V. Decentralized Court (Nov. 3, 2021, 6:21 PM) https: // www.reddit. com/r/ethereum/comments/4gigyd/decentralized_court/?st=jk5uaa08&sh=eae1485f.

6   Kanashevsky V.A. International transactions: legal regulation (2016).

7   Majorina M.V. On collision of law and "wrong", renovation of lex mercatoria, smart contracts and blockchain arbitration, Lex Russica (Russian Law), 7 (2019).

WHAT IS BLOCKCHAIN?

Before turning to the analysis of the legal relationships arising from the application of blockchain to the resolution of disputes in arbitration, we need to define what blockchain is.

Blockchain refers to a decentralized, distributed database containing information about all validated transactions involving a particular asset and based on cryptographic algorithms[8].

The analogy with blockchain is a necklace, where each bead is a "block" or record of action. This necklace cannot be destroyed. Thus, blockchain is an indestructible digital record of action. The reliability of this system has allowed it to be used to improve the efficiency of monetary transactions and information exchange among individuals, corporations and even the public sector[9].

As Max I. Raskin wrote, blockchain is simply a decentralized ledger for recording digital data in a verified time-stamped manner without the need for a trusted third-party[10]. According to Joseph Bambar, blockchain provides more "security, traceability and transparency of records, as well as lower operational costs"[11]. In this regard, blockchain platforms are protected from threats because

---

8   Savelyev A.I. Some legal aspects of using smart contracts and blockchain technologies under the Russian law, Law, 5 (2017).

9   Blockchain: Enigma. Paradox. Opportunity (Oct. 29, 2021, 12:41 PM), https://www2.deloitte.com/content/dam/Deloitte/xe/Documents/technology/Blockchain.pdf

10   Max I. Raskin. Realm of the Coin: Bitcoin and Civil Procedure (Nov. 1, 11:17 AM) https://ir.lawnet.fordham.edu/cgi/viewcontent.cgi?referer=https://www.google.com/&httpsredir=1&article=1418&context=jcfl

11   Blockchain: A Practical Guide to Developing Business, Law, and Technology Solutions (Oct. 28, 2021, 1:18 AM) https://www.mheducation.ca/

they store information on multiple servers, that can be changed if at least 51% of the information is adjusted[12].

The point of a blockchain as follows. Every action performed in the system is encoded and recorded as a block of data. Then blocks are accumulated, as a result of which a chain of data is formed. Herein lies the key idea of blockchain, as the blocks formed in a result of transactions are inseparably connected with each other, which eliminates the possibility of data modification in the original block. Each new block in the transaction chain is an additional confirmation of previous block trustworthiness and the blockchain as a whole.

As a Bank of England official rightly pointed out in an interview, blockchain is "a technology that allows individuals who do not know each other to share a record of data".[13] It is impossible to surreptitiously tamper with the data within this system, so it is recognized as resistant to corruptive factors.

Initially originated as a platform for mining and storing cryptocurrency transactions, blockchain has been implemented in various market instruments, in the insurance sector, etc.[14] Unfortunately, where there are economic relations, there's legal disputes, frequently merging into litigation.

---

blockchain-a-practical-guide-to-developing-business-law-and-technology-solutions-9781260115871-can

12   Max I. Raskin. Realm of the Coin: Bitcoin and Civil Procedure (Nov. 1, 2021, 11:17 AM), https://ir.lawnet.fordham.edu/cgi/viewcontent.cgi?referer=https://www.google.com/&httpsredir=1&article=1418&context=jcfl .

13   Bank of England works with Anomali to improve threat intelligence capabilities (Nov. 4, 2021, 12:15 AM) https://www.bankofengland.co.uk/news/2017/february/boe-works-with-anomali-to-improve-threat-intelligence-capabilities .

14   In addition, blockchain has become popular in law-related areas, such as smart-contracts and notary actions. In particular, the main notarial acts that can be performed using blockchain technology are the following: proof of existence, proof

As disputes arising from blockchain-based relationships clearly have significant specificity, the choice of appropriate legal remedies and tools to protect the interests must be appropriate.

The legal community has found a solution to this problem in such form as blockchain arbitration.

BLOCKCHAIN ARBITRATION: WHAT'S THE POINT?

Blockchain arbitration has appeared in legal theory and practice not long ago, but the idea has attracted attention among scholars. By the way, nowadays, that idea still needs to be developed.

What are advantages of the proposed idea that it managed to conquer the minds of digital law researchers in a short period of time? Firstly, it is efficiency, which means the reduction of time costs (as the automated system processes data and transmits the final result many times faster than a human does) and the reduction of financial costs (certainly, if a dispute is considered on an online platform in a simplified procedural form, the costs which the parties incur in a classical arbitration case are not generated). Second, confidentiality and security of the data.

Meanwhile, no unambiguous understanding of the legal nature of blockchain arbitrage is currently formulated in science.

---

of ownership and document ownership transfer (A Blockchain-Based Digital Notary: What You Need To Know (Nov. 11, 2021, 1:12 PM), https://www.forbes.com/sites/forbestechcouncil/2019/11/12/a-blockchain-based-digital-notary-what-you-need-to-know/?sh=52ae6ce54557).

See also Blockchain Use Cases for Notary (Nov. 6, 2021, 10:43 PM) https://4irelabs.com/cases/notarization-in-blockchain/.

M.A. Rozhkova defines blockchain arbitration, as well as online arbitration, as a kind of classical arbitration, taking into account the "complication" of these mechanisms by digital technologies and the specificity of the subject matter of disputes submitted for resolution[15]. Other scholars thinks that blockchain arbitration is just a way of conducting litigation using blockchain technology[16].

Despite on various ideas and mechanics for the construction and operation of blockchain arbitrage, but CodeLegit and Kleros are considered the most widespread and developed.

The first ideas for smart-contract arbitration were developed based on the CodeLegit. This concept is looks like traditional arbitration. Initially, the parties enter into a smart-contract that contains an arbitration clause to resolve disputes under the Blockchain Dispute Resolution Arbitration Rules[17]. Once a smart-contract containing an arbitration clause is entered into, the contract is entered into an arbitration library. The arbitration library provides an opportunity for parties to suspend performance under a smart-contract due to a breach of contract by one party or improper performance under the

---

15   Rozhkova M.A. On the automation of online arbitration and online resolution of commercial and consumer disputes, E-commerce and related areas (legal regulation): collection of articles (2019).

16   Arbitration Center of the National Chamber of Entrepreneurs of the Republic of Kazakhstan "Atameken" (Nov, 7, 2021, 5:45 PM) https://aca.kz/news/view/predlagaem-oznakomitsa-so-statej-francuzskih-uristov-o-robotizirovannom-arbitrazei18ni18n.

17   The Blockchain Arbitration Rules are a set of rules agreed to by the parties in their legal contract. The advantage of the rules is speed, because they are tailored to work together with the Arbitration Library, and all communication is done via email or any other form of electronic communication.

The typicality of blockchain arbitration under the CodeLegit model and traditional arbitration is also due to the fact that the Blockchain Arbitration Rules were built on the basis of the UNCITRAL Model Rules.

contract[18]. The arbitration library also serves as a channel of communication for parties to a smart-contract with arbitrators.

In case of a dispute, the party who consider its rights have been violated triggers the Arbitration Library by invoking the Pause and Send to Arbitrator function. The smart-contract is then suspended and the arbitration library sends a notice of arbitration to the appointing authority, which is CodeLegit.

After the suspension, an aggrieved party initiates arbitration proceedings by sending a relevant message through the CodeLegit platform. After receiving notification of the arbitration, the platform automatically selects arbitrators to resolve the dispute. Just as in traditional arbitration, the blockchain arbitrator must complete a declaration of independence and impartiality, as well as give his or her consent to the dispute. However, the person appointed as a blockchain arbitrator should understand both how to resolve the dispute and how blockchain technology and smart contracts work, which makes the selection of arbitrators much more difficult.

Upon receipt of the information by the arbitrator, the arbitrator shall invite the parties to a hearing, if the parties deem it necessary. After the appointment of the arbitral tribunal, the claimant and the respondent shall exchange procedural documents, which shall also be sent to the arbitrators. All communication shall be in electronic form. Hearings may be held in person or through the use of information technology (e.g., videoconferencing)[19].

When the parties have concluded their oral pleadings, the arbitrator shall retire to render an award, after which the case shall be deemed concluded.

---

18   It is also possible to renew, modify and terminate a smart contract using the arbitration library.

19   The use of information systems that allow a dispute to be heard remotely is a preferable option because it allows the case to be heard in the shortest possible time and at a lower cost and to achieve the goal of the arbitration, which is the ultimate goal of the arbitrator.

Depending on the award, CodeLegit calls one of the functions available after the award in the arbitration library. After receiving the appropriate message from CodeLegit, the smart contract automatically executes the appropriate award[20]. The award may also be sent to the parties by e-mail and, if necessary, it is sent in written form by post[21].

The second popular model of blockchain arbitration is called Kleros. It's a decentralized protocol designed to resolve disputes arising from smart-contracts, involving independent arbitrators.

A condition for resolving a dispute using Kleros is the inclusion in the smart-contract of a clause on the use of this system when a dispute arises. In the event of a dispute, information in the form of a code is sent to the platform, where the arbitrators are selected from among users of the system[22]. The selection system is based on the method of random number generation; those who have a higher number of tokens are more likely to be selected as arbitrators[23].

Once the arbitrators have been selected, each of them shall evaluate the available evidence and, by way of a vote, render an award. However, the list of awards is limited to the parties and the arbitrators may not choose an award

---

20   The admissibility of on-chain award is also a subject of discussion, but is not considered in this study due to the limited volume.

21   CodeLegit (Oct. 15, 2021, 2:34 AM) http://codelegit.com/.

22   It should be noted here that not every user of the system can be elected as an arbitrator; only the person using the tokens that certify their rights can be an arbitrator.

23   Lesaege Cl., Ast F. Kleros: Short Paper (Nov. 10, 2021, 12:15 AM) https://kleros.pdf.

other than the one proposed[24]. Once voting is completed, the system counts the votes[25].[26]

Meanwhile, described models are far from perfect. Thus, in relation to CodeLegit, it is worth noting that this system is just some form of online arbitration; therefore, the interpretation of blockchain arbitration in this concept cannot claim for its independence. After all, it is true that a traditional arbitration can also hear a case via videoconferencing[27] and mark it on the blockchain system; creating a separate body for this purpose does not seem justified.

As far as the Kleros model is concerned, it is worth noting that it inherently has great features stemming from legal relations arising from blockchain. However, this system is also not devoid of conceptual flaws because, firstly, it doesn't focus enough attention on the application of technological solutions in dispute resolution, secondly, it resembles in fact a special blockchain-based arbitrator selection system and decision-making method, without focusing significant attention on the specifics of dispute resolution, which also raises the

---

24   For example, in the case of a contract of sale, options may include "refund to the buyer", "provide the seller with an additional period for correcting defects in the goods", and "transfer funds to the seller".

25   Kleros (Nov. 2, 2021, 1:34 PM) https://kleros.io/ru/#solution.

26   In this regard, it is worth noting that the decision-making is based on an algorithm based on the concept of "Schelling point", which means "a decision that people tend to use to coordinate their behavior (in the absence of communication between the parties or in a situation where neither party can be sure of the truth of the other's statements) because that decision seems natural or relevant to them" (Buterin V. Schellingcoin: A minimal-trust universal data feed (Oct. 29, 2021, 6:31 PM) https:// blog. ethereum. org/2014/03/28/ schellingcoin-a-minimal-trust-universal-data-feed/).

27   At the same time, when considering a dispute using videoconferencing, we are not saying that there is a videoconference arbitration.

question of whether it should be defined specifically as a form of blockchain-based arbitration.

Without going into the details, it should be noted that the decribed concepts consider the functionality of blockchain in a rather limited way, resulting in an understanding of blockchain arbitration only as a subset of online arbitration, while it appears that blockchain arbitration, in order to take its place in the legal system and to assert its right to exist, should become, in some way, an independent artificial intelligence-based dispute resolution provider[28]. Moreover, all the prerequisites for this are in place.

Conceptually, blockchain arbitration should focus not only on the application of blockchain to the adjudication and resolution of cases, but also on decision-making using this technology (possibly with the use of a supervising arbitrator). Blockchain arbitration should represent a kind of transition to artificial intelligence and information technology justice with minimal human involvement in the resolution of a dispute[29], as blockchain, given its functional properties, allows the fullest possible implementation of this technology[30].

---

28   Indeed, objectively, it is necessary to distinguish between online and digital arbitration. We believe that in the case of blockchain arbitration, it is the latter that should be referred to.

29   This position is also contained in other sources (Arbitration Center of the National Chamber of Entrepreneurs of the Republic of Kazakhstan "Atameken" (Nov. 11, 2021, 7:54 AM) https://aca.kz/news/view/predlagaem-oznakomitsa-so-statej-francuzskih-uristov-o-robotizirovannom-arbitrazei18ni18n).

30   However, in this case we are inevitably faced with issues of admissibility of the use of artificial intelligence in the administration of justice, including the ethical component of the problem. Grubtsova S.P. draws attention to this problem, considering the example of the French Republic, the admissibility of information technologies in the administration of justice, concluding that "...prohibiting fully automated decision-making in arbitration, the French "Law on programming", in fact, follows the

BLOCKCHAIN ARBITRATION: THEORETICAL AND PRACTICAL PROBLEMS

Despite the simplicity and efficiency of blockchain arbitration, there are a number of questions remain. In particular, can a blockchain arbitration award be recognized and enforced under the rules of the 1958 New York Convention on the Recognition and Enforcement of Foreign Arbitral Awards[31]? Whether an arbitration clause in the form of a code spelled out in a smart contract meets the requirements of Article II of the New York Convention on the written form of the arbitration agreement etc.

Let's consider each of them separately.

First problem is determining the applicable law and selecting the competent forum.

In order to have the place of dispute resolution and applicable law determined, the parties should include in the smart contract an arbitration agreement which shall contain dispute resolution procedure, the place of dispute resolution and the applicable law. Given that many smart contract disputes will be the first of their kind, the parties should describe in detail which law and procedural rules will be applied to resolve the dispute.

How, meanwhile, should one proceed if the parties have not identified the competent forum and the applicable law? In the absence of a choice of competent forum, the answer is fairly straightforward: the dispute will be

---

philosophical concept that "justice can only be human-made" (Grubtsova S.P. On some issues of artificial intelligence technology application and automated, Arbitration Law Review, 2 (2021).

31   UN Convention on the Recognition and Enforcement of Foreign Arbitral Awards (New York, 10 June 1958).

submitted to domestic courts under the lex fori rules. The choice of applicable law in such a case would be subject to the conflict-of-laws rules.

However, what should the parties do in the case of non-arbitrability of the dispute in one of the countries? Unfortunately, the New York Convention keep silence on those matters. Nowadays, there are no mechanism to resolve such disputes and, therefore, the non-arbitrability of the dispute in one country may lead to the denial in recognition of the award[32].

Second, the specific nature of blockchain-based arbitration undoubtedly distorts the content of the basic principles of arbitration, which raises the question of whether national judges are currently prepared to recognize and enforce the decisions with derogations from the basic principles of the 1958 New York Convention. This problem is particularly acute in relation to the use of Kleros technology for the resolution of blockchain-related disputes.

It is well known that the fundamental principle of arbitration proceedings is the adversarial rule, comprising the right to be heard in the dispute[33]. Thus, depriving a party of the opportunity to present its arguments on the substance of the dispute under consideration may be regarded as a violation of article V, paragraph 1 (b), of the 1958 New York Convention and may subsequently lead to a refusal to enforce the award.

Meanwhile, the following mechanism may smooth the contradictions. There is no doubt about the thesis that if a party in the process has not exercised

---

32   We believe that the pro-arbitration approach can be a solution to this dilemma, but it appears that many states at this stage of their development are not prepared to apply it so broadly to uncharted areas.

33   Article 22(4) of the ICC Arbitration Rules (2012) refers to a party's ability to be heard in a case. This language is also reflected, in one form or another, in many rules of arbitral institutions, such as Article 14.4(i) of the LCIA Arbitration Rules (2014); Article 17 of the CIArb Arbitration Rules (2015) reflects this language as a right to a reasonable opportunity to present its case in the arbitral proceedings.

by its own will the procedural rights belonging to it (including the right to be heard), this should not serve as a basis for recognizing the arbitration award as defective. We believe that the current regulatory framework for blockchain arbitration should consider a party's right to present its position in court as exercised at the moment of sending to the blockchain arbitration relevant explanations (both in the form of a procedural document and in the form of a transaction on the blockchain platform).

Closely related to this is the issue of enforcement of awards made by electronic tools. For example, to what extent is it permissible for an award to be in electronic form alone, in the form of a digital code, without any hard copy, and if so, what is the applicable standard for deciding whether or not such an award should be enforced? There was also a question of electronic signature admissibility to sign an award, since it was also unclear whether judges in domestic jurisdictions would be ready to recognize such awards. At this point, it appears that if the approaches of arbitral institutions are too conservative, the process will be unduly delayed and costly, and if too innovative, it may result in the setting aside of awards.

Next, there is the issue of data privacy. While blockchain certainly protects data as much as possible from outside interference, it does not prevent interested parties from adjusting software codes, which could lead to distortion of primary digital data and improper case resolution. Another aspect of confidentiality relates to the fact that in fully computerized interactions between counterparties to transactions, data leakage into the public domain cannot be ruled out.

Some authors have also pointed to the problem of the validity of the arbitration clause[34]. At present, the question of whether an arbitration clause in

---

34   This problem is pointed out in the Kluwer Arbitration Blog (Is Online Dispute Resolution The Future of Alternative Dispute Resolution? (Oct. 23, 2021, 9:15 PM) http://arbitrationblog.kluwerarbitration.com/2018/03/29/online-dispute-resolution-future-alternative-dispute-resolution/).

the form of a code in a smart-contract meets the requirements of the 1958 UN Convention on the Recognition and Enforcement of Foreign Arbitral Awards, in particular Article II, paragraph 2, can be rightly ranked among the most contentious issues related to the regulation of cross-border dispute resolution using blockchain technology[35]. However, it seems that these concerns are groundless.

The problem appears from established practice that a smart contract (including an arbitration clause contained therein) may be concluded entirely in a programming language, overlaid in a natural language and a programming language, or in a hybrid form.

In theory, there is a ground that a smart-contract is not a contract in the classic sense because it doesn't meet the requirements of US and European law[36]. This position is justified by the fact that a smart-contract is a software code that defines the order of actions in a blockchain.

M. Kaulartz and J. Heckman concur with this position, pointing out that "... the programming code in a smart-contract does not serve to express the expression of will. A smart-contract cannot be equated with a written document which reflects the content of the expression of the will of the parties. It merely implements the terms of the contract"[37]. In their view, parties to a contract may decide that their relationship will be governed by a smart-contract which performs the function of a written contract. In this case, the software code would be used to express the will.

---

35   Darcy W.E. Allen, Aaron M. Lane, Marta Poblet. The Governance of Blockchain Dispute Resolution, Harvard Negotiation Law Review, 25 (2019).

36   Smart-Contract (Oct. 22, 2021, 3:14 PM) https://rspp.ru/upload/iblock/2f9/ IPChain%20Smart-Contracts.pdf .

37   M. Kaulartz, J. Heckmann. Smart Contracts - Anwendungen der Blockchain-Technologie (Oct. 21, 2021, 11:15 AM) https://www.degruyter.com/document/ doi/10.9785/cr-2016-0923/html .

However, this approach doesn't stand up to criticism. Certainly, the conclusion of a smart contract using blockchain technology is a rather specific way of entering into a contract. In the meantime, do we define the possibility of entering into a contract (including an arbitration clause, which undoubtedly has a contractual basis) exclusively in classical written form? Are we not interpreting that provision expansively? And, in this sense, there is no difference between, for example, the conclusion of an agreement through the exchange of emails and through blockchain because, in either case, there is a deliberate expression of the will of the parties, which can be ascertained.[38]

Furthermore, it is necessary to bear in mind the principle of validity (favor validitatis, in favorem validitatis), which consists in applying to the arbitration agreement the law by virtue of which the arbitration agreement will be valid[39].

In this light, the argument that a blockchain-based arbitration clause may be invalidated is, is incorrect, especially since a model arbitration clause can be pre-established in a blockchain. The draft clause set out in the CodeLegit rules could be used as such:

_____

38   In the case of blockchain, such acceptance can be traced back to software code.

39   The necessity of applying the principle of validity when determining the validity of an arbitration clause is pointed out in A.I. Kolomiets' dissertation. Thus, the author writes that "... the provisions [of the New York Convention] are not only fully compatible with the principle of favor validitatis, but it appears that the Convention must be interpreted in the following way. Allowing the parties to choose the law ("the law to which the parties have subjected the agreement") states the parties' purported intention to subject the arbitration agreement to the law under which it would be valid. Moreover, Article V (1) (a) does not direct the courts not to recognize an award on the grounds stated ("may be refused..."), thus nothing in the article prevents the courts from recognizing and enforcing awards (and arbitration agreements), thereby following the principle of validity. (Kolomiets A.I. Validity of the arbitration agreement according to the law of Russia and foreign countries, 48 (2018)).

"Any dispute, controversy or claim arising out of or in connection with the performance of obligations under a contract shall be submitted to arbitration in accordance with the Blockchain Arbitration Rules. Unless otherwise stipulated, the case shall be heard by a single arbitrator by default and the hearing will be conducted via videoconferencing in English"[40].

A WAY FORWARD

Smart-contracts require new ways of dispute resolution. Its development assumes close cooperation between a lawyer on the one hand and computer, mathematical and cryptographic experts on the other hand. Blockchain arbitration will enable, firstly, to agree on the rules and the jurisdictional body that will consider disputes arising from the execution of a smart contract; secondly, to provide the parties with the possibility of suspending the execution of a smart contract, in case a party discovers a breach of contract or other non-performance; thirdly, to preserve all the advantages of a smart-contract, because the dispute does not necessarily have to be taken to court, but can be resolved by an experienced arbitrator or directly by an independent system.

As William Kirtley of Aceris Law noted: "A number of organizations around the world are trying to use blockchain for a variety of applications. So, I expect more arbitration using cryptocurrencies and blockchain in the coming years"[41].

---

40   CodeLegit White Paper on Blockchain Arbitration (Oct. 21, 2021, 1:12 AM) https://www.academia.edu/36257030/CodeLegit_White_Paper_on_Blockchain_Arbitration .

41   Aceris-law successfully resolves ICC arbitration involving the cryptocurrency industry (Nov. 5, 2021, 5:17 PM) https://www.international-arbitration-attorney.com/en/aceris-law-successfully-resolves-icc-arbitration-involving-the-cryptocurrency-industry/.

Some of our message to future researchers and enforcers concerns the admissibility of blockchain arbitration of disputes using artificial intelligence alone, with a de facto complete removal of humans from the decision-making process. We dare to suggest that blockchain arbitration will develop into a fully automated dispute resolution system. In our view, however, the specifics of blockchain itself prompts a distinction between traditional arbitration and its use of information technology (including blockchain) and blockchain arbitration itself.

Meanwhile, the further development of blockchain arbitration will depend on two factors. The first is the possibility of adopting an international document that unifies approaches to cross-border disputes arising from digital relationships[42]. The second factor is the willingness of states to recognize blockchain arbitration judgments.

Of course, blockchain arbitration now seems to be a new and unexplored phenomenon, but once options were perceived with distrust as well. Therefore, we want to believe that national legislators and law enforcers will not obstruct the way of informatization and digitalization of society and will recognize the admissibility of such an institution as blockchain arbitration with all its specific features and peculiarities, while the international community can develop universal acts, which will facilitate the search for a compromise and the search for an optimal solution.

---

42   It should be noted that unification may be carried out in the following ways: through the development and adoption of an independent instrument of an international legal nature (for example, a convention), through the conclusion of bilateral and multilateral agreements between the parties, through the signing of protocols to existing conventions, as well as through the development and subsequent implementation of Unidroit and UNCITRAL rules into national law.

After all, as Jacques Fresco correctly observed, "if technology doesn't free people from routine, so that they can pursue the higher goals of humanity, then all technological progress is meaningless.[43]"

REFERENCES

Aceris-law successfully resolves ICC arbitration involving the cryptocurrency industry (Nov. 5, 2021, 5:17 PM) https://www.international-arbitration-attorney.com/en/aceris-law-successfully-resolves-icc-arbitration-involving-the-cryptocurrency-industry/.

Arbitration Center of the National Chamber of Entrepreneurs of the Republic of Kazakhstan "Atameken" (Nov, 7, 2021, 5:45 PM) https://aca.kz/news/view/predlagaem-oznakomitsa-so-statej-francuzskih-uristov-o-robotizirovannom-arbitrazei18ni18n

A Blockchain-Based Digital Notary: What You Need To Know (Nov. 11, 2021, 1:12 PM), https://www.forbes.com/sites/forbestechcouncil/2019/11/12/a-blockchain-based-digital-notary-what-you-need-to-know/?sh=52ae6ce54557.

Bank of England works with Anomali to improve threat intelligence capabilities (Nov. 4, 2021, 12:15 AM) https://www.bankofengland.co.uk/news/2017/february/boe-works-with-anomali-to-improve-threat-intelligence-capabilities.

Blockchain: A Practical Guide to Developing Business, Law, and Technology Solutions (Oct. 28, 2021, 1:18 AM) https://www.mheducation.ca/blockchain-a-practical-guide-to-developing-business-law-and-technology-solutions-9781260115871-can.

Blockchain-based justice system (Nov. 5, 2021, 11:28 AM), https://hightech.fm/2017/10/31/blockchain-smart-contracts.

---

43   Quotes of famous personalities (Nov. 9, 2021, 5:51 PM) https://ru.citaty.net/temy/tekhnologii/.

Blockchain: Enigma. Paradox. Opportunity (Oct. 29, 2021, 12:41 PM), https://www2.deloitte.com/content/dam/Deloitte/xe/Documents/technology/Blockchain.pdf.

Blockchain Use Cases for Notary (Nov. 6, 2021, 10:43 PM) https://4irelabs.com/cases/notarization-in-blockchain/.

Buterin V. Schellingcoin: A minimal-trust universal data feed (Oct. 29, 2021, 6:31 PM) https://blog.ethereum.org/2014/03/28/schellingcoin-a-minimal-trust-universal-data-feed/.

Buterin V. Decentralized Court (Nov. 3, 2021, 6:21 PM) https://www.reddit.com/r/ethereum/comments/4gigyd/decentralized_court/?st=jk5uaa08&sh=eae1485f.

CodeLegit (Oct. 15, 2021, 2:34 AM) http://codelegit.com/.

CodeLegit White Paper on Blockchain Arbitration (Oct. 21, 2021, 1:12 AM) https://www.academia.edu/36257030/CodeLegit_White_Paper_on_Blockchain_Arbitration.

Darcy W.E. Allen, Aaron M. Lane, Marta Poblet. The Governance of Blockchain Dispute Resolution, Harvard Negotiation Law Review, 25 (2019).

Grubtsova S.P. On some issues of artificial intelligence technology application and automated, Arbitration Law Review, 2 (2021).

ICC Arbitration Rules 2012 and ICC Friendly Dispute Resolution Rules 2001 (ICC Publication No. 850R) (Oct. 21, 2021, 12:15 PM) http://base.garant.ru/2571573/

Is Online Dispute Resolution The Future of Alternative Dispute Resolution? (Oct. 23, 2021, 9:15 PM) http://arbitrationblog.kluwerarbitration.com/2018/03/29/online-dispute-resolution-future-alternative-dispute-resolution/.

Kanashevsky V.A. International transactions: legal regulation (2016).

Kaulartz M., Heckmann J. Smart Contracts - Anwendungen der Blockchain-Technologie (Oct. 21, 2021, 11:15 AM) https://www.degruyter.com/document/doi/10.9785/cr-2016-0923/html

Kaufmann-Kohler G., Schultz T. The Use of Information Technology in Arbitration (Oct. 28, 2021, 3:31 PM), https://lk-k.com/wp-content/uploads/The-Use-of-Information-Technology-in-Arbitration.pdf.

Kleros (Nov. 2, 2021, 1:34 PM) https://kleros.io/ru/#solution.

Kluwer Arbitration Blog (Is Online Dispute Resolution The Future of Alternative Dispute Resolution? (Oct. 21, 2021, 2:54 AM) http://arbitrationblog.kluwerarbitration.com/2018/03/29/online-dispute-resolution-future-alternative-dispute-resolution/.

Kolomiets A.I. Validity of the arbitration agreement according to the law of Russia and foreign countries, 48 (2018).

LCIA Arbitration Rules (2014) (Oct. 28, 2021, 4:55 PM) https://www.lcia.org/Dispute_Resolution_Services/lcia-arbitration-rules-2014.aspx#Article%2014.

Lesaege Cl., Ast F. Kleros: Short Paper (Nov. 10, 2021, 12:15 AM) https://kleros.pdf.

Majorina M.V. On collision of law and "wrong", renovation of lex mercatoria, smart contracts and blockchain arbitration, Lex Russica (Russian Law), 7 (2019).

Quotes of famous personalities (Nov. 9, 2021, 5:51 PM) https://ru.citaty.net/temy/tekhnologii/.

Raskin M. Realm of the Coin: Bitcoin and Civil Procedure (Nov. 1, 11:17 AM) https://ir.lawnet.fordham.edu/cgi/viewcontent.cgi?referer=https://www.google.com/&httpsredir=1&article=1418&context=jcfl.

Raval S. Decentralized Applications. Blockchain technology in action 139 (2017).

Rozhkova M.A. On the automation of online arbitration and online resolution of commercial and consumer disputes, E-commerce and related areas (legal regulation): collection of articles (2019).

Savelyev A.I. Some legal aspects of using smart contracts and blockchain technologies under the Russian law, Law, 5 (2017).

Smart-Contract (Oct. 22, 2021, 3:14 PM) https://rspp.ru/upload/iblock/2f9/IPChain%20Smart-Contracts.pdf.

Theory of Future Decentralized Arbitration System (Oct. 28, 2021, 10:12 AM), https://geektimes.ru/company/jincor/blog/292033/.

UN Convention on the Recognition and Enforcement of Foreign Arbitral Awards (New York, 10 June 1958)

JURISPRUDENCE OF CONSENT IN DATA PROTECTION LAWS IN THE AGE OF BIG DATA

Author:

Gorremutchu Mahith Vidyasagar

INTRODUCTION

The notion of informational autonomy or self-determination is controlling over one's personal data, which means it is the individuals' "right to determine which information about themselves will be disclosed, to whom and for which purpose" (Terwangne, 2013, p. 4). The phrase 'control' not entirely means one's decision over the use of their data, but to the possible extent the "right to be aware of their fate, to get informed about who knows what about you and for what to do" (Terwangne, 2013, p. 4). In this 21st century, which is driven by technology, personal information is most commonly used to shape the desired modes of behavior, target personal activities, or outline personality profiles (Eberle, 2001, p. 972), by the Big Data titans like Amazon, Apple, Facebook, Google, and Netflix etc., at the same time governments also possess unprecedented information concerning each of its citizens (Eberle, 2001, p. 965). The informational self-determination, which is the domain of privacy and data protection (Custers et al., 2018, p. 247) is the autonomy of the individual to disclose their personal data to those private as well as public entities and their subsequent use of such data. This flow of data is regulated by the data protection regulations or laws (Bhardwaj, 2018, p. 101).

Data protection regulations are the principles tailored to protect the individuals' personal information by limiting how such information can be collected, used and disclosed (Bygrave, 2002, p. 2). The data protection legislations across the world use consent as a mechanism that authorizes the use of personal and sensitive data (Taylor & Paterson, 2020, p. 72). In the context of informational self-determination, consent can often be described as that "each person should have a right to determine for himself when, how and to what extent information about him or her is communicated to others" (Custers et al., 2018, p. 247). This right is a foundation for numerous contemporary data protection regulations (Poscher, 2017, p. 129) and even protected by granting constitutional status. The first and foremost one is the 1983 avant-grade decision of the Federal Constitutional Court of Germany, which declared the right to informational self-determination as the right to data protection and is protected under the Constitution of Germany (Rouvroy & Poullet, 2009, p. 45).

Similarly, the European Courts expanded the scope of privacy granted under Article 8 of the European Convention on Human Rights (ECHR) and recognized and declared informational self-determination as the right to protection of personal data (Terwangne, 2013, p. 5). The essence of this interface centers around the jurisprudence developed by the Court of Justice of the European Union (CJEU) on privacy and data protection (Brkan, 2019, p. 864). The decisions of the CJEU clearly show its acknowledgment of the right to protection of personal data even before the adoption of the Charter of the Fundamental Rights of the European Union (Poscher, 2017, p. 130). It is the first international instrument that recognizes the right to protection of personal data as a fundamental right and Article 8 of the charter epitomizes the same (Brkan, 2019, p. 864).

From a non-European perspective it is visible that data protection is codified as a fundamental right in Germany and Europe (Poscher, 2017, p.

131). Usually, in data protection regulations, the respect for informational self-determination or right to data protection is manifested by consent (Taylor & Paterson, 2020, p. 72), which facilitates individual autonomy and choice (Bhardwaj, 2018, p. 101). However, there are different voices around the notion of consent in data protection regulations. These debates, which are otherwise referred to as the consent paradox (Bergemann, 2018) doubted the inclusion of consent in data protection laws.

This paper emphasizes the importance of preserving consent for the protection of information privacy and individual autonomy in this digital world. For that purpose, the second part of the paper looks into the importance of consent in protecting privacy and autonomy in data protection from a jurisprudential lens. Whereas, the third-part looks into the shortcomings of the consent framework. Fourth part highlights some of the alternatives proposed and their criticisms. For advocate better incorporation of consent framework, part five concludes with the consequences of having ineffective consent in data protection regime.

THE PARALLELISM OF AUTONOMY, PRIVACY, AND CONSENT IN DATA PROTECTION

In the context of data protection, informed consent is "the requirement to obtain the data subject's consent before processing his or her personal data" (Jarovsky, 2018, p. 447). It relies on the paradigm of 'notice' and 'consent' (Yeung, 2017, p. 125). Notice entails that the individual parting with the personal information (data subject) should be informed by the data collecting entity (data controller or data fiduciary) what type of data it intends to collect, and how such data will be processed and used subsequently (Bhardwaj, 2018, p. 103). Likewise, the principle of consent "stipulates that personal data can only be collected and used pursuant to the data subject's consent" (Bhardwaj, 2018, p. 104). The welcoming definition for informed consent can be found in Europe's most appreciated data protection regulation – General Data Protection Regulations (Regulation (EU) 2016/679). It defines consent as "any freely given, specific, informed and unambiguous indication of the data subject's wishes by which he or she, by a statement or by a clear affirmative action, signifies agreement to the processing of personal data relating to him or her" (EU GDPR, art. 4(11)). It is not an exaggeration to say that "[c]onsent to personal data-processing practices become quite a mundane activity in the digital world" (Custers et al., 2018, p. 247). But the haunted question is, what makes consent so vital in data protection?

As an expression of free choice, consent is tightly interlinked with personal autonomy. In fact, consent is the most intuitive method that ensures protection of individual autonomy (Westin, 1967). This individual autonomy "implies the ability to reflect wholly on oneself, to accept or reject one's values, connections, and self-defining features, and change such elements of one's life at will" (Christman, 2015). This approach has its roots in Gerald Dworkin's definition (Dworkin, 1998):

> Autonomy is conceived of as a second-order capacity of persons to reflect critically upon their first order preferences, desires, wishes, and so forth and the capacity to accept or attempt to change these in light of higher-order preferences and values. By exercising such a capacity, persons define their nature, give meaning and coherence to their lives, and take personality for the kind of person they are. (p. 20)

From the definition, the notion of autonomy is premised on two core elements: the ability to reflect on one's own preferences and the ability to accept or attempt to change them (Jarovsky, 2018, p. 451). Simply speaking, it is the "capacity or liberty to make decisions, free from external control" (McLean, 2010, p. 40). Digitization created a situation where there exists 'cradle-to-grave' information. This information can be applied for multiple purposes, once it is available and having control over such personal information is nothing but controlling an individual (Eberle, 2001, p. 965). In such a scenario, autonomy over personal data gives an individual the ability to exercise control over the method in which their information is collected and used. Informational autonomy is crucial for human development. Cohen remarked that "informational autonomy comports with important values concerning the fair and just treatment of individuals within society" (Cohen, 2000, p. 1423).

Recognizing autonomy and individuals' right to make choices impacting their lives, is one of the most primary conceptualizations of privacy (Solove, 2002). This shows the existence of clear parallels between the notions of privacy and that of autonomy (McLean, 2010, p. 3). This can be understood further from the privacy definition of Alan Westin. According to him, privacy is "the claim of individuals, groups or institutions to determine for themselves when, how, and to what extent information about them is communicated to others" (Westin, 1967, p. 7) Which means, from the lens of data protection, privacy is the right of an individual to determine when and in which boundaries their data is disseminated (Poscher, 2017, p. 132), and unauthorized use of such data would lead to an infringement of this right. Another deduction that can be drawn from Ruth Gavison claim on the function of privacy (Gavison, 1980, p. 423) is, "privacy creates the environment through which informational autonomy can be exercised" (Forde, 2016, p. 137). So, one can understand that both the concepts of privacy and autonomy in data protection safeguards the ability and the right to make self-determining decisions over personal data albeit in slightly different ways (McLean, 2010, p. 3).

In data protection laws, these two supporting concepts can only be preserved through consent. From the words of Ewa Lugger and Tom Rodden, "[t]he human agency involved in the act of consenting to the disclosure of personal information, whether explicit or implied, 'is the primary means for individual to exercise their autonomy and to protect their privacy'" (Luger & Rodden, 2013). This statement shows the importance of consent in facilitating individual autonomy, privacy and choice over personal data. Analyzing from the lens of jurisprudence, consent plays a prominent role in one's life by way of effecting both their moral and legal obligations and rights (Müller & Schaber, 2018, p. 1). Daniel Solove wrote "Consent is an under theorized concept that is crucial for privacy and many other areas of law.... Activities that would otherwise be illegitimate are made legitimate by consent" (Solove, 2013, p. 1894). That is the reason why the liberal political theorists starting from Locke appreciated the view that the foundation of entire politico-legal order lies in consent. Which means, the contours of consent are not just within the law but it gets expanded towards the "basis of legal authority and perhaps to the essence of legal order itself" (Beyleveld & Brownsword, 2007, p. 3).

The population of this modern world habituated "to a culture which is based on liberty; the freedom of individuals to act as they choose, albeit within certain limits..." (McLean, 2010, p. 1). Hence, States should facilitate autonomy, which is the ability to determine the shape of one's life and to make their own decisions. Atkin says: "Autonomy in the liberal tradition, is generally understood as self-determination: the freedom to pursue one's conception of the good life" (Atkins, 2000, p. 74). So, the laws should be in such a way that they maximize individual freedom. This maximization approach serves two purposes: "first, it acknowledges the respect due to autonomy and second, it allows for the development of the concept of privacy, within which individuals are free from State scrutiny and control" (McLean, 2010, p. 1). This respect to autonomy and development of privacy in data protection can only be achieved by the notion of consent. Maclean scholarly points, "[t]he legal rules of consent are founded upon the right to autonomy and the principle of (respect for) autonomy" (Maclean, 2000, p. 277).

When it comes to data protection laws, consent as a manifestation of self-determination builds on the notion of autonomy (Efroni et al., 2019, p. 353). The prominence of consent can be understood as a "very central tool in concretize autonomy, as information is frequently available in digital form, thus presenting a quality of abstraction that might distract us from its personal character and its potential to trigger privacy harm" (Jarovsky, 2018, p. 452). The data protection regulations deal with the collection, usage and processing of individual personal data by the governments as well as the private entities. Therefore, data processing practices require consent as it ensures that the individual has made knowledge decisions over their own personal data and also ensures that these are respected. It is only valid when the consent is informed. This informed consent contains an essential aspect – "the person who is asked for consent should be properly informed of what exactly he or she is consenting to and is to some extent (made) aware of the consequences such consent may have" (Custers et al., 2018, p. 248).

From the above discussion it is clear that the theoretical way of executing autonomy in the context of information privacy is an ex ante procedure of notice and consent, because the data subject is involved expressly and a rational position is required from it with respect to its personal data collection (Jarovsky, 2018, p. 452). However, the degree of involvement of the consent in the data protection rules is disputed because of the shortcomings associated with it. Different authors have raised doubts on the effectiveness of this tool. The following section discusses these shortcomings.

OTHER SIDE OF CONSENT IN THE INFORMATIONAL AGE

Although, there has been a wider consideration of consent as an efficient mechanism to protect the personal information (Reidenberg et al., 2015, p. 489), it faces certain criticisms. It has to be remembered that the criticisms of consent are as old as consent in data protection itself (Lynskey, 2015). The shortcomings and limits that have been raised against consent by these criticisms are discussed in this section.

The first one in the line of discussion is, it is difficult to provide information relating to personal data. Big Data analytics permit the collection of personal data, which will be analysed for the purposes not mentioned in advance and may be different from the initially notified ones (Mantelero, 2014, p. 645). The Big Data developments (exponentially more data, more real-time data and more diverse datasets) and the data mining across domains provide opportunities for the discovery of unanticipated relations and patterns in the data (Custers et al., 2018, p. 251). In the words of Ira Rubinstein: "firms that rely on data mining may find it impossible to provide adequate notice for the simple reason that they do not (and cannot) know in advance what they may discover" (Rubinstein, 2013, p. 79). This data mining happens so swiftly that most people are not aware of both the scale and the speed of these transactions (Richards & King, 2014, p. 405). The use of data is re-contextualized with the combination of data across various domains and time, which in some instances goes beyond the scope of original consent. This change in the context of consensual data collection, and less or no possibility of truly informing the consequences of permitting the data use, means that the validity of informed consent is lost.

Second, because of the obstacles associated with it, the informed consent models are unsuccessful in offering adequate protection to the people (Solove, 2013, p. 1880). Usually, people do not read the privacy policies because they are "commonly long, textual explanations of data practices, most frequently written by lawyers to protect companies against legal action" (Kelley, 2010). Although the privacy policies are drafted in compliance with the legal standards, they still fail to achieve 'conscious data disclosure behaviour' (Monteleone, 2015, pp. 75-76). These lengthy privacy policies take too long (information overload) to read while at the same time there are too many of them (consent overload) (Schermer et al., 2014, p. 177). It has been estimated by McDonald & Cranor that if the people have to read all the privacy policies that they have encountered, it would take nearly 244 hours annually (McDonald & Cranor, 2008). This consent overload leads to consent desensitization, which means the people are simply consented to the consent request they have come across with. Subsequently, it devalues consent and lowers the level of data protection (Schermer et al., 2014, p. 178).

Sometimes, even if people do read privacy policies, the information provided in them is too difficult to understand. Because, in most of the circumstances the language of the privacy policies is standardized and extremely legal or filled with technical terms (Solove, 2013, p. 1884), which is difficult to comprehend for the understanding capacity of an average data subject (Barocas & Nissenbaum, 2014, p. 59). While it seems obvious that an abbreviated plain language would be helpful to read and ease the understanding of privacy policies, the hidden details carry the most significance (Toubiana & Nissenbaum, 2011). Higher the complexity reduces, higher the information missing (See Solove, 2013, p. 1886; Koops, 2014, p. 252). If the privacy policy does not contain essential information, the decision of the data subject will be considered inferior, in fact, invalid (Jarovsky, 2018, p. 450). Although people read and understand privacy policies and are in a position to take informed decisions, they are not offered the free choice on the basis of their preferences.

The reason for this lack of free choice is, the privacy policies are framed in a way of take-it-or-leave-it offers (Custers et al., 2018, p. 253). The "companies require personal data collection as a condition to provide basic services, leaving the data subject with no real choice besides accepting it or – giving up the service" (Jarovsky, 2018, p. 450). So, if consent is refused, the access to that particular website or service provided on the internet is denied at the outset or strictly hindered. In addition, the individuals have little to no room for negotiation (Schermer et al., 2014, p. 117) as they have to consent to the standard privacy policies (Austin, 2014, p. 143). Moreover, once the data subject is consented it is renewed rarely. "As a result, consenting once often implies consent 'forever' (i.e., until it is actively withdrawn), even though the consent may rapidly get outdated (i.e., no longer match the initial preferences of a user)" (Custers et al., 2018, p. 252).

Third, in the context of Big Data, there is no guarantee that consent withholding, (i.e., refusing to disclose personal data) ensures privacy protection. The right to be let alone, which is a facet of right to privacy as advocated by Warren & Brandeis in their seminal essay (Warren & Brandeis, 1890), is not possible to achieve with respect to Big Data. Whether the data subjects consented voluntarily to disclose their personal information or not, the techniques of Big Data analytics entail the identification of patterns of behaviour and personal characteristics (Carolan & Spina, 2015, p. 172). Which means, with the Big Data developments it is even possible to make predictive analysis of individuals' personal characteristics although they neither disclose nor consented to disclose their information (Crawford & Schultz, 2014, p. 94).

These predictions seem pretty accurate. For instance, based on the 'likes' of a person on Facebook, a wide range of highly volatile personality traits can be predicted very accurately (See Kosinski et al., 2013). Such kind of activities result in information asymmetry, which supports unintended data disclosures (Carolan & Spina, 2015, p. 171), and disrupts the effectiveness of withholding consent.

Fourth, the difficulties in withdrawing consent of the data subject. In the context of data processing, the withdrawal of consent is an important aspect of 'right to be forgotten.' The European Commission refers to this right to be forgotten as "the right of the individuals to have their data no longer processed and deleted when they are no longer needed for legitimate purposes. This is the case, for example, when processing is based on the person's consent and when he or she withdraws consent" (Terwangne, 2013, p. 2). This digital right to be forgotten provides data subjects with the right to erasure of their personal data when they withdraw consent for their personal data processing. However, in practice, it is not possible to withdraw consent. As a result of which, the obligation erasing the data created by the right to be forgotten in the context of personal data might be hard to comply with or may theoretically be ineffective. Even if the consent is withdrawn, it is not possible to delete the personal data of an individual because prior to the withdrawal of consent itself, the personal data might be spread across various domains.

These criticisms declared that the model of informed consent in Big Data environment is an assumption that individuals are having autonomous decision making pertaining to their personal data (Soh, 2019, p. 67) and contemporary data protection scholars have suggested alternative models. Some of these proposed models have advised for lesser consent inclusion. Nonetheless, replacing consent with these alternative models would diminish the informational self-determination, which is the foundation of data protection laws. These proposed alternatives and their drawbacks are discussed in the following section.

REPLACEMENT OF CONSENT IN DATA PROTECTION LAWS

The unease towards consent at the centre of data protection framework has raised voices suggesting that the principles of consent should be replaced with other alternatives for achieving better rational and autonomous decisions as well as enhancing the individual privacy. One such solution advocated by Tene & Polonetsky is 'relaxing' the principles of data minimisation and consent, and providing stronger access and transparency rights to the individual (Tene & Polonetsky, 2013, p. 263). According to them, access to their personal data should be provided to the individuals in a usable format and allow them to utilise the applications of third-party to analyse and draw conclusions from their own data (Tene & Polonetsky, 2013, p. 264). The authors also suggested that the organisations should be more transparent in disclosing their data bases and decisional criteria for processing the personal data, which would help to curb unethical data processing and sensitive data usage and enable the individuals to have knowledge on how their information is used and to alter their decisions affecting their life for the better (Tene & Polonetsky, 2013, p. 270).

In recent times, there has been a new proposal of shifting consent to the principle of accountability (See Policy and the Resarch Group of the Office of the Privacy Commissioner of Canada, 2016; Matthan, 2017), which transfers the burden of privacy harms to individual data, onto the data controllers. Accordingly, the principle requires that data controllers are responsible for the data in their possession and held liable if any harm happens to the data subject arising from the data collected or used by them (Cate et al., 2014, p. 21). The accountability principle proposed by Rahul Matthan contemplates severe liability on the data controller, which includes significant financial penalties in case of proven harm (Matthan, 2017, p. 8). The most intriguing assurance of this accountability approach is that despite being an alternative to the consent framework, the proposal provides for a right to withdraw consent for processing certain data (Matthan, 2017, p. 6). This right to opt-out is an inherent aspect of consent (Bhardwaj, 2018, p. 107).

Nevertheless, these alternatives are not far from criticism. It has been acknowledged by Allan and further enunciated by Daniel Solove – accepting the fact that consent enables freedom in decision-making and abridging it for protecting privacy is inherited with inconsistencies (Solove, 2013, p. 1896). It has been opined that principles based on privacy protection framework cannot advance on the foundation that individuals are not capable of taking rational decisions. If the aim of the law is to protect individual privacy then it cannot be accomplished by removing the individuals' autonomy over their personal data (Bhardwaj, 2018, p. 107). Also the solution of Tene & Polonetsky supports innovation against privacy, which is problematic. As rightly criticized by Cohen that privacy is not something that can always be "traded off against other goods" (Cohen, 2012, p. 148). Waving of privacy results in "less creativity and impinge upon the development of selfhood" (Solove, 2013, p. 1895). It has to be kept in mind that any benefits of innovation should further develop individual autonomy but not come at the cost of it.

In addition, any stress laid on access rights to personal data, transparency or accountability is positioned on ex-post corrective action. Which means, the data subjects are provided with rights only after their personal data has already been collected, used, processed and apparently disseminated across various domains or hosts. This lack of checks and balances at the time of data collection would result in the disappearance of certain other essential data protection principles (Solove, 2013, p. 1895). The proponents of the above alternatives, in their support, have envisaged this but mostly argued that along with consent, data minimisation principles and purpose limitation act to limit the potential of big data (Tene & Polonetsky, 2013, pp. 242, 259; Matthan, 2017, pp. 22-23).

Similarly, Custers et. al., in their essay, also suggested simplifying consent in order to address the challenges posed by the current consent framework in the data protection regime (Custers et al., 2018, p. 254). One such solution is representing the information in a simplified process by way of privacy icons (Holtz, Zwingelberg, & Hansen, 2011, p. 279; see (Efroni et al., 2019, pp. 357-

358). It has been assumed that this kind of privacy indication would take less time for consent and would be clear for the user (Custers et al., 2018, p. 254). However, the icons are not a 'silver bullet' because of the challenges they pose (Efroni et al., 2019, pp. 358-359). They might reduce the information overload but the issues of explicit consent still persist. Another approach is focussed on reducing the issue of consent overload (Custers et al., 2018, pp. 254-255). According to this, policies and risks, which are acceptable and unacceptable will be formally specified in the privacy profile of the individual. By matching the individual preference against the privacy policy of the website, acceptability of the conditions to the users could be derived (Broenink, et al., 2010, pp. 72-81). If there is a match, consent could be derived from the user and if it is not matched it would show where the policies actually differ. This kind of approach seems to reduce the number of consent acts but individuals are still likely to face problems with the take-it-or-leave-it policy environment.

In order to address all the relative issues of informed consent Schermer et. al., proposed a fair transaction model (Schermer et al., 2014). This model suggested less informed and legal consent requests by allowing implied consent for personal data processing in certain situations. According to this model, consent is only required where it involves serious risks or effects to the individual who consents and it is not required when there is fair use of personal data. In order to make this model work, the authors pose two different questions: i) what actions or inactions constitute consent; ii) what 'fair use' of personal data is (Schermer et al., 2014). However, the authors did not provide complete answers to these questions. In practice it is not feasible to achieve common consensus among people on both the questions. The notion of privacy changes from individual to individual according to the circumstances. So it is not advisable to consider certain kinds of online actions as implied consent of the individual. At the same time, deciding what amounts to fair data processing will be Greek and Latin. Because the fairness of data processing differs from situation to situation and depends on the type of personal data processed. There is also a possibility that States may take advantage over the personal information of the individual citing it as fair data use.

CONCLUSION: WHY CONSENT SHOULD BE PRESERVED

The existing literature clearly emphasised the privacy and predictive harms posed by the Big Data (See Crawford & Schultz, 2014, pp. 96-105; Tene & Polonetsky, 2013, pp. 251-256; Tene & Polonetsky, 2011-2012, p. 65; Paterson & McDonagh, 2018, pp. 6-9), and how uncontrolled data collection and use of personal information poses threats to individual freedom (Eberle, 2001, pp. 969-978). The problems with the current consent framework are legitimate but lowering or relaxing the requirements of consent will create more complex problems. It creates disturbances to informational privacy. As stated by Daniel Solove "privacy self-management [informational privacy] takes refuge in consent" (Solove, 2013, p. 1880). Cohen emphasized, "[t]he values of informational privacy are far more fundamental" (Cohen, 2000, p. 1423). The predictions and inferences of Big Data compromises the individual identity by enabling institutional surveillance (Richards & King, 2014, p. 396). Anonymization of data has already failed in protecting privacy. That's why Schwartz & Solove called it an 'anonymity myth' (Schwartz & Solove, 2011, p. 1836). Paul Ohm pointed that "[r]eidentification science disrupts the privacy policy landscape by undermining the faith that we have placed in anonymization" (Ohm, 2010, p. 1704). Along with this, the resulting picture of data aggregation, which is typically shaped by various actors over long period of time (Solove, 2001, p. 1432), can be very invasive in private life (Grafanaki, 2017, p. 806) and poses serious risk to privacy and data protection rights (Monteleone, 2015, p. 71).

This invasion into private life by tracking the footprints that one left knowingly or unknowingly on the digital platforms will increase perils to individual autonomy "because one's capacity and facility for choice requires a degree of freedom from monitoring, scrutiny, interference, and categorization by others" (Grafanaki, 2017, p. 809). This autonomy protected by privacy is "vital to the development of individuality and consciousness of individual choice in life.... [T]his development of individuality is particular in democratic societies, since qualities of independent thought, diversity of views, and non-conformity are considered desirable traits for individuals" (Solove et al., 2006, p. 38). This kind of autonomy is the cornerstone of democratic society (See Cohen, 2000, p. 1426). That is the reason why, instead of searching for alternatives it is better to design measures that could strengthen the consent framework thereby upholding the informational autonomy and privacy of an individual.

REFERENCES

Atkins, K. (2000). Autonomy and the subjective character of experience. Journal of Applied Philosophy, 17(1), 71-79.

Austin, L. M. (2014). Enough about me: Why privacy is about power, not consent (or harm). In A. Sarat (Ed.), A world without privacy: What law can and should do? (pp. 131-189). Cambridge University Press.

Barocas, S., & Nissenbaum, H. (2014). Big data's end run around autonomy and consent. In J. Lane, V. Stodden, S. Bender, & H. Nissenbaum (Eds.), Big data, and the public good: Frameworks for engagement (pp. 44-75). Cambridge University Press.

Bergemann, B. (2018). The consent paradox: Accounting for the prominent role of consent in data protection. In Hansen, K. Marit, N.-F. Eleni, F.-H. Igor, & Simone (Eds.), Privacy and identity management (pp. 111-131). Springer International Publishing.

Beyleveld, D., & Brownsword, R. (2007). Consent in the law. Hart Publishing.

Bhardwaj, K. (2018). Preserving consent within data protection in the age of big data. National Law University Delhi Student Law Journal, 5, 100-110.

Brkan, M. (2019). The Essence of the Fundamental Rights to Privacy and Data Protection: Finding a Way through the Maze of CJEU's Constitutional Reasoning. German Law Review, 20(6), 864-883.

Broenink, G., Hoepman, J. H., Hof, C., Kranenburg, R., Smits, D., & Wisman, T. (2010). The privacy coach: supporting customer privacy in the internet of things. Pervasive 2010 Conference Workshop on What can the Internet of Things Do for the Citizen.

Bygrave, L. A. (2002). Data protection law: Approaching its rationale, logic and limits. Kluwer Law International.

Carolan, E., & Spina, A. (2015). Behavioural sciences and EU data protection law: Challenges and opportunities. In A. Alemanno, & A. L. Sibony (Eds.), Nudge and the law: A European prespective (pp. 161-178). Hart Publishing.

Cate, F. H., Cullen, P., & Schönberger, V. M. (2014). Data protection principles for the 21st century: revising the 1980 OECD guidelines. Oxford Internet Institute, Oxford University Press. Retrieved from https://www.oii.ox.ac.uk/archive/downloads/publications/Data_Protection_Principles_for_the_21st_Century.pdf

Christman, J. (2015, January 9). Autonomy in moral and plitical pilosophy. Stanford Encyclopedia Philosophy Rechive. Retrieved from http://plato.stanford.edu/archives/spr2015/entries/autonomy-moral/

Cohen, J. E. (2000). Examined lives: Informational privacy and the subject as object. Stanford Law Review, 52(5), 1373-1438.

Cohen, J. E. (2012). Configuring the networked self: Law, code, and the play of everyday practice. Yale University Press.

Crawford, K., & Schultz, J. (2014). Big data and due process: Towards a framework to redress predictive privacy harms. Boston College Law Review, 55(1), 93-128.

Custers, B., Dechesne, F., Pieters, W., Schermer, B., & van der Hof, S. (2018). Consent and privacy. In A. Müler, & P. Schaber (Eds.), The Routledge Handbook of the Ethics of Consent (pp. 247-258). Routledge.

Dworkin, G. (1998). The theory and practice of autonomy. Cambridge University Press.

Eberle, E. J. (2001). The right to information self-determination. Utah Law Review, 2001(4), 965-1061.

Efroni, Z., Metzger, J., Mischau, L., & Schirmbeck, M. (2019). Privacy icons: A risk-based approach to visualisation of data processing. European Data Protection and Law Review, 5(3), 352-366.

Forde, A. (2016). The conceptual relationship between privacy and data protection. Cambridge Law Review, 1, 135-149.

Gavison, R. (1980). Privacy and the limits of law. The Yale Law Journal, 89(3), 421-471.

Grafanaki, S. (2017). Autonomy challenges in the age of big data. Fordham Intellectual Property, Media & Entertainment Law Journal, 27(4), 803-868.

Holtz, L. E., Zwingelberg, H., & Hansen, M. (2011). Privacy policy icons. In J. Camenisch, S. F. Hübner, & K. Rannenberg (Eds.), Privacy and identity management for life (pp. 279-285). Heidelberg: Springer.

Jarovsky, L. (2018). Improving consent in information privacy through autonomy-preserving protective measures (APPMs). European Data Protection Law Review, 4(4), 447-458.

Kelley, P. G., Cesca, L., Bresee, I., & Cranor, F. L. (2010). Standardizing privacy notices: An online study of the nutrition label approach. Proceedings of the 28th International Conference on Human Factors in Computing Systems, CHI'10,, (pp. 1573-1582).

Koops, B. J. (2014). The trouble with European data protection law. International Data Privacy Law, 4(4), 250-261.

Kosinski, M., Stillwell, D., & Graepel, T. (2013). Private traits and attributes are predictable from digital records of human behaviour. PNAS, 110(15), 5802-5804.

Luger, E., & Rodden, T. (2013). An informed view on consent for UbiComp. Proceedings of the 2013 ACM International Joint Conference on Pervasive and Ubiquitous Computing, Ubicomp'13, (pp. 529-538).

Lynskey, O. (2015). The Foundation of EU data protection (1st ed.). Oxford University Press.

Maclean, A. R. (2000). Now you see It now you don't: Consent and the legal protection of autonomy. Journal of Applied Philosophy, 17(3), 277-288.

Mantelero, A. (2014). The future of consumer data protection in the E.U. Re-thinking the "notice and consent" paradigm in the new era of predictive analytics. Computer Law & Security Review, 30(6), 643-660.

Matthan, R. (2017). Beyond consent: A new paradigm for data protection. Takshashila Discussion Document. Retrieved from http://takshashila.org.in/wp-content/uploads/2017/07/TDD-Beyond-Consent-Data-Protection-RM-2017-03.pdf

McDonald, A. M., & Cranor, L. F. (2008). The cost of reading privacy policies. I/S A Journal of Law and Policy for the Information Society, 4(3), 543-568.

McLean, S. A. (2010). Autonomy, onsent and the law. Routledge-Cavendish.

Monteleone, S. (2015). Addressing the failure of informed consent in online data protection: Learning the lessons from behaviour aware regulation. Syracuse Journal of International Law and Commerce, 43(1), 69-119.

Müller, A., & Schaber, P. (2018). The ethics of consent: An introduction. In A. Müller, & P. Schaber (Eds.), The Routledge Handbook of the Ethics of Consent (pp. 1-5). Routledge.

Ohm, P. (2010). Broken promises of privacy: Responding to the surprising failure of anonymization. UCLA Law Review, 1701-1777.

Paterson, M., & McDonagh, M. (2018). Data protection in an era of big data: The challenges posed by big personal data. Monash University Law Review, 44(1), 1-31.

Policy and the Resarch Group of the Office of the Privacy Commissioner of Canada. (2016). Consent and privacy: A discussion paper exploring potential enhancements to consent under the personal information protection and electronic documents act. Retrieved from https://www.priv.gc.ca/media/1806/ consent_201605_e.pdf

Poscher, R. (2017). The right to data protection: A no-right thesis. In R. A. Miller (Ed.), Privacy and power: A transatlantic dialogue in the shadow of the NSA-affair (pp. 129-141). Cambridge University Press.

Reidenberg, J. R., Russel, N. C., Callen, A. J., Qasir, S., & Norton, B. T. (2015). Privacy and harms and the effectiveness of the notice and choice framework. I/S Journal of Law and Policy for the Information Society, 11(2), 485-524.

Regulation (EU) 2016/679 of the European Parliament and of the Council of Apr. 27, 2016   on the protection of natural persons with regard to the processing of personal data on   the free movement of such data and repealing Directive 95/46/EC (General Data Protection   Regulations)   O.J. 2016 (L 119/1).

Richards, N. M., & King, J. H. (2014). Big data ethics. Wake Forest Law Review, 49(2), 393-432.

Rouvroy, A., & Poullet, Y. (2009). The right to informational self-determination and the value of self-development: Reassessing the importance of privacy for democracy. In S. Gutwirth, Y. Poullet, P. De Hert, C. Terwangne, & S. Nouwt (Eds.), Reinventing data protection? (pp. 45-76). Springer.

Rubinstein, I. S. (2013). Big data: The end of privacy or new beginning? International Data Privacy Law, 3(2), 74-87.

Schermer, B. W., Custers, B., & Van der Hof, S. (2014). The crisis of consent: How stronger legal protection may lead to weaker consent in data protection. Ethics and Information Technology, 16(2), 171-182.

Schwartz, P. M., & Solove, D. J. (2011). The pii problem: Privacy and a new concept of personally identifiable information. New York University Law Review, 86(6), 1814-1894.

Soh, S. Y. (2019). Privacy nudges: An alternative regulatory mechanism to informed consent for online data protection behaviour. European Data Protection Law Review, 5(1), 65-74.

Solove, D. J. (2001). Privacy and power: Comuper and metaphors for information privacy. Stanford Law Review, 53(6), 1393-1462.

Solove, D. J. (2002). Conceptualizing privacy. California Law Review, 90, 1087-1154.

Solove, D. J. (2013). Privacy self-management and the consent dilemma. Harvard Law Review, 126(7), 1880-1903.

Solove, D. J., Rotenberg, M., & Schwartz, P. M. (2006). Privacy, information, and technology. Aspen Publishers.

Taylor, M. J., & Paterson, J. M. (2020). Protecting privacy in India: The roles of consent and fairness in data protection. The Indian Journal of Law and Technology, 16, 71-102.

Tene, O., & Polonetsky, J. (2011-2012). Privacy in the age of big data: A time for big decisions. Stanford Online Law Review, 63, 63-69.

Tene, O., & Polonetsky, J. (2013). Big data for all: Privacy and user control in the age of analytics. Newyork Journal of Technology and Intellectual Property, 11(5), [xxvii]-274.

Terwangne, C. (2013). The right to be forgotten and the informational autonomy in the digital environment. European Commission, Joint Research Centre. Retrieved from https://publications.jrc.ec.europa.eu/repository/bitstream/JRC86750/jrc86750_cecile_fv.pdf

Toubiana, V., & Nissenbaum, H. (2011). An analysis of Google log retention policies. The Journal of Privacy and Confidentiality, 3(1), 3-26.

Warren, S. D., & Brandeis, L. D. (1890). The right to privacy. Harvard Law Review, 4(5), 193-220.

Westin, A. (1967). Privacy and freedom. Atheneum.

Yeung, K. (2017). 'Hypernudge': Big data as a mode of regulation by design. Information, Communication & Society, 20(1), 118-136.

CYBER STALKING IN CYBER CRIME: AN ORCHESTRATED THREAT TO CYBER SECURITY IN THE LABYRINTH OF LAW

Author:

Nabanita Sen

ABSTRACT

Once Roger Revelle quoted-

"Ever since men began to modify their lives by using technology they have found themselves in a series of technological traps".

The cyber space of digital life is indeed ubiquitous with novel technologies drawing inexorably into their clutches. The new emerging technologies initiated computer-oriented crimes involving a computer and a network affecting national and overseas security. These internet enabled crimes know no boundaries, either physical or virtual commit cyber attacks across the world. Internet is vulnerable to intrusion and attacks are resilient to prevent and respond often leaving the perpetrators of crime to go scot-free. Cybercrime is mushrooming rapidly with posing threats to victims worldwide assuming an exponential growth in form of multi pronged attack often fashioned as transnational crime. Attempts of malicious cyber activities in the form of cyber intrusions, data breach or cyber attack has assumed immense risk to national and international safety and security. In the domain of security and legal concerns, protection is considered as an internal issue whereas security seems to be an external problem. Cyber stalking denotes online harassment or online abuse mostly committed against women and conceiving dismaying proportions along with devastating effect on victims portray deplorable and distressing scenario of cybercrime landscape. The Federal Bureau of Investigation (FBI) is the leading investigative agency for various cyber intrusions and cyber attacks. The Information Technology Act, 2000 suggested for setting up of cyber crime police stations add to the measure of mitigation and prevention. Indian Penal Code, 1860 penalizes number of cyber crimes. Both these enactments are overlapping with same nomenclature and same ingredients. The Communication Convergence Law provides regulatory framework to facilitate the convergence of cyber crime in India. Cyber crime with its international dimension should ensure that legal protection is harmonized internationally. Specialized global agencies like World Intellectual Property Organization (WIPO) and Internet Corporation of Assigned Name and Numbers (ICANN) deal with various challenges of cyber crimes. The United Nations Commission on International Trade Law adopted the Model Law on electronic commerce also worth mentioning in this respect. In spite of recent spurt of legislations worldwide; cyber crime is escalating day by day. National Crime Record Bureau (NCRB) reveals surge of 61% in cases registered under cyber stalking and bullying of women and children in 2020. The Legislature should be more sensitized with regard to cyber crimes especially cyber stalking bearing enduring impact on victims. Uniform legislation of cyber crime with enhanced punitive provisions is the need of the hour with rapid reporting can put a check to the crime and thereby contribute to the efforts against the emerging cyber threats. The present study attempts to examine concepts, typologies, modes used by cyber stalkers, cyber victimization along with proposing ways to thwart the menace. With shared risk comes shared responsibility for ensuring safety and security of global economy from high-tech organized and sophisticated criminal activity in the cyber epoch. We can, we will!!

Keywords: Cyber crime, Stalking, Cyber threat, Cyber security, Technology

INTRODUCTION

The advancement of technology strikes as being 'game changer' along with brainstorming impression of robotics, artificial intelligence (AI), block chain technologies, augmented reality (AR), Internet of Things and smart phone revolution ushering drastic digital transformation. Internet promotes virtual space of meet for individuals around the globe involved in cyber relationship enabling exchanging conversations and electronic transactions through electronic data interchange. Technology and internet has wreaked havoc facilitating cyber crimes beyond domestic jurisdiction. The phenomenal progress of technology has posed disastrous challenges to criminal jurisprudence in the form cyber crimes encompassing unauthorized use of technology and furthering anonymity. Internet penetration is proliferating briskly paving way to various emerging forms of traditional crimes and criminality. Cybercrime relates to all criminal activities committed with nefarious intention in cyberspace, including critical networks, involving 'cyber contraventions' and 'cyber offences' amounting to succor illicit ends. Contravention is generic in nature whereas offence is specific. Apart from specific target attacks on individuals or businesses, cyber crimes have assumed sophisticated form of targeting repositories of data with innovative use of technology.

Over time, stalking has garnered substantial concern in social media. Stalking finds its root of origin in crime, change and culture placing itself on the edge of law slipping from mental illness to deviance to crime across time and place (Wykes, 2007). Individuals remain worried about violent crimes (Povey et al., 2005) which happen to be unremitting, unpredictable and unambiguous component of culture (Wykes, 2007). Stalking is a worn phenomenon, bearing detrimental socio-economic and psychological consequences, prevalent in societies for centuries. Stalking implies intrusive repeated behavior amounting to crime with paradoxical status intended to threaten, harass and defame the victim spotted. In common parlance; the term 'stalking' implies activities of harassing or threatening an individual to cause acute trepidation and engenders reactive responses from exasperation and frustration to distress and fear (Dardis & Gidyez, 2017, 2019; Menard & Pincus, 2012; Dutton & Winstead, 2006). Cyber stalking using electronic communication mode seems to be sophisticated extended version of traditional stalking using technology in a felonious manner. Online and physical stalking harassment embraces a continuum of distressing behaviors involving unwanted and persistent phone calls, messages or emails, intrusive face to face contact, posting online false information about the victim, physical or electronic verbal threats and acts of aggression or violence (Dardis & Gidyez, 2017, Dutton & Winstead, 2006). The magnitude of such criminal activity has assumed exponential growth resulting in devastating ramifications for perturbed victims. The finding of various studies reports that females are significant targets for online stalking attacks but in contrary Pathe and Mullen (2002) states stalking as not the exclusive crime to perturb dignified bigwigs and celebrities. Majority of available literature is restricted only to the notion of stalking (Dardis & Gidyez, 2019) and exploring psychological effect on victim but the present study extends to convey the legal regime of this modish form of criminality. This paper aspires to address various dimensions of criminal jurisprudence in cyber/online stalking and sketch proposed measures to be implemented to curb the threat.

As specified by NCRB (National Crime Records Bureau), the number of reported national cybercrime cases has surged from 44,735 to 50,035 with Maharashtra recording considerable count in cyber stalking cases against women succeeded by Andhra Pradesh (Rai, 2021).

REVIEW OF LITERATURE

Cyber stalking disrupts privacy of individuals while seeking its aura in cyber culture. Cyber stalking seems to be the universal cardinal Gordian knot and a magnifying social hitch in the societal matrix (Report on Cyber stalking, 1999; CyberAngels, 1999, Ellison & Akdeniz, 1998) that often goes undivulged ("Cyber Crime in India," 2004). The extant research studies reported on frequent coexistence of digital and traditional form of stalking harassment (Dardis & Gidyez, 2017). In accord with a study by the Working to Halt Online Abuse (2003) reveals that majority of instances of online/cyber stalking begins with an e-mail and maximum cyber stalkers or harassers are intimate partners or schoolmates who are known to victims (Short et al., 2015). There are obtrusive instances which divulge the factuality that stalkers are persons of close intimate contact with their targeted victims. It implies controlling co-relation between two prevalent patterns of stalking. Dardis and Gidyez (2019) focused on poor self control in online as well as in offline stalking. Marcum et al. (2014) studied and assessed relationship between execution of online/cyber stalking and low self control. Tending to appraise online deviant behavior, low self control transpires to be decisive factor in this regard. Individuals owned to low self control appears to have invariant traits like irascible, impulsive, self obsessed, risk seeing, parochial attitude and fond of physical tasks (Fissel et al., 2021). The implications involved in cyber stalking erode self determination with indecisive attitude as a quirk in response to the marked effect of online harassment. Hence, victims of online/cyber stalking encounter psychological and physical consequences (Short et al., 2015) to the same extent as offline stalking. Despite diverse protruding criminological research, however, the findings are not universally acknowledged for definition of traditional physical stalking with dearth in literature accessible pertaining to activities of online/cyber stalking (Pittaro, 2007).

According to the Report on Cyber Stalking (1999), victims of online/cyber stalking were quite reluctant to report such crime as they thought that authorities would hardly pay heed to their complaints. However, trail of such happening has long lasting intense impact with deep-seated psychological pain. In a study by Davis, Coker and Sanderson (2002) established that physical and psychical impression about stalking were not gender based. Nonetheless, social and psychological sequels are inter-related (Mishra & Mishra, 2002). Furthermore, Kamphuis and Emmelkamp (2000) studied psychological aspects and observed social seclusion, emotional immaturity, indexterity and inability to manage with failed relationships as common with traditional physical stalking too. The driving factors that trigger the offence of cyber harassment bear gloom-ridden consequential impact coupled with long-standing response on well being of victims vexed.

STALKING GOES ONLINE: CYBER STALKING

Cyber stalking reflects reproduction of activities that resembles the pattern similar in traditional physical stalking. This implies an extension of traditional stalking, however, involving high-tech modus operandi (Pittaro, 2007a) while committing the crime. Cyber stalking, essentially, involves a virtual eye with geotags and webcams to retain firm rein on activities of the targeted victim. According to Tokunaga and Aune (2017), the clandestine nature of digital technology has shaped it as universal means to expedite stalking. In the words of Wykes (2007), cyberspace subsists as an interactive community which is 'continuous with and embedded in other social spaces' (Miller & Salter, 2000). Cyber space experiences communication and reciprocation of cyber cultural exchange of activities among its players. Over the last few years, terminologies such as 'crime', 'stalking' and 'cyber' observed to be placed together in various studies and reports of relevance. Cyber stalking activities encompasses tracing locations, trawling for personal information, video surveillance, tracking conversations, phone calls, eaves dropping and GPS spoofing (Tokunaga & Aune, 2017). Technology based stalking through internet and email is acknowledged as online harassment or cyber stalking that adheres to varied modes of electronic and digital communication with an endeavor to harass or terrorize victims. According to Emma Ogilvie et al. (2000) cyber stalking can be explicated as use of digital communication counting internet, emails, cell phones and pagers bearing an intention to harass, threaten, coerce and daunt a victim focused. Cyber stalking supervened as an electronic version of traditional stalking that abuse, threatens, intimidates, molests and apprehends a victim causing defamation and humiliation leaving deep scars of trauma having enduring impact. Technology is abused for committing time worn crimes in a novel manner at low cost, high speed, wide access and anonymity. With the ease of communications, identity of stalkers committing crime is concealed that triggers cyber stalker to execute his online obscene gesture constituting cyber harassment furtively. Unfortunately, cyber stalking has gained momentum involving new technology through exploiting internet and threatening behavior to induce fear and distress in mind of targeted victims.

Traditional physical/ fleshy stalking and novel cyber stalking can be distinctively classified based on geographical proximity, nature, risk, predictability, anonymity familiarity and intimacy with victim. In the matter of geographical proximity; physical stalking requires physical confrontation which engulfs instigating a third party to pester a victim becomes difficult whereas in cyber stalking physical confrontation is irrelevant to accomplish the predetermined purpose as the third party can be easily instigated to harass victims. In terms of nature; physical stalking records personal communion between stalker and victim whereas cyber stalking abets stalkers to commit crime with anonymity to shield his/her identity. In matters of risk; physical stalking involves high risk of stalkers being charged for harassment or threat portrayed through his activities whereas cyber stalking proposes less risk for the stalker as he was unlikely to be caught hold of. In terms of familiarity with victims; physical stalking involves interpersonal relationship where victim is a celebrity, neighbor or relative of stalker whereas cyber stalking pertains to choosing victims randomly from social networking forums with limited available knowledge. Regarding predictability; physical stalking easily traces to identify the stalker as he follows victim regularly to threaten and harass him whereas cyber/online stalking is unpredictable with nah involvement of physical confrontation. In terms of anonymity, physical stalking recognizes the stalker whereas cyber stalking promotes concealment of identity. With regard to intimacy; physical stalking can assess intention of stalkers whereas cyber stalking misleads victims through deceptive behavior of fake promises creating delusional beliefs in mind of victim.

The pestering activities of stalkers are precipitated by preordained events that pave way for delusional disorders posing threat to public health. Rekha Sharma, the Chairperson of the National Commission for Women, at a virtual event notes that online harassment including cyber stalking towards women has surged by 500%, last year (Prasad, 2021)

Cyber stalking reflects reproduction of activities that resembles the pattern similar in traditional physical stalking. This implies an extension of traditional stalking, however, involving high-tech modus operandi (Pittaro, 2007a) while committing the crime. Cyber stalking, essentially, involves a virtual eye with geotags and webcams to retain firm rein on activities of the targeted victim. According to Tokunaga and Aune (2017), the clandestine nature of digital technology has shaped it as universal means to expedite stalking. In the words of Wykes (2007), cyberspace subsists as an interactive community which is 'continuous with and embedded in other social spaces' (Miller & Salter, 2000). Cyber space experiences communication and reciprocation of cyber cultural exchange of activities among its players. Over the last few years, terminologies such as 'crime', 'stalking' and 'cyber' observed to be placed together in various studies and reports of relevance. Cyber stalking activities encompasses tracing locations, trawling for personal information, video surveillance, tracking conversations, phone calls, eaves dropping and GPS spooring (Tokunaga & Aune, 2017). Technology based stalking through internet and email is acknowledged as online harassment or cyber stalking that adheres to varied modes of electronic and digital communication with an endeavor to harass or terrorize victims. According to Emma Ogilvie et al. (2000) cyber stalking can be explicated as use of digital communication counting internet, emails, cell phones and pagers bearing an intention to harass, threaten, coerce and daunt a victim focused. Cyber stalking supervened as an electronic version of traditional stalking that abuse, threatens, intimidates, molests and apprehends a victim causing defamation and humiliation leaving deep scars of trauma having enduring impact. Technology is abused for committing time worn crimes in a novel manner at low cost, high speed, wide access and anonymity. With the ease of communications, identity of stalkers committing crime is concealed that triggers cyber stalker to execute his online obscene gesture constituting cyber harassment furtively. Unfortunately, cyber stalking has gained momentum involving new technology through exploiting internet and threatening behavior to induce fear and distress in mind of targeted victims.

Traditional physical/ fleshy stalking and novel cyber stalking can be distinctively classified based on geographical proximity, nature, risk, predictability, anonymity familiarity and intimacy with victim. In the matter of geographical proximity; physical stalking requires physical confrontation which engulfs instigating a third party to pester a victim becomes difficult whereas in cyber stalking physical confrontation is irrelevant to accomplish the predetermined purpose as the third party can be easily instigated to harass victims. In terms of nature; physical stalking records personal communion between stalker and victim whereas cyber stalking abets stalkers to commit crime with anonymity to shield his/her identity. In matters of risk; physical stalking involves high risk of stalkers being charged for harassment or threat portrayed through his activities whereas cyber stalking proposes less risk for the stalker as he was unlikely to be caught hold of. In terms of familiarity with victims; physical stalking involves interpersonal relationship where victim is a celebrity, neighbor or relative of stalker whereas cyber stalking pertains to choosing victims randomly from social networking forums with limited available knowledge. Regarding predictability; physical stalking easily traces to identify the stalker as he follows victim regularly to threaten and harass him whereas cyber/online stalking is unpredictable with nah involvement of physical confrontation. In terms of anonymity, physical stalking recognizes the stalker whereas cyber stalking promotes concealment of identity. With regard to intimacy; physical stalking can assess intention of stalkers whereas cyber stalking misleads victims through deceptive behavior of fake promises creating delusional beliefs in mind of victim.

The pestering activities of stalkers are precipitated by preordained events that pave way for delusional disorders posing threat to public health. Rekha Sharma, the Chairperson of the National Commission for Women, at a virtual event notes that online harassment including cyber stalking towards women has surged by 500%, last year (Prasad, 2021)

EXTENT AND MAGNITUDE

Cyber stalking does not ensue to be distinct, independent crime of its kind but entangles other offences in its periphery. A survey was conducted comprising of Fortune 1000 corporate houses perceived an annual growth rate of 64% in cyber attacks executed through Internet (Bagchi & Udo, 2003). Cyber stalking transpires to be societal ill (Fissel, 2021) assuming substantial proportion in recent times. The magnitude to which criminal justice system reciprocates and regulates cyber stalking literally devolves on the extent of its pursuing traditional activities corresponding to stalking in reality (Ogilvie, 2000).

In 2020, India noted 50,035 cases of cyber crime; reporting 972 cyber stalking or cyber bullying of women and children cases with an escalation of 11.8 per cent in alike offences along with an elevation in cyber crime rate displaying as 3.7 per cent within the country over the preceding year ("India reports 11.8%", 2021). Pawan Duggal articulates that India's existing laws cannot adequately deal with the menace labeled as cyber stalking (Duggal, 2017). With gaining momentum of criminological concern, apropos cyber stalking, stalker's behavior and activities need to be scrutinized in greater depth (Desai & Jaishankar, 2007).

STALKER'S MOTIVES AND METHODS

Stalking often goes disdained and disregarded but acts as a harbinger towards commission of any misconduct. The inducing motives behind majority cases of stalking are generally sham and stalled relationships, vengeance, abomination and psychological ailments such as obsession, misapprehension and sexual harassments. Anonymity tendered by internet often act as power source to instigate cyber stalkers to threaten and harass victims online. Wykes (2007) relates victimization with power transfer for the purpose of controlling crime from state to individual. Conforming to a study by Emma Ogilvie of Australian Institute of Criminology (Ogilvie, 2000); states initiating relationship, fixing an existing relationship, traumatizing or threatening an individual amounts to an incitement to commit the crime of cyber stalking. Previous intimacy has potential likelihood of magnifying risks of violence involved in stalking. However, studies indicate 'age' no way significant prognosticator in cyber stalking perpetration (Marcum et al., 2014, 2017). Further studies reveal that predominantly such cases are heterosexual and below 1% happen to be homosexuals in nature. In a study by Meloy et al. (1998) divulges stalkers to be from more mature age level having greater educational achievements compared to other offender population. Cyber stalkers are conventionally adroit at computer technology skill sets to abuse the confidential available online information of their targeted victims. Conventionally, the psychological aspect behind stalking behavior primarily focus on obsessive love disorder, sexual harassment, jealousy, erotomania, internet addiction, sexual deviation, personality deviation and psychiatric dysfunction, retribution etc.

Obsession and attraction can make the love obsessional stalker suffer from other delusional disorders whereas others suffer from no delusions but they simply love their subjects fanatically in an obsessive way (Kamath, ed., 2005). Erotomaniac delusion relates to a belief wherein stalker assumes the victim (who are celebrities) to be passionately in love with him. Jealousy bears a firm cause of stalking especially between ex-partner and the present partner. Revenge and hatred are recorded under stalker's motive which does not imply that targeted victim being the cause of hatred for stalker but by victimizing him through internet the stalker expresses his feeling of hatred. Sexual harassment often enlisted as the vital motive behind maximum stalking cases. Ready accessibility with easy approachability of information strikes as being significant concern for the widespread of cyber stalking. However, vast confidential information of individuals available on the internet furnishes the stalker with contact numbers, residential addresses and security passwords, financial data that often forms to be the genesis of pain and peril in life, livelihood, reputation, physical and emotional well being of an individual. Social media forums are fecund grounds for cyber harassments.

IMPACT ON VICTIMS

Marked footprints of cyber/online stalking assumes terrifying ordeal to victims encountering such harassment. In order to place a discrete behavior under cyber stalking; threat, harassment, intruding privacy and exudation of information seem to be dominant imperative of such crime. Unfortunately, the targeted victim of stalking is spotted by present or former spouse/intimate partner (Bjorklund et al., 2010; Melton, 2000, 2007; Baldry, 2002; Walby & Allen, 2001; Mullen et al., 2000; Tjaden & Thoennes, 1998; Walker & Meloy, 1998). Often victims are found to have some prior connection with stalkers and online/cyber stalking being no exception to it. This prior relationship affects police responses to the crime committed. Cases of stalking embracing previous sexual intimates presupposes enhanced plausibility of violence when there remains strong emotional attachment to victims of crime (Bjorklund et al., 2010; Mullen et. al., 2000). The horrendous practice of cyber crime of the utmost savagery against women is delineated as dreadful crime yet under-reported and often manifested through cyber stalking. Psychological trauma and social impairment shatter victims of online/cyber stalking introspectively and corporeally too.

In consequence of interminable harassment, victims time and again exhibit behavioral changes and psychosocial disfigurement. A cyber stalked victim is exposed to a slew of harassment with no bruises and bleeds but debilitated from within.

LEGAL PROTECTION

Nearly all advanced nations are lagging behind in matter of laws addressing cyber stalking positioned either as non-existent or in its budding phase. During 1999, cyber stalking law was first enacted by California State of US to control and combat the menace. The law enforcement authorities were quite reluctant to the crime of online/cyber stalking as being not designated under heinous crime endangering life and liberty along with threatening one's freedom. Nonetheless, abhorrent and grave the crime of cyber harassment pertaining to stalking is.

In Crime in India Report, 2017; National Crime Records Bureau (NCRB) first ever has included cyber stalking and cyber bullying of women under cyber crimes against women recording maximum incidents in Maharashtra (Singh, 2019). Section 67, Information Technology Act, 2000 imposes criminal liability on publishing or conveying an obscene subject material that is lascivious in nature. Comprehensibly, this section deals with punitive provisions for publication or transmission of sexually explicit stuffs through digital mode. Henceforth, when the stalker posts or sends an obscene matter or content, to the baited victim through electronic media, is subjected to punishment with 5 years of imprisonment and fine of Rs.1 lakh. If the episode repeats; punishment for the stalker, to endure such an act through time, would call for imprisonment of 10 years and fine of Rs. 2 lakh. Furthermore Section 500 of Indian Penal Code, 1860 concerns with punishment for defamation and as well applies to cases relating to online/cyber stalking in India. When stalker fabricates or forges any confidential fact of the targeted victim with an intention to publish or post an obscene message or comment on electronic media, amounts to a crime, punishable with imprisonment for a term which might extend to 2 years, fine or both. Indian Penal Code, 1860 and Information Technology Act, 2000 does not explicitly explore issues of online/cyber stalking but attempts to punish the offenders of such crime. Vijay Mukhi and Karan Gokani observed to enhance the penalty provided under existing provisions taking into consideration the wellbeing of the victim[1]. Moreover, cyber stalkers should be charged and prosecuted under Article 21 of Indian Constitution as his repellent behavior of intruding into the private space violates right to life entwined with right to personal liberty and right to privacy of the victim. Section 66A, added by Information Technology Amendment Act, 2008 was eventually struck down by the honorable Apex Court as unconstitutional in Shreya Singhal versus Union of India[2] addressing the reason as vagueness in words of provision in the Section. The Criminal Amendment Act, 2013 added Section 345D to IPC, after the Delhi Gang Rape Case (Nirbhaya Case), which defines stalking and takes into consideration cyber stalking besides physical stalking. Surprisingly, the criminal amendment of 2013, initiated by Justice Verma Committee proposed stalking laws in India. This section extends widened scope to 'stalking' and designates it as an offence. However, if male perpetrator engages in any unbidden activity, he shall be charged with and convicted of offence under Section 509 IPC (Indian Penal Code). This section entails words, gesture or sound intended to outrage modesty or virtue of women by intruding upon her privacy but that needs to be spoken, seen and heard respectively. Hence, cyber stalkers usually evade the charges and penalty imposed upon him by this section with the plea that gesture of harassment are not spoken for cyber behavior/activity amounting to crime. Indian Computer Emergency Response Team (CERT-IN) has been identified, by Information Technology (Amendment) Act, 2008, as the focal agency to deal and tackle cyber security threats.

In Indian scenario, the first reported cyber stalking case was filed in 2001 was by Ritu Kohli. Delhi police arrested Manish Kathuria for impersonating Ritu Kohli in an internet chat room by chatting illegally using her name, obnoxious language and residential phone number while beguiling people

---

1   Vijay Mukhi & Karan Gokani, Observations on the Proposed Amendments to the IT Act 2000, AIAI.

2   AIR 2015 SC 1523 /(2013) 12 SCC 73

to gossip with her over phone. Kathuria was formally charged for outraging modesty of Ritu Kohli under IPC. This glaring event initiated amendment exigency of the Information Technology Act in 2008. Following the next humiliating Vinupriya's case, the culprit posted obscene photographs of victim who was a 21-year old student from Salem, Tamil Nadu. The first photograph posted on June 23, 2016 followed by the derogatory practice again on June 26, triggered terror in mind of Vinupriya and she hanged herself on June 27. In furtherance, the chilling case of Vijay Nair, pioneer and director of OML (Only Match Louder) reports horrendous experience of being cyber stalked by female stalker since 2015. With reference to law, men cyber stalking women are charged under Section 354 of Indian Penal Code but the reverse scenario doesn't apply which puts the safety of men at stake. Information Technology Act (IT Act) though addresses offences relating to publication of obscene content but does not overtly consider cyber stalking, mail jacking, morphing faces on nude bodies.

CONCLUSION

Technology has sown seeds of high-tech crimes through emerging trends that promoted ample opportunities to perpetrators to control and abuse their targeted victims. Easy internet accessibility has recorded surge in cyber harassment cases on social networking website, chats rooms and over emails. The web being gateway to illicit activities leading to cyber crime while concealing identity of offender contributes to an increase in crime rates across the globe. In an effort to validate the statement, Aarti Kalra, sociologist once poignantly remarked anonymity on internet assumes to be an intrinsic lure for cyber-stalkers (Ghosh, 2010). Recent years have witnessed an exponential escalation in technology based crime with cyber stalking barging in one's private domain. Cyber stalking provides a striking example of novel form of tech-based crime assuming global significance that calls for an immediate response in both legal and mental well being domain. The deep gulf in legislative approach regarding the association of other related crimes with cyber stalking ought to be done away with. Framing of a discrete legislation on cyber staking takes pre-eminence.

Public education and awareness regarding self-protection as promoted by various protective agencies such as Cyber Angels and WHOA (Working to Halt Online Abuse) ought to be the stratagem and precautionary initiative to control the plague of cyber stalking. Using specific software programs to restrict receiving of contents or blocking the emails from unfamiliar and unacknowledged person might be constrictive approach towards restraining such abuses. Concerted effort between the enforcement agencies along with Internet Service Protocol (ISP) can go a long way to curb cyber stalking misdeeds. The baleful practice of online stalking has jeopardized freedom of individuals by restricting their cyber movement ornamented with cyber phobia for maintaining cyber security.

TASK AHEAD

To prevent occurrence and re-occurrence of cyber/ online stalking entails comprehensive outlook to protect safety and freedom of cyber users from multi-pronged ambush. However, multitudinous conspicuous loopholes in legal framework abet perpetrators escaping prosecution and accountability for their abusive behavior must probe further. The present prevailing piece of enactment (Information Technology) should be proposed to undergo major and minor amendments along with inclusion of a distinct new section or segment on cyber stalking issue to acclimate to progressive lenses of cyber world. There remains an indispensable and demanding need to legislate a discrete law with a legal definition of cyber/online stalking as there happen to be no distinct section under Indian Information Technology Act to define cyber stalking as a crime to be designated as heinous. Incidentally ambiguity remains regarding exact number of veracious cases being filed against online/ cyber stalking crime as there persists an established practice to associate the crime of online/cyber stalking with other crimes namely sharing pornographic material, hate crimes, threat, abuse, harassment. Initiating compelling need to accentuate co-occurrence of cybercrime offences, with the exigency to discern and succor people more vulnerable to victimization and re-victimization, on priority. Uniform cyber laws both at national and international level should be framed to control the crime of stalking assuming alarming proportions worldwide. The mode for combating online/cyber harassment, wherein an Internet Service Provider (ISP) can contact the stalker to pause his/her conduct or can directly lock their accounts, should be publicly obvious enough. Individuals before exploring an unauthorized domain should be well versed to the technical pros and cons with due diligence to maintain security and restraints of confidential information which could be misused by stalkers. General awareness schemes of ensuring privacy in cyber space to inculcate sense of safety behaviors to avoid being victimized and re-victimized should be conceived.

Designing and implementing cyber stalking preventive, awareness and educative programs may quell orientation and delusion regarding stalking. These programs should attempt to publicly educate community members on behaviors that constitute gentle and overtly grave activities resulting in cyber stalking. Coping strategies to quash deleterious effects of online/cyber stalking pertaining to emotional distress that the victim undergoes should be devised. Allied liaison between the enforcement authority and Government at international level should be promoted. Punitive measures for cyber stalkers to be rigorous envisaging distress and deplorable plight of victims in issue. This might be an endeavor to put cyber stalking crime at low ebb. Imparting regular trainings to upgrade technical traits along with published concept manuals and handbooks indicating potential and devastating impact of online/cyber stalking should be conveyed to personnel and law enforcement authorities for upholding the utmost gravity of the transnational crime. Conscientious inquisition and prosecution of cyber stalkers should be strictly effectuated. This clamors for an integrated regulatory legal approach through global integration and co-ordination to safeguard privacy from being publicized. We can and we will!!!

REFERENCES

Bagchi, K., & Udo, G. (2003). An analysis of the growth of computer and internet security breaches. Communication of the Association for Information Systems, 12(46), 129.

Baldry, A.C. (2002). From domestic violence to stalking: The infinite cycle of violence. In J. Boon & L. Sheridan (Eds.), Stalking and psychosexual obsession: Psychological perspectives for prevention, policing and treatment (pp. 83-104). Chichester, UK: Wiley.

Bjorklund, K., Hakkanen-Nyholm, H., Sheridan, L., & Roberts, K. (2010). The prevalence of stalking among Finnish University students. Journal of Interpersonal Violence, 25, 684.

CyberAngels. (1999). Retrieved from http://cyberangels.org. Accessed 28 October 2021

Cyber Crime in India. (2004). Cyber stalking-online harassment. Retrieved from https://www.indianchild.com/cyber-stalking.htm. Accessed 28 October 2021.

Dardis, C.M., & Gidyez, C.A. (2017). The frequency and perceived impact of engaging in in-person and cyber unwanted pursuit after relationship break-up among college men and women. Sex Roles: A Journal of Research, 76(1-2), 56-72.

doi: 10.1007/s11199-016-0667-1

Dardis, C.M., & Gidyez, C.A. (2019). Reconciliation or retaliation? An integrative model of postrelationship in-person and cyber unwanted pursuit perpetration among undergraduate men and women. Psychology of Violence, 9(3), 328-339. doi:10.1037/vio0000102

Davis, K.E., Coker, L., & Sanderson, M. (2002). Physical and mental health effects of being stalked for men and women, Violence Vict, 17(4), 429

Desai, M., & Jaishankar, K. (2007, February). Cyber stalking victimization of girl students: An empirical study. Paper presented at the second International and sixth biennial Conference of the Indian society of Victimology at Chennai, India, 1-23.

Duggal, P. (2017, May 13). The Scary Reality of Cyberstalking: The Law Can't Protect Us (Yet). The Quint. Retrieved from https://www.thequint.com/amp/story/voices/opinion/ the-dark-world-of-cyberstalking-and-how-the-law-cant-protect-us. Accessed 28 October 2021.

Dutton, L. B., & Winstead, B.A. (2006). Predicting unwanted pursuit: Attachment, relationship satisfaction, relationship alternatives, and break-up distress. Journal of Social and Personal Relationships, 23(4), 565-586.

doi: 10.1177/0265407506065984

Ellison, L., & Akdeniz, Y. (1998). Cyber-stalking: The regulation of harassment on the internet (Special Edition: Crime, Criminal Justice and the Internet). Criminal Law Review, 2948. Retrieved from https://www.cyber-rights.org/documents/stalking. Accessed 28 October 2021.

Fissel, E. R., Fisher, B.S., & Nedelec, J.L. (2021). Cyberstalking perpetration among young adults: An assessment of the effects of low self-control and moral disengagement. Crime & Deliquency, 67(12), 1935-1961.

doi: 10.1177/0011128721989079

Ghosh, A. (2010, August 22). Cyber stalking: Loopholes abound. The Economic Times. Retrieved from https://m.economictimes.com/special-report/cyber-stalking-loopholes-abound/articleshow/6389491.cms?_oref=cook. Accessed 27 October 2021.

India reports 11.8% jumps in cyber crime in 2020: NCRB data. (2021, September 16). Business Today. Retrieved from https://www.businesstoday.in/latest/economy/ story/india-reports-118-jumps-in-cyber-crime-in-2020-ncrb-data-306890-2021-09-16. Accessed 26 October 2021.

Kamath, N. (Ed.). (2005). Laws relating to Computers, Internet and E-commerce (2nd ed.). Delhi: Universal Law Publishing Co. Pvt. Ltd.

Kamphuis, J.H., & Emmelkamp, P.M.G. (2000). Stalking-A contemporary challenge for forensic and clinical psychiatry. British Journal of Psychiatry, 176, 206-209.

Marcum, C. D., Higgins, G.E., Ricketts, M.L. (2014). Juveniles and cyber stalking in the United States: An analysis of theoretical predictors of patterns of online perpetration. International Journal of Cyber Criminology, 8(1), 47-56.

Marcum, C. D., Higgins, G.E., Nicholson, J. (2017). I'm watching you: Cyberstalking behaviors of university students in romantic relationships. American Journal of Criminal Justice, 42(2), 378-388.

Meloy, J. R., & Gothard, S. (1995). Demographic and clinical comparison of obsessional followers and offenders with mental disorders. American Journal of Psychiatry, 15(2), 258-263.

doi: 10.1176/ajp.152.2.258

Melton, H. (2000). Stalking: a review of the literature and direction for the future. Criminal Justice Review, 25, 246-262.

Melton, H. C. (2007). Predicting the occurrence of stalking in relationships characterized by domestic violence. Journal of Interpersonal Violence, 22, 3-25.

Menard, K. S., & Pincus, A.L. (2012). Predicting overt and cyber stalking perpetration by male and female college students. Journal of Interpersonal Violence, 27(11), 2183-2207. doi:10.1177/0886260511432144

Miller, D. & Slatter, D. (2000). The Internet: An Ethnographic Approach. Oxford: Berg.

Mishra, A., & Mishra, D. (2002). Cyber Stalking: A Challenge for Web Security. In L.J. Janczewski & A.M. Colarik (Eds.), Cyber Warfare and Cyber Terrorism (pp.216-226). doi:10.4018/978-1-59140-991-5

Mullen, P. E., Pathe, M., & Purcell, R. (2000). Stalkers and their victims. Cambridge, UK: Cambridge University Press.

Ogilvie, E. (2000). Cyberstalking. Trends & issues in crime and criminal justice. Australian Institute of Criminology, Canberra, 166, 0817-8542. Retrieved from https://www.aic.gov.au/publications/tandi/tandi166. Accessed 25 October 2021.

Pathe, M., & Mullen, P. (2002). The victim of stalking. In J. Boon & L. Sheridan (Eds.), Stalking and psychosexual obsession: Psychological perspectives for prevention, policing and treatment (1, pp. 1-22). Chichester, UK: Wiley.

Pittaro, Michael L. (2007). Cyber stalking: An analysis of Online Harassment and Intimidation. International Journal of Cyber Criminology (IJCC), 1(2), 181.

Pittaro, Michael L. (2007a). Cyber stalking: An analysis of Online Harassment and Intimidation. International Journal of Cyber Criminology (IJCC), 1(2), 181.

Povey, D., Upson, A. & Jannson, K. (2005). Crime in England and Wales: Quarterly Update to June 2005, Statistical Bulletin 18/05. London: Home Office.

Prasad, A. (2021, April 6). Beware! Cyber stalking is on the rise during the pandemic. Times of India. Retrieved from https://m.timesofindia.com/life-style/spotlight/beware-cyberstalking-is-on-the-rise-during-the-pandemic/amp_articleshow/81924158.cms. Accessed 26 October 2021.

Rai, S. (2021, September 18). UP 'cybercrime capital' with over 11,000 cases, Maharashtra has most cases of cyberstalking. The Times of India. Retrieved from https://m.timesofindia.com/city/meerut/up-cybercrime-capital-with-over-11k-cases-maha-has-most-cases-of-cyberstalking/articleshow/86302510.cms. Accessed 27 October 2021.

Report on Cyberstalking. (1999, August). Cyber-stalking: A new challenge for law enforcement and industry. A Report from the Attorney General to the Vice President. Retrieved from http://www.usdoj.gov/criminal/cybercrime/cyberstalking.htm. Accessed 27 October 2021.

Short, E., Guppy, A., Hart, J.A. & Barnes, J. (2015). The Impact of Cyberstalking. Studies in Media and Communication, 3(2), 29. Retrieved from http://dx.doi.org/10.11114/smc.v3i2.970. Accessed 10 November 2021.

Singh, V. (2019, October 23). 30% jump in 'crimes against state': NCRB. The Hindu. Retrieved from https://www.thehindu.com/news/national/30-jump-in-crimes-against-state-ncrb/article29771116.ece. Accessed 26 October 2021.

Tjaden, P., & Thoennes, N. (1998). Stalking in America: Findings from the National Violence against Women Survey. Washington, DC: US Department of Justice.

Tokunaga, R.S., & Aune, K. S. (2017). Cyber-defense: A taxonomy of tactics for managing cyberstalking. Journal of Interpersonal Violence, 32(10), 1451-1475.

Walby, S., & Allen, J. (2001). Domestic violence, sexual assault and stalking: Findings from the British Crime Survey (Home Office Research study), London, Home Office, 276

Walker, L.E., & Meloy, J.R. (1998). Stalking and domestic violence. In J.R. Meloy (Ed.), The psychology of stalking: Clinical and forensic perspectives, San Diego, CA: Academic Press, 139:161.

Working to Halt Online Abuse. (WHO). (2003, May 25). Online harassment/ Cyberstalking statistics. Retrieved from http://www.haltabuse. org/resources/stats/index. shtml. Accessed 28 October 2021.

Wykes, M. (2007). Constructing crime: Culture, stalking, celebrity and cyber, Crime Media Culture, 3(2), 158-174. doi:10.1177/1741659007078541.

THE ISSUES OF LEGAL REGULATION OF APPLICATION OF AI IN IN CRIMINAL PROCEEDINGS

Authors:

Rusman Galina Sergeevna

Popova Elizaveta Igorevna

The current state of development of artificial intelligence technology provides new opportunities for the transformation of various spheres of human activity. Criminal proceedings are one of the types of providing access to justice for citizens and therefore must respond to the changes taking place in the modern world as soon as reasonably possible. In this regard, scientists are increasingly turning in their research to the use of information technology, especially artificial intelligence (hereinafter the "AI"), capable of performing heuristic functions, which previously could only be performed by humans.

The introduction of modern technologies, in particular AI, opens up new perspectives for further improvement of criminal proceedings, significantly increasing the chances of effective investigation of crimes and, consequently, giving a fair verdict.

At the same time, the need to optimize certain processes of investigation criminal cases and criminal trial through the use of AI technologies, ensuring the constitutional right of citizens to access to justice, criminal procedural proving, providing of forensic examination appropriate legal regulation.

Of primary importance is the criminal procedural legislation, which regulates the peculiarities of admissibility of evidence. Most noticeable in the legal regulation of the possibilities of application of AI in forensic activities are normative acts of the relevant specialized departments.

At the present time in the Russian Federation there is no clear regulation of the possibility of the application of AI in criminal proceedings in general and in the course of forensic examinations in particular. At the same time, legal regulation is especially important due to the emergence of completely new and obsolescence of existing technologies.

In the second half of the twentieth century in Soviet criminalistics, in conjunction with the emergence of "legal cybernetics" began a theoretical discussion about the problem of replacing the human expert by a computer, which received two main directions. Tkachev A.V. (2018) notes that according to the first point of view - the human expert will not be removed from the process of forensic examination, because his participation in the research as a guarantee of the correct operation of automated systems in the process of examination. With any degree of automation, there will still be room for value judgments. According to the second position, a human being as a participant in criminal proceedings will be excluded from the forensic examination, provided that the process of expert research is fully automated. Forensic examinations will become a reference activity, similar to checking with the assistance of the criminal records information system.

Nowadays, "legal cybernetics" and the above-mentioned positions have found their place in modern legal science and continue to develop. Thus, their development at the present stage is expressed in the process of combining "legal cybernetics" and "legal informatics" with information law.

Although at the moment it has not been possible to create a fully independent intelligent program, namely strong AI, artificial neural networks, the so-called weak AI, are already quite successful.

H. F. Gusarova (2018) defines AI as:

A digital reproduction of the processes of conscious activity of humans and society as a whole in terms of creative processing and reasoning based on non-trivially formalized information under the time and resource constraints of uncertainty and incomplete input data, creating cybernetic objects that can independently set goals and achieve them with quality not below the average specialist, capable in the future to replace existing activities and professions. (p.8)

Considering AI as a significant prospect of modernizing the sphere of criminal proceedings, we must remember that the use of any modern technology should help to improve the efficiency of justice and the quality of evidence, the level of access to justice for citizens.

It is necessary to understand what is meant by the term "artificial intelligence" in the legislation of the Russian Federation. In accordance with paragraph "a" of Article 5 of Decree 490 of the President of the Russian Federation of 10.10.2019 N 490 "On the development of artificial intelligence in the Russian Federation" artificial intelligence is:

A set of technological solutions that allows simulating human cognitive functions (including self-learning and finding solutions without a predetermined algorithm) and obtaining results when performing specific tasks that are comparable to at least the results of human intellectual activity. The complex of technological solutions includes information and communication infrastructure, software (particularly those using machine learning methods), processes and services for data processing and search for solutions (Analytical Center under the Government of the Russian Federation, 2021).

The participation of the expert, as a subject of criminal proceedings, is due to the need to apply special knowledge to solve questions that have arisen during the crime investigation and criminal trial.

The main advantages of the application of AI in criminal proceedings, which make us take up the problem of its legal regulation, are increasing the accuracy, objectivity and reliability of evidence. At the same time, participants in criminal proceedings should not rely only on the results obtained through its application. AI should be a useful tool for a person, as a participant in criminal proceedings, during certain procedural actions.

A number of researchers point to the advantage of AI in making decisions instead of a judge. They argue that AI is not subject to the negative influence of emotions on decision-making, is able to adhere strictly to the rules established by law, and reduces the probability of corrupt actions. AI makes decisions based on the analysis of a lot of data, in particular information describing the participants in the case. It is worth noting that AI operates with significantly larger volumes of arrays than a human can process. This advantage is especially important when working with data from the storages of public services, such as criminal cases, which for a long time remained unsolved for some reason or another, or when working with the archive of court cases and legal reference systems. This is especially important because AI can process data significantly faster and consider enormously more information than a human judge (Voskobitova L.A., 2019).

Thus, researchers believe that the rational use of modern technologies, based on AI in criminal proceedings will unify and systematize investigative and judicial practice, increase the speed and efficiency of investigative actions and procedural decision-making, as well as significantly reduce the number of human errors that take considerable time to correct (Zazulin A.I., 2020).

The use of AI in the field of criminal procedural activities has become most widespread in the course of expert research due to a number of advantages.

1. Increased level of objectivity of the results of the expert's thinking activity, conducted on the basis of scientific data, professional knowledge and experience, using scientifically validated techniques, procedurally formalized in the form of an expert opinion (Bushuev V.V., 2007).

Expert activity, regardless of specialization, is characterized by: legal and research nature; independence of the expert in the choice of research methods, techniques and forensic means as well as expert initiative, i.e., ability of the expert to self-directed decisive action beyond the task defined by the investigator or the court, and the assessment of the expert report by participants of criminal proceedings and the court.

At the same time, special attention should be paid to the process of formation of the inner conviction of the forensic expert, as the main component of his intellectual activity.

Bushuev V.V. (2007) defines the inner conviction of the forensic expert as "the result of his thinking activity, carried out through mental comparison of the properties of the investigated object (objects) with the properties of another object (objects) on the basis of scientific data, using proven scientifically based techniques to establish the factual data relevant to the criminal case" (p. 82).

According to Bushuev V.V. (2007) the use of information technology contributes to the objectivity of the internal conviction of the forensic expert, but the main role is still played by psychological mechanisms of cognitive activity.

The inner conviction of the forensic expert substantiates the decision-making, the commission of specific practical actions by him during the forensic research, i.e., acts as a certain moral and psychological guarantee.

The conclusions of the forensic expert, formulated by him on the basis of the expert research conducted through the application of his special knowledge, and his inner conviction of their correctness are the basis of the forensic expert's report.

2. Increasing the visibility, objectivity, reliability and quality of the forensic expert's report.

Zhuravlyov I. L., Sokolov A. Yu. And Kadejshvili A. A (2017) point out that the neural network algorithm of the face identification "Vocord Video Expert" can work with photo and video images with low resolution and increased noise. The integration of the face recognition in this software is intended to make it easy and affordable for forensic experts to select the necessary range of features.

3. Increasing the efficiency of search, collection, processing, storage, analysis, issuance and transfer of information with minimal effort, cost and time.

For example, the method of analyzing a large amount of data (Big Data) finds its application in the form of providing an opportunity to instantly get data, calculate a number of necessary indicators, and process the available data (Grigorev A.V., Grigorenko M. A. and Pecheritsa E.V., 2019).

When solving diagnostic tasks, the use of computer technologies relieves the forensic expert from the routine operations of describing the course of the research and processing the report.

Along with the listed advantages, a number of disadvantages of application of AI are also noted:

1. AI does not fully meet the requirements of scientific validity since the principle of operation of AI is far from the basic foundations of a particular forensic science (Popov V.L., 2020).

This is especially important because only those methods and means that meet certain requirements can be used in forensic examination.

"No system with AI can and will fully meet the requirement of transparency. Here, it should be understood that a system with AI is an object with a complex architecture that does not allow it to be understood "light-mindedly" (Kartashov I.I. and Kartashov I.I., 2021, p. 85).

Kholopov A.V. (2020) believes that a significant disadvantage of neural network-based AI systems, which almost exclude their use in criminal proceedings, is that if the neural network has performed calculations and produced a decision, the process and logic of making such a decision cannot be rechecked. In other words, there is no reflexivity in making such a decision, and it is impossible to implement the principle of verification, i.e., to check the objectivity and impartiality of a decision's logic.

Popov V.L. (2020) considers this on the example of the forensic portrait examination. When using AI, science cedes all of its functions to computer code, the principle of which is far from the basic foundations of any particular forensic science. The machine code carries out the analysis on the basis of the entered images of a large number of people at different periods of life. And on the basis of this the computer as if works out certain regularities, which can be explained only at the level of mathematical algorithm, but in no way can be translated under the regularities of basic forensic science - habitoscopy, which defines this type of forensic examination.

Ivanov A. I., Gazin A. I., Kachaikin E. I. and Andreev D. Y. (2016) point out that, apart from the above, there is no neural network forensic research of handwriting today because forensic experts still have quite little confidence in artificial neural networks. Although the artificial neural network analyzes 480 parameters of handwriting, and the forensic expert about 30, but also forensic expert has a lot of previous experience in this kind of work. Such neural network forensic research should give additionally its probabilistic characteristics together with the solution, not just classification.

2. AI in its learning process can never cover all possible scenarios and variants of its future functioning and, like humans, is capable of making mistakes (Bakhteev D.V., 2019).

AI learns from its environment using Big Data technology, i.e., processing large amounts of data. This approach allows AI to make further decisions based on what it has been able to learn previously. In turn, this makes the development of AI unpredictable since AI will make decisions that developers and later users could not have foreseen. At the same time, there is a high probability that situations will arise in practice where in the process that begins with the development and ends with the direct use of AI, people have done everything "right", but AI learns the "wrong thing" nevertheless (Kartashov I.I. and Kartashov I.I., 2021).

3. It is impossible to achieve absolute effectiveness of AI. Various errors can occur, including so-called "hardware" errors and false matches.

At the modern stage of development of forensic examination there is the so-called "hardware" error, which is inherent in the forensic expert report because of his use of new methods of examination, computer technologies, technical means of work with traces, etc. That increases the role of the human factor in the prevention of expert errors, in the correct formulation of his conclusions based on inner conviction.

4. Without forensic expert correction and evaluation, the use of AI may entail negative criminal law consequences.

Returning to AI technologies used in automated fingerprinting information systems, "even the most advanced Automated Fingerprint Identification System (AFIS) is capable of making mistakes" (Edzhubov L.G., 1999, p. 141). They can produce false matches when comparing hand papillary ridge pattern.

Despite the fact that the use of AI in criminal proceedings is becoming more and more widespread, the legislation has not been able to keep up with the changing realities. For this reason, there are gaps in the legal regulation of the admissibility of the use of AI technologies in criminal proceedings.

Thus, the activity of a forensic expert in criminal proceedings is regulated by procedural legislation and therefore additional restrictions are imposed on the software used in forensic expert practice.

The forensic expert, in accordance with the Russian legislation, bears criminal responsibility for giving false forensic expert's opinion, including its scientific validity, objectivity, comprehensiveness, completeness and reliability, and, consequently, for the study itself. Therefore, the forensic expert must justify the choice of research algorithm to solve a particular forensic expert task. Participants of criminal proceedings should always understand and know on what the conclusions of AI are based. Otherwise, the forensic expert will be responsible for the research, which he has no control and cannot evaluate.

Morhat P.M. in his works analyzes the positions of foreign authors and together with them come to the conclusion that special attention should be paid to the objective importance and role of emotions in the activities of judges, among other factors that objectively require human participation in criminal proceedings. The specified position is due to the fact that the making of the final decision in the case requires from the judge both formal knowledge of the law and a certain level of "cognitive and emotional competence", which AI systems do not yet possess. Consequently, researchers agree that the lack of an emotional component in judicial cases handled by AI systems will have a significant adverse effect on judicial decisions. Namely, that the decisions will be too formalized and straightforward, and will not take into account the importance of people's emotional and motivational sphere (Voskobitova L.A, 2019).

In order to address the above gaps in the legal regulation of the admissibility of the use of AI technologies in criminal proceedings, it is proposed:

1. To study all possible risks that can only be assumed at the current stage of technology development, as well as take into account the specifics of the application of AI in various areas of human activity.

Emelkina N. L. (2019) believes that in forensic activities AI can only be used "if its implementation ensures transparency, including the availability and comprehensibility of raw Big Data and the use of only those types of neural networks for which an external audit can find out the recognition criteria for certain aggregates" (p. 53). In addition, it is necessary to create conditions for transparency, impartiality and non-discrimination in the algorithms.

2. To find an optimal balance between a fully automatic decision and a human decision. In this regard, the researchers propose to "legislate a general prohibition on decisions by law enforcement entities generating legal consequences for citizens based solely on automated data processing, since even a highly developed model that reproduces human thinking is capable of committing an error with negligible probability" (Ushakov R.M., 2020, p. 67).

Researchers pay special attention to two conditions: one must not replace the objective necessity with maximalism, and one must not show excessive humanism both AI systems and the results of their application. These conditions are due to the fact that AI will never be identical to the human mind and must remain a means of human activity (Uzhov F.V., 2017).

AI at the current stage does not possess the necessary amount of knowledge, is not sufficiently intelligent, and cannot replace a highly qualified lawyer or forensic expert. However, we should not forget that the lawyer, in accordance with the rapidly changing global trends, should be aware of modern technologies that can change "the image of the law, affect its regulatory potential and efficiency, and a balanced approach is necessary when introducing the electronic form of criminal proceedings in domestic criminal proceedings" (Sementsov V.A., 2019, p. 27).

To date, theoretical studies identify two main options for the development of criminal proceedings, provided the application of AI in it. The first option is the use of AI as an auxiliary tool to facilitate the effective work of the investigator, judge and other participants of criminal proceedings. This way has already found its application in practice, and for a long time will remain the most probable in the future. At this stage of the development of AI system, it can act as consultants, and if it conducts the investigation of a criminal case and administer justice, then it can act as programs with the direct participation of a person as a subject of criminal proceedings. In addition, artificial neural networks can be used in the production of procedural actions and the subsequent adoption of procedural decisions (Solomatina A.G., 2020).

The second version of the path is expressed in the complete replacement of AI functions of the investigation, court and other participants in criminal proceedings, thereby leaving them without jobs, as well as possible loss of human control over AI systems. Although this way will probably never be implemented in reality, but it is worth providing a possible solution to this problem. Researchers suggest that if developers create AI systems capable of affecting people's future lives, they should also provide ways to curb its uncontrolled behavior that can have a negative impact (Solomatina A.G., 2020).

3. To develop a different from the traditional "anthropocentric" concept of the subject of crime, based on the specific characteristics of AI. Accordingly, "alternative types of liability, such as, deactivation, reprogramming or vesting the status of a criminal, which will serve as a warning for all participants of legal relations" (Khisamova Z.I. and Begishev I.R., 2019, p. 571), as well as the possibility of endowing AI "with limited legal personality in terms of endowing autonomous AI with responsibility for the caused harm and negative consequences" (Khisamova Z.I. and Begishev I.R, 2019, p. 572), are proposed.

Also, Khisamova Z.I. and Begishev I.R (2019) note that such changes in the legislation are due to the fact that the legal personality of AI "cannot be equated to the human or to the legal status of a legal entity. A human being, with legal status, acts on the basis of thought processes, guided by subjective beliefs. An AI, in turn, acts independently, having no consciousness or feelings" (p. 570).

Thus, to date, from the point of view of domestic criminal legislation, it is impossible to endow AI with a set of rights and obligations and, as a consequence, to recognize it as a subject of law. In accordance with article 19 of the Criminal Code of the Russian Federation only a physical person - a person who is sane, capable of realizing the actual nature and public danger of their actions (inaction) and directing them is subject to criminal liability.

Researchers offer the following theoretical definition of the new subject of legal proceedings, which should be improved in accordance with the further development of technology and the law. "Electronic person - a carrier of artificial intelligence (machine, robot, program), possessing a mind similar to the human, the ability to make conscious and not based on the algorithm of decisions laid down by the creator of such machine, robot, program, and by virtue of this endowed with certain rights and obligations" (Uzhov F.V., 2017, p. 359).

In addition, it will be necessary to define the rights, the protection of which may be necessary for this kind of the subject. At the moment, it is assumed that they will be conditioned by the factor of the existence of the carrier and the factor of the results of his "intellectual" activity, namely these are the right to inviolability and the right to authorship. The right to the inviolability is expressed in the fact that any modification of an AI medium will only be possible with the permission of the relevant authority. The right to authorship is that the carrier of AI will own the rights to any results of intellectual activity created without direct human involvement (Uzhov F.V., 2017).

4. To adjust legislation, including the rules of criminal procedure, to allow for their unambiguous interpretation and clarification of the meaning of the norm, and further translate them into machine-readable form (Markovicheva E. V., 2019).

Tests of AI judicial algorithms for AI (the digital judge) to make the final decision are taking place all over the world. For example, AI has found applications for data analysis in the administration of justice in France, the United Kingdom and the United States of America. However, in France, AI systems have found application only within the civil law, while in the UK and the US both in civil and criminal cases. Researchers at the University of Pennsylvania and the University of Sheffield, based on an analysis of 584 cases of the European Court of Human Rights, created AI capable of deciding a case that is 79% the same as the decision rendered by the ECHR. It is worth mentioning separately that the head of this project, Nicholas Aletras, concluded that he did not think that AI could replace lawyers, or even judges. But he believes, however, that the system being developed by researchers at the University of Pennsylvania and the University of Sheffield could be found useful by them because it can quickly identify those characteristics of the case that are most likely to lead to an unambiguous final decision. In addition, Nicholas Aletras noted that AI system could also be a very useful tool for detecting cases that violate the European Convention on Human Rights (Alexandrov A.S., Andreeva O.I. and Zaytsev O.A., 2019).

Fairly noted was the Roy L. Ferman at Harvard Law School, Lawrence Lessing, the fact that the use of AI systems entails new challenges for the legislature and judiciary. In particular, he points out that although AI is capable of displacing a huge portion of the practice of law, the algorithms on which AI functions are unpredictable. For example, there are AI algorithms designed to process Big Data that are trained and then produce results that no one puts into them. AI can't replace absolutely everything in a trial with its functionality, but the parties involved don't need it. Consequently, it is necessary to leave it to the judge to intervene in such an AI application process and, if necessary, to guide it and the proceedings according to the correct scenario (Alexandrov A.S., Andreeva O.I. and Zaytsev O.A., 2019).

According to the European Commission for the Efficiency of Justice, which adopted the Charter on Ethical Principles for the Use of Artificial Intelligence in Judicial Systems, AI should help improve the quality and efficiency of the courts. At the same time, it must be implemented responsibly and not violate the European Convention on Human Rights and the Convention for the Protection of Personal Data.

The charter outlines five basic principles:

- The principle of respect for fundamental rights - the development and implementation of artificial intelligence must not violate fundamental human rights;

- The principle of non-discrimination - preventing discrimination against individuals and groups from occurring or intensifying;

- Quality and security - judgments and data must be processed in a technically secure environment, on the basis of verified sources and using models developed by specialists in several scientific disciplines;

- The principle of openness, impartiality and honesty - the data processing methods must be accessible and understandable for third-party verification;

- The principle of user control - users must have the right of choice and the necessary information. (Alexandrov A.S., Andreeva O.I. and Zaytsev O.A., 2019, p. 204)

From the mentioned provisions of the Charter on the ethical principles of the use of AI in judicial systems, it follows that the judge should be able to review the decision that has been proposed by AI algorithms and make his own decision. In turn, participants in criminal proceedings should be empowered to appeal directly to the court and to appeal a decision made by AI judicial algorithms.

The most promising directions for replacing humans with AI systems in criminal proceedings can be considered:

(a) Rapid response to a crime signal from any technical communication channel from any source;

(b) The use of "Big Data", record-keeping systems, in determining the identity of the offender and his motives;

(c) The implementation of machine interaction in establishing indicia of crime;

(d) Preparation of draft charges, judicial decisions, etc. (Alexandrov A.S., Andreeva O.I. and Zaytsev O.A., 2019, p. 204)

5. To increase the scientific level of forensic examination, the level of qualification of forensic experts and the level of training of scientific personnel.

"T. F. Moiseeva once again draws attention to the competence of the forensic expert, acquired in the process of his training, is the key to the eradication of forensic expert errors" (Yarmak K.V., 2015, p. 12).

Undoubtedly, in the near foreseeable future no modern technology, even AI, will be able to replace humans in the sphere of criminal proceedings, completely determining its legally significant decisions. At this stage of development, the role of AI is to help the participants of criminal proceedings and reduce human subjective errors to a minimum. In turn, the human controls the work of AI and analyzes the results obtained.

Even now, the use of the latest technologies, including AI, provides significant assistance to forensic experts, facilitating the very process of examination, comparison, accelerating the processing of information and increasing the accuracy of the results obtained. Automation of the aforementioned processes is already having a favorable effect on improving the quality and efficiency of forensic examinations.

Human thinking activity is non-standard, it is characterized by abstract thinking, creativity and creativity. During an expert examination, the forensic expert is guided by experience, including experience based on past mistakes, special knowledge, and inner conviction. Only a human is able to directly implement and realize a creative approach to the selection of methodology and methods of forensic research, the production of forensic examination. (Sharypova, T.N. and Kolesnik, D.D., 2019).

Undoubtedly, the determining factors in giving a forensic expert opinion are the professional experience and special knowledge of the forensic expert, i.e., his competence, and technology is only a means to improve the efficiency of the expert, automating the processes of decision preparation.

For example, by creating forensically significant conclusions, AI helps the forensic expert, allowing him, taking into account all the other available data, to make the final decision much easier.

At the same time, AI cannot fully independently give an answer to the questions put by the investigator or the court to the forensic expert or give an assessment of the forensic investigation. That is, the decisions issued by AI at this stage of development have no legal force, but contribute to the administration of justice and accelerate the process of criminal proceedings.

Thus, the sphere of criminal proceedings in the Russian Federation is developing in line with global trends. The main direction of development of this sphere is the need to introduce modern technologies in forensic science and forensic examination as its practical implementation.

In the course of forensic examination, the leading position should be taken not by AI, but by human development from the position of cognitive, moral and creative aspects. At the same time, there should be the development of various automated systems as tools in the process of cognition. Hence, it follows that it is necessary to pay special attention and increase the scientific level of forensic examination, the level of qualification of forensic experts, and the level of training of scientific personnel (Mailis N. P., 2015).

It is worth noting once again that the real possibilities of AI in the criminal process have yet to be explored and settled.

Human and AI systems should not exclude each other from the process of forensic examination, but on the contrary - mutually complement each other, as the forensic expert controls the work of AI and analyzes the results obtained. As a result, the principles of criminal law will be completely rethought, in particular the institutions of the subject and subjective side of the crime. In order for AI to have competence similar to that of a humane forensic expert in the future, it is necessary to work not only on the development of AI technologies, but also on the improvement of legal regulation of AI, which will probably allow to determine its procedural status.

V.V. Momotov believes that:

> Artificial intelligence system will never be able to get into the depths of the human psyche, artificial intelligence can assess the circumstances of the case only in terms of formal logic, and that is why artificial intelligence will never be able to fully understand the facet of the case, as in many cases, such as family cases and, especially, criminal cases, a lot of irrationals rather than formal-logical (Council of Judges Russian Federation, 2020).

One can only agree with Belkin R.S. (1997):

> Thus, the conclusion of the discussion was that humans and AI
> systems should not mutually exclude, but mutually complement
> each other. Man sets a global goal, formulates problems and solution
> options, and determines general courses of action with the help of
> computer systems, while intelligent systems allow to exclude or
> minimize subjective human errors and facilitate the performance of
> routine, uncreative operations (p.41).

Thus, we can conclude that the introduction of modern technology opens up new prospects for the further development of forensic activities and, as a result, significantly increases the chances of effective crime investigation and a fair verdict.

REFERENCES

Alexandrov A.S., Andreeva O.I. and Zaytsev O.A. (2019). On Development Prospects of the Russian Criminal Proceeding in the Context of Digitalization. Vestnik Tomskogo gosudarstvennogo universiteta, (448), 199–207. (in Russian)

Analytical Center for the Government of the Russian Federation. Neurotechnology and artificial intelligence. (2021). https://digitech.ac.gov.ru/technologies/neurotechnology_and_artificial_intelligence/ (in Russian)

Bakhteev D.V. (2019). Risks and ethical-legal models of using artificial intelligence systems. Legal research, (11), 1-11. (in Russian)

Belkin R.S. (1997). Criminalistics course: in 3 t. Criminalistic means, receptions and recommendations. Moscow: Yurist, (3), 480 p. (in Russian)

Bushuev V.V. (2007). On the concept, formation and value of the internal conviction of the judicial expert in criminal proceedings. Forensic Expertise, (4), 80-84. (in Russian)

Council of Judges Russian Federation. Prospects for the use of artificial intelligence in the judicial system of the Russian Federation: speech by the Chairman of the Council of Judges of the Russian Federation V.V. Momotov at the plenary session. (2020). http://ssrf.ru/news/lientanovostiei/ 36912/ (in Russian)

Edzhubov L.G. (1999). Statistical. fingerprinting. Methodological problems /. L.G. Edzhubov (ed.). Moscow: Gorodets, Formula prava, 184 p. (in Russian)

Emelkina N. L. (2019). Artificial intelligence in criminal proceedings. Criminal policy at the present stage: state, trends, prospects, 49-54. (in Russian)

Grigorev A.V., Grigorenko M. A. and Pecheritsa E.V. (2020). Modern directions for the development of information technologies in the court production. National security and strategic planning, (1), 118-124. (in Russian)

Gusarova, N. F. (2018). Introduction to the theory of artificial intelligence. SPb: ITMO University, 62 p. (in Russian)

Ivanov A. I., Gazin A. I., Kachaikin E. I. and Andreev D. Y. (2016). Automation of graphologic examination based on teaching large artificial neuronal nets. Models, systems, networks in economics, technology, nature, and society, (1 (17)), 249-257. (in Russian)

Kartashov I.I. and Kartashov I.I. (2021). Artificial intelligence: criminal and procedural aspects. Current issues of the state and law, 5(17), 75-89. (in Russian)

Khisamova Z.I. and Begishev I.R. (2019). Criminal liability and artificial intelligence: theoretical and applied aspects. Vserossiiskii kriminologicheskii zhurnal. 13(4), 564-574. (In Russian)

Kholopov A.V. (2020). A person in the conditions of digitalization of law: problems and ways of development. Legal Science, (6), 8-12. (in Russian)

Mailis N. P. (2015). Improvement of forensic and didactic activities with the use of innovative technologies. Bulletin of Economic Security, (2), 12-15. (in Russian)

Markovicheva E. V. (2019). To the question of the introduction of electronic criminal case in the Russian criminal process. Criminal Procedure and Criminalistics: Theory, Practice, Didactics, 220-224. (in Russian)

Popov V.L. (2020). Problems and prospects of using neural network technologies in the forensic trials on transport. Transport Law and Security, 3 (35), 65-75. (in Russian)

Sementsov V.A. (2019). The digitalization of domestic criminal proceedings: evolutionary approach. Legal Bulletin of the Kuban State University, 3, 24-28. (in Russian)

Sharypova T.N., Kolesnik, D.D. (2019). Information technologies in forensic examination. Alleya nauki, 2(1), 945-948. (in Russian)

Solomatina A.G. (2020). Admissibility of the use of artificial intelligence in criminal proceedings. Vestnik Moskovskogo universiteta MVD Rossii, (3), 97-99. (in Russian)

Tkachev A.V. (2018). On the use of digital expert research in the investigation of crimes. Tactics and methods of investigation of crimes: theory, practice, innovations, 150-153. (in Russian)

Ushakov R.M. (2020). Big data technology as a direction of development of criminalistic technique: prospects for application in the context of their lawfulness. Ural Journal of Legal Research, 2(9), 54-69. (In Russian)

Uzhov F.V. (2017). Legal personality of Artificial Intelligence. Gaps in Russian legislation, (3), 357-360. (in Russian)

Voskobitova L.A (2019). Criminal Justice and Digital Technology: Compatibility Issue. Lex Russica. (5), 91-104. (in Russian)

Yarmak K.V. (2015). Preventing of expert errors in the light of the using of modern technologies in the forensic examinations. Vestnik Moskovskogo universiteta MVD Rossii, (3), 10-15. (in Russian)

Zazulin A.I. (2020). Functions of Digital Information and Technologies in Criminal Proceedings. Siberian Law Review, 17(1), 75-82. (in Russian)

Zhuravlyov I. L., Sokolov A. Yu. and Kadejshvili A. A. Efficiency of identification and verification of persons by a neural network at low quality of pictures. Encyclopedia of forensic science, (2), 76-87. (in Russian)

THE USE OF SMART CONTRACTS IN BUSINESS ACTIVITY

Authors:

David Gabriel Dutra Martins

Luane Silva Nascimento

Anna Carolina Pinho

ABSTRACT

This study aims to describe how smart contracts are made and the legal certainty of using them on business contracts. For this, the study concepted the smart contract, as well its characteristics and the difference between smart contract and e-contract. It described the legal certainty of smart contract and how they can be used on business transactions. Besides, the research explained the importance of blockchain, ethereum and cryptocurrency at the smart contract. At last, it was described how smart contracts are applied in the legal universe and demonstrated their advantages as self-execution and clauses' immutability. For this work, the bibliographic research and deductive method were used. The study concluded that the inexistence of law causes legal insecurity which represents an obstacle to spread the use of smart contracts.

Keywords: Business Activity, Technologies, Security.

INTRODUCTION

This paper was organized based on the explanation of the smart contract concept and its distinctions with regard to other types of electronic contracts, such as the e-contract, since the so-called technological revolution has presented several tools to simplify, make feasible and democratize several activities of human life, which inevitably led to the inclusion of the contract, one of the oldest institutes of Law.

In the first chapter the concept of smart contracts was presented, which consists of contracts whose terms are reduced to programming languages that execute the commands that were contracted automatically.

Moreover, it was also shown that although the existence of a smart contract does not depend on its insertion in a blockchain, its use became much more attractive after the emergence of this technology. Along these lines, it was found that the blockchain is a decentralized data storage network, similar to a ledger, with the difference that there is no central authority able to change any of the data stored on the network.

The most widely used blockchain for smart contracts has been Ethereum, which was created in 2014 by Vitalik Buterin precisely with the goal of spreading the use of these resources, such as smart contracts, tokens, decentralized organizations, and other applications.

In the second chapter, the need for security in business transactions established through technology was demonstrated, thus, asymmetric cryptography has also been shown as a great ally, because it is essential to ensure security for users, however, the lack of regulation has been a major obstacle, as in the case of the Securities and Exchange Commission not considering a crypto-asset as a security due to the uncertainty of regulation leading to insecurity for the crypto economy.

In the third chapter, in turn, it was shown that, despite the obstacles that still exist for greater diffusion of the technology in the business environment, day after day the use of blockchain has been disseminated in various areas of law, especially in business activities, in notary and intellectual property records, however, the potential of this technology combined with smart contracts has been extremely broad, from cost sharing contracts to Decentralized Finance (DeFi).

The research was conducted through bibliographic research, under the deductive method, whose problem was centered on the investigation of the legal (in)security present in smart contracts and how this can influence its diffusion in the business environment. From this, the objectives of conceptualizing smart contracts and explaining the applicability of programming and blockchain networks in the legal universe in business practice were stipulated.

Finally, it was found that the potential for use of the technologies presented is great, moreover, that the regulation of this new economy (crypto economy) can help popularize its use, since it will represent legal certainty to the user.

SMART CONTRACTS: GENERAL CONCEPTION

The beginning of this discussion permeates the contractual universe, therefore, for a better understanding of smart contracts, we will first make a brief note about contracts, since they are the essence of the discussion. According to Diniz[1], a contract is a kind of legal transaction that results from an agreement of wills between two or more parties, precisely when these parties intend to create, modify or terminate rights in accordance with the legal order, creating in its content an individual legal rule capable of regulating the relationship created between the parties, furthermore, establishing rights and obligations, whose noncompliance is capable of generating sanctions and penalties, provided that it is a valid legal transaction.

---

1   DINIZ. Maria Helena Diniz. Curso de Direito Civil Brasileiro. São Paulo-SP. Saraiva Jur, 2020.

Article 104 of the Brazilian Civil Code[2] provides for the assumptions of validity of a legal transaction, which are: to be performed by a capable agent, having as purpose a lawful, possible, determined or determinable object, in a form prescribed or not defended by law[3].

Therefore, as the contract is a legal transaction, in order for it to be legally valid it is necessary to comply with the three essential requirements, which are subdivided into subjective, objective and formal[4] and which make up the Ponteana Ladder of existence, validity and effectiveness.

Although the Brazilian legislation contemplates contracts whose solemnity is a validity requirement, such as the real estate purchase and sale contract that requires the form of a public deed for goods whose value is higher than thirty minimum wages, there is no form required in the Brazilian legal system for the formation of smart contracts, there is not even specific legislation to regulate them, therefore, there is no obstacle regarding the validity of a smart contract, provided that the validity requirements exposed above are observed and it is possible to prove its authenticity and integrity, as well elucidated by Jimene[5] when discussing the admission of electronic documents as documentary evidence of legal acts and facts, according to the provisions of the Code of

---

2   BRAZIL. Law n° 10.406, January, 10th, 2002. Establishes the Civil Code. Diário Oficial da União: section 1, Brasília, DF, year 139, n. 8, p. 1-74, January, 11th, 2002. PL 634/1975.

3   Art. 104. The validity of a juristic act requires: I - a capable agent; II - a licit, possible, determined, or determinable object; III - a form prescribed or not defended by law.

4   DINIZ, 2020.

5   JIMENE, Camilla do Vale, BLUM, Renato Opice. O valor probatório do documento eletrônico, São Paulo: Sicurezza, 2010.

Civil Procedure, provided they have the peculiar characteristics of authorship and veracity.

Nick Szabo[6] was a pioneer when writing about smart contracts, comparing them to a vending machine, due to its characteristic of formalizing and executing a certain contract autonomously from pre-determined commands, since the deposit of the amount required by the buyer would be enough for the machine to confirm the payment and deliver the chosen product without the need for the presence, in loco, of a person in the sales position.

Szabo[7] further conceptualizes the smart contract as a set of promises and protocols in which the parties make promises and fulfill them. Currently these protocols are written in programming language and can be inserted in a blockchain[8], in which case they will be automatically executed as the parties confirm the fulfillment of their obligations.

It should be noted that the term "smart" is used because of the ability of the program, whose contractual terms were written, to execute the promises

---

6   SZABO, Nick. Formalizing and Securing Relationships on Public Networks, 1997. First Monday, Available at <https://firstmonday.org/ojs/index.php/fm/article/view/548/469>. Article.

7   SZABO, Nick. Smart Contracts: Building Blocks for Digital Markets, 1996. Available at <https://www.fon.hum.uva.nl/rob/Courses/InformationInSpeech/CDROM/Literature/LOTwinterschool2006/szabo.best.vwh.net/smart_contracts_2.html/>. Article.

8   A blockchain is a simple chronological database of transactions recorded by a network of computers. Each blockchain is encrypted and organized into a smaller data set called a "block". Each block contains information about a certain number of transactions, the reference of the previous block in the blockchain, and the answer to a mathematical puzzle, which is used to validate the information contained in each block. Each computer on the network contains a copy of the blockchain, and these computers synchronize the information periodically to ensure that they all contain the same information.

contained therein from the confirmation of the programmed commands and without the need for a relationship with a trusted third party between the parties, therefore, it is enough that both parties trust the code and the network used to write and insert the contract that will be signed between them, regardless of their location.

The discussion about the concept of smart contract has sharpened in recent years, and from it, Josh Stark[9] pointed out two distinct definitions for smart contract, namely, Smart Contract Code and Smart Legal Contract. The first term is used by professionals linked to programming and computer science to define the technology related to the code or program inserted in the blockchain capable of executing commands written in programming language, the second term is related to the legal conceptualization of the use of smart contract code for the formalization of a legally valid contract capable of being protected by law.

For Pinheiro[10] "[...] smart contract can be understood as the set formed by the contract and the software used in its execution. [...]". Authors such as Divino[11], on the other hand, restrict the concept of smart contract considerably:

> *[...] unilateral or bilateral legal business, almost inviolable, imperative, previously agreed upon in writing or verbally, reduced to the appropriate computer language (algorithms)*

---

9   STARK, Josh. Making Sense of Blockchain Smart Contracts. Coindesk, 2016. Available at < https://www.coindesk.com/making-sense-smart-contracts/>. Article.

10   PINHEIRO, Luís de Lima. Smart Contracts e Direito Aplicável. Discussões sobre Direito na Era Digital, cord. Ana C. Pinho. 1ª ed. Rio de Janeiro: GZ, 2021, p. 503 – 527.

11   DIVINO, Sthéfano Bruno Santos. Smart Contracts: Conceitos, Limitações, Aplicabilidade e Desafios, 2018, p. 2788. Article

and expressed in a digital term that will represent ipsis litteris the previously agreed upon, stored and executed in a decentralized database (Blockchain), to manage it autonomously and automatically from its formation to its termination - including conditions, terms, charges, and eventual clauses of civil liability - with the aid of software and hardware, without the interference of third parties, aiming at reducing transaction costs and eventual legal expenses, provided that legal and economic principles compatible with the contractual relationship established are applied.

However, this is a very restricted concept, since it is not necessary to aim for the reduction of transaction costs and eventual legal expenses in order to form the smart contract, although, in fact, the reduction of transaction costs and eventual legal expenses may be considered advantages of a smart contract compared to traditional contracts, however, they are not essential features for the formalization of the smart contract, moreover, furthermore, nothing prevents the smart contract code from being written for another network instead of a blockchain network, since the factor that makes a contract be considered smart is its ability to perform the terms adjusted without the need for human interference, therefore, it is the machine intelligence that differentiates a simple contract from a smart contract, thus, it becomes restrictive to conceptualize the smart contract together with the technology used contemporaneously with the text considering that technology is in constant evolution.

Therefore, from a broader perspective, one can see that the smart contract is an unilateral, bilateral or more than two parts in a legal transaction, whose terms are reduced to a computer language expressed in a computer program capable of managing it autonomously and automatically.

Having made these initial conceptual considerations, it is important to elucidate the distinctions between smart contracts and e-contracts.

Electronic contracts or e-contracts are formed by electronic means of communication, especially the internet. Anderson Schreiber[12] argues that the e-contract could not be considered another contractual genre, but only a means of electronic contracting, in this sense Bandeira[13] corroborates by providing that "[...] smart contracts do not consist in a new type or contractual species; but in a technological means for contract formation [...]" [Author's translate].

Thus, any contract formed by electronic means could be considered an e-contract, whether they are adhesion contracts, whose signature is the acceptance issued by the contracting party through the website or computer program, or the contracts inserted in platforms that enable the reliable collection of the electronic signature.

That said, it can be said that every smart contract is an e-contract, but not the opposite, because the smart contract has unique features that are not applicable to any electronic contract, which will be analyzed below.

The smart contract needs to be written in algorithms or other computer language of a certain software to dictate and execute the terms of the agreement, thus creating a computer program through the smart contract code, on the other hand, other electronic contracts do not need such technological complexity, it is enough that they are formed by electronic means.

In the wake of Divino[14] an essential feature of the smart contract is that it is autonomous, that is, once its protocols are programmed, the contract performs

---

12   SCHREIBER, Anderson. Contratos Eletrônicos e Consumo, REVISTA BRASILEIRA DE DIREITO CIVIL. ISSN 2358-6974. Volume 1, p. 88-110, Jul./Sept. 2014.

13   BANDEIRA. Paula Greco. Os Smart Contracts no Direito Contratual Contemporâneo. Discussões sobre Direito na Era Digital, coord. Ana C. Pinho. 1ª ed. Rio de Janeiro: GZ, 2021, p. 557-575.

14   DIVINO, Sthéfano Bruno Santos. Smart Contracts: Conceitos, Limitações, Aplicabilidade e Desafios, 2018. Article.

its programming regardless of the will of the parties, however, it is not to be forgotten that not every e-contract has this feature, only the smart one.

Once the smart contract code is inserted in a blockchain it will not be possible to make any amendments considering the level of technological advancement today, that is, it is not possible to have an amendment term capable of modifying the terms written in a smart contract, however, in other electronic contracts this will be possible by simply inserting the amendment term in the same platform and collecting the signatures of the parties.

Thus, it can be said that the e-contract is a genus of which the smart contract is a species and, for a better understanding of the subject, it is necessary to situate the noble reader in relation to the blockchain, bitcoin and ethereum.

In the line of Aaron Wright and Primavera de Filippi[15], blockchain is a platform that works as a distributed database with chronological records of transactions recorded by a network of computers, in which each blockchain is encrypted and organized into a set of smaller blocks that contain the information about a certain number of transactions accompanied by information from previous blocks and the answer of a mathematical puzzle, called hash, which is used to validate the data associated with each block.

Each computer has a copy of this blockchain that is synchronized with the other copies of the network periodically to ensure that everyone has the same database so that no one can defraud the network without requiring more effort than the potential reward for defrauding it.

So, for Aaron Wright and Primavera de Filippi:

> *A blockchain is simply a chronological database of transactions recorded by a network of computers. Each blockchain is encrypted and organized into smaller datasets*

---

15   WRIGHT, Aaron; DE FILIPPI, Primavera. Decentralized Blockchain Technology and the Rise of Lex Cryptographia, 2015. Articlce.

referred to as "blocks". Every block contains information about a certain number of transactions, a reference to the preceding block in the blockchain, as well as an answer to a complex mathematical puzzle, which is used to validate the data associated with that block. A copy of the blockchain is stored on every computer in the network and these computers periodically synchronize to make sure that all of them have the same shared database

Thus, in the wake of the authors, one can state that a blockchain is equivalent to the ledger of a notary's office, since everything that is done in that program will be recorded, however, unlike the latter, there is no need for a server endowed with public faith to validate that information, because these are validated by anyone who uses the network, thus ensuring the authenticity of the information since it is confirmed by thousands of people who have no interest in it.

Mazzola and Lundgren[16] teach "[...] it is literally a chain of blocks in which data of any nature is stored. It is as if the technology were a big digital ledger, where all kinds of transactions are registered [...]". This technological innovation is of utmost importance to smart contracts, however, its utility is infinitely greater, for those authors "[...] the potential for use of this technology is practically infinite [...]".

After that, the concept of cryptocurrency will be exposed, which, according to Brandão[17] is a digital representative of values, whose issuance is not linked to a central authority of currency issuance, nor intertwined with a common fiat

---

16   MAZZOLA, LUNDGREN. Blockchain e Propriedade Intelectual: Impactos Práticos da Tecnologia. Discussões sobre Direito na Era Digital, cord. Ana C. Pinho. 1ª ed. Rio de Janeiro: GZ, 2021, p. 529 – 546.

17   BRANDÃO. Pedro Ramos Brandão. Criptomoeda: o Bitcoin. 2020. Article.

currency, but is accepted as a means of payment and can be stored in a digital wallet.

Bitcoin, in turn, is a cryptocurrency that was created by a person, or group of people, using the pseudonym Satoshi Nakamoto[18], programmed in open-source code in a peer-to-peer system, in which there is no central server or authority able to control its issue, which in turn is done through a process called mining. Mining is a process that involves the computational ability to solve a mathematical problem while processing the transactions made on the network.

The revolutionary potential of this technology provokes discussions in several areas of scientific knowledge, from programmers and economists to political scientists. With this in mind, Fernando Ulrich[19] conceptualizes bitcoin for the legal universe as an intangible asset, as follows:

> [...] Bitcoins, as a monetary unit, are best considered an intangible good that, in certain markets, have been accepted in exchange for goods and services. We could say that these transactions constitute an exchange, and never a sale with payment in cash, as currency in each jurisdiction is defined by force of law, and is the exclusive prerogative of the state.

Ethereum, in turn, was created by Vitalik Buterin and consists of a blockchain platform that is equivalent to bitcoin, however, was not created with the intention of becoming digital currency, because its main function is the use of smart contracts. In this sense, authors Mazzola and Lundgren

---

18   NAKAMOTO, Satoshi. Bitcoin: A Peer-to-Peer Eletronic Cash System, 2008.

19   ULRICH, Fernando Ulrich. Bitcoin - A moeda na era digital. São Paulo-SP, Instituto Ludwig Von Mises Brasil, 2014.

state that in addition to the implementation of smart contracts, the Ethereum network enabled "[...] the creation of voting systems, registration of property titles and, potentially, registration of any type of information and/or object, especially in the digital environment. The platform's currency is called ether and is used to reward the platform's miners, as well as being the platform's medium of exchange to enable the use of smart contracts. Undoubtedly, it is the largest smart contract platform today as it is able to perform the full turing, according to Gavin Wood[20].

Conceição[21] argues that within ethereum it is possible to create smart contracts written in high-level computer language, which are converted to EthereumVM bytecode, after which it will be inserted into the ethereum blockchain to be executed.

That said, it is salutary for the popularization of smart contracts that the security of blockchain networks be duly proven, because it is undeniable the revolution that the use of this technology can bring to the legal universe, which will be demonstrated below.

SECURITY IN SMART CONTRACTS

It is known that technology is present in contemporaneity, so much so that any breakdown in the system and the lack of connection leads to financial losses and a real chaos in the business world, as it happened on October 04, 2021, when a problem in the WhatsApp, Instagram and Facebook systems caused an absence of communication in an interval of approximately 7 (seven)

---

20   WOOD, Gavin, ethereum: A secure decentralised generalised transaction ledger, 2017. Article.

21   CONCEIÇÃO. Tomás Morgado de Carvalho Conceição. Validation of Smart Contracts Through Automated Tooling. 2019.

hours, costing Mark Zuckerberg more than 6 billion dollars and the position of 4th richest in the world to Bill Gates[22].

This insecurity leads, therefore, to conservatism and a certain resistance in the adoption of technologies for the execution of contracts. Nowadays, there is a very important security tool used in several technological sectors, namely cryptography, therefore, understanding cryptography is fundamental to study the security system of smart contracts.

Firstly, we must emphasize the difference between steganography and cryptography, since they are two different techniques, in which steganography seeks to hide a message without obscuring its content. Cryptography, on the other hand, differs from steganography and, according to Fiarresga[23], its true role is to hide the information so that, even if someone intercepts the message, they will not be able to understand it.

A curious fact is that Herodotus reported how Histieu transmitted a certain message to Aristagoras telling that Histieu shaved the head of an individual and wrote the message on his scalp, then waited for the individual's hair to grow back and sent him to meet Aristagoras, In this situation, this would represent steganography, you see, in this example, if the individual was intercepted and the interceptor shaved his head, he would have no difficulty in understanding the meaning of the message that Histieu sent to Aristagoras.

Otherwise, according to Fiarresga, cryptography uses several ciphers throughout time, varying according to their sophistication. It should be noted that only in the second half of the last century asymmetric ciphers started to

---

22   Available at: https://economia.uol.com.br/noticias/redacao/2021/10/04/ mark-zuckerberg-perde-us-7-bilhoes-queda-facebook.htm. Access in october, 12th, 2021.

23   FIARRESGA, Victor Manuel Calhabrês. Criptografia e Matemática. 2010. Thesis (Master in Mathematics for Teachers) – Faculdade de Ciências, Universidade de Lisboa, Belas, 2010.

be used, which means that from that moment on the key used to encrypt a message would no longer be the same as the one used to decrypt it, since two keys started to be used, one of them public and used to encrypt the message and the other private, which has the function of decrypting the message.

About asymmetric cryptography, Pereira and Nascimento[24] "in this asymmetric model, the public key can be shared among all members who will make the communication, however, the private key is kept secret [...]" [Author's translate].

Sanas[25] exposes that this type of cryptography with asymmetric cipher is used in blockchain networks such as bitcoin and ethereum granting a higher level of security for the user who has two keys, one public, which is used to identify his wallet on the network and another private, which has the function of authorizing access to his wallet.

Another security tool that blockchain networks offer the user is consensus (mining), which consists in confirming the movements made on the network in a decentralized manner, through the solution of a mathematical equation. Now, imagine a person wants to transfer a certain amount of bitcoins to another, in which case the transaction will go through the validation process (consensus) before it is confirmed by the network, thus preventing fraudulent transactions, whether in an attempt to manipulate the network with duplicate transactions or hacker attacks in order to alter information recorded in the blockchain.

Having exposed the main technical security tool, not only of smart contracts and the so-called crypto-economy, a brief study will be made on the

---

24   PEREIRA, Pedro Paulo Prudente e NASCIMENTO. Luane Silva. Inovações, Instrumentos e Ferramentas Tecnológicas no Direito. Discussões sobre Direito na Era Digital, cord. Ana C. Pinho. 1ª ed. Rio de Janeiro: GZ, 2021, p. 593 – 616.

25   SANAS, Caio Fernando. O Futuro dos Contratos: Pontencialidade e Desafios dos Smart Contracts no Brasil. Volta Redonda-RJ, Editora Jurismestre, 2021.

legal security related to smart contracts. A priori, it is necessary to consider that there are no legal impediments for the use of smart contracts, since for the existence of a legal business it is enough that the requirements of article 104 of the Civil Code of 2002 are observed, moreover, there is no legal form prescribed by law for the formation of these contracts, therefore, it is perfectly possible that an agreement is formalized by means of a smart contract, in this line, "implications were found as to the validity and effectiveness of legal business instrumented in smart contracts, especially with the claim that the principle of the social function of the contract is an obstacle to the validity [...]"[26].

One should not forget that the social function of contracts is provided for in article 421 of the Brazilian Civil Code and, therefore, it must also be observed in smart contracts, since it is a general clause of contract law.

Thus, although Efing and Santos[27] have concluded that the principle of the social function of contracts would prevent the implementation of smart contracts in Brazil, the authors did not consider all the possible functions of this technology, because even if the insertion of the smart contract in the blockchain makes it immutable, nothing prevents that, provided that prior to the insertion in the blockchain, mechanisms to control the execution of the contract are programmed, or even that a reverse operation can be performed to correct any error in execution.

Precisely in order to make this situation possible, it was suggested "the figure of the 'Judge as a Service', a kind of arbitrator with technical powers

---

26   SANAS, 2021, p. 91.

27   EFING, A. C., SANTOS, A. P. Análise dos Smart Contracts à luz do Princípio da Função Social dos Contratos no Direito Brasileiro. REVISTA DO PROGRAMA DE PÓS-GRADUAÇÃO EM DIREITO (Mestrado em Direito e Desenvolvimento Sustentável) Direito e Desenvolvimento, ISSN 2236-0859, João Pessoa, v. 9, n. 2, p. 49-64, aug./dec. 2018.

to reverse or change transactions performed through smart contracts on the Blockchain [...]"[28].

But it is worth noting that throughout the research were not found authors who support the idea of changing transactions, however, this does not make less impactful the figure of the judge as a service, in this sense, Sanas explains that the use of smart contracts for alternative dispute resolution is easy to develop and can increase efficiency and reduce transaction costs.

Judge as a Service is very similar to the figure of the arbitrator, already consolidated in Brazilian law through Law 9.307/96[29], which allows the parties to elect the arbitration court to resolve conflicts, in accordance with the provision of Article 2 of that law, in verbis:

> *Art. 2 The arbitration may be of law or of equity, at the discretion of the parties.*
>
> *§ 1st The parties are free to choose the rules of law that will be applied in the arbitration, provided they do not violate good customs and public order.*
>
> *§ 2nd The parties may also agree that arbitration be based on general principles of law, usages and customs, and international rules of trade.*

---

28   GONÇALVES, CAMARGOS. Blockchain, Smart Contracts e 'Judge As a Service' no Direito Brasileiro. Anais do II Seminário Governança das Redes e o Marco Civil da Internet, org. Fabrício B. P. Polido, Lucas C. dos Anjos & Luíza C. C. Brandão, Belo Horizonte: Instituto de Referência em Internet e Sociedade, 2017, p. 207-211.

29   BRAZIL. Law 9.307 de 1996. Brasília, DF: Presidency of the Republic. Available at: http://www.planalto.gov.br/ccivil_03/leis/l9307.htm. Access in: october, 26th, 2021.

§ 3rd The arbitration involving the public administration
will always be in law and will respect the principle of publicity.

In addition, the Civil Code after the changes introduced by Law 13,874/2019[30] safeguards the compliance with the principle of minimum intervention and the exceptionality of contractual revision in private relations, thus strengthening the principle of pacta sunt servanda.

In this sense, even before the Economic Freedom Law (13.874/2019)[31] came into effect, the Brazilian courts have already decided for the application of the principle of the autonomy of the will and the mandatory force of the agreements (pacta sunt servanda) to business contracts, as per the content of REsp 936. 741/GO under the Rapporteur of Minister ANTONIO CARLOS FERREIRA, in the FOURTH GROUP, whose judgment was held on 03/11/2011 and published in the DJe 08/03/2012, as well as in special appeals 1910582, 1644890, 1799627, 1691008, 1441620, 1409849 and 1413818 all judged by the Superior Court of Justice.

Therefore, the apparent conflict between the immutability feature of smart contracts and the principle of the social function of the contract and even the rebus sic standibus clause does not prove to be a major obstacle for its use.

Nevertheless, considering the applicability of smart contracts in foreign trade transactions, the immutability of smart contracts is not an obstacle in the eyes of international law, since, according to Pinheiro (2021), the autonomy of the will is a principle of Private International Law common to most national systems.

---

30   Article 421, § sole.

31   BRAZIL. Law 13.874 from 2019, Establishes the Bill of Rights for Economic Freedom. Brasília, DF: Presidency of the Republic. Available at: http://www.planalto. gov.br/ccivil_03/_ato2019-2022/2019/lei/L13874.htm. Access in: october, 26th, 2021.

APPLICABILITY OF BLOCKCHAIN PROGRAMMING AND NETWORKS IN THE BUSINESS ACTIVITY

The blockchain technology and smart contracts have been generating impact on the world economy due to its popular use with cryptocurrencies, however, there are countless other activities common to the legal universe that can be impacted by the use of this technology.

This is what is inferred from the intelligence of Sanas apud Santa Cruz "the more crypto active products consolidate, the smarter contracts will also consolidate, I think they are very closely linked [...]"[32].

Thus, it is possible to state that smart contracts have great potential to overcome the problem of distrust between the parties, due to their attributes of self-execution and immutability, which represents a very important differential in the business environment, especially.

Moreover, as demonstrated elsewhere, the blockchain can be compared to a ledger, due to its feature of immutability of the information entered and authenticated, thus, in view of this immutability and granting of legal security to formalized acts, the use of blockchain has also significantly impacted the notarial activities in Brazil, so much so that the National Council of Justice (CNJ) through Provision No. 100, of May 26, 2020, regulated the practice of electronic notarial acts using the e-Notary system, which is able to perform notarial acts digitally.

Also, in 2020 the Notarchain project emerged, which aims to allow the validation and authentication by the notaries of documents in digital form

---

32   2021, p.131.

through Provision No. 100/2020[33], with this, the Brazilian College of Notaries intends to make each notary's office a validation node of the e-Notary network and, for this, has been using the Hyperledger Fabric blockchain.

It also highlights the practicality that blockchain technology grants to the procedure of registering works for the protection of intellectual property, for Mazzola and Ludgren "[...] The registration of creations in blockchain allows, therefore, robust proof of authorship and the exact moment of creation of original works[34]".

The use of this technology cumulated with smart contracts would make possible automatic applications for licensing the use of works by third parties, with automatic remuneration for the artist, outside the intellectual property branch, it would also be possible to write off in fiduciary alienation, For example, as from the confirmation of the payment by the smart contract, the smart contract would automatically, without the need for human intervention, proceed with the write-off procedure at the real estate registry, which would undoubtedly represent the celerity of the procedures and debureaucratization of the system.

Moreover, it is also worth mentioning that the Internet of Things is invogue, which in the words of Santos et al[35] "is nothing more than an extension of the current Internet, which allows everyday objects (whatever they may be), but with computing and communication capabilities, to connect to the Internet."

---

33   BRAZIL.CNJ. Provision n° 100, may, 26th, 2020. Provides for the practice of electronic notarial acts using the e-Notary system, creates the Electronic Notary Registration-MNE and makes other provisions. Available aat: https://atos.cnj.jus.br/atos/detalhar/3334. Access in: october, 18th, 2021.

34   2021, p. 534

35   SANTOS et. al. Internet das Coisas: da Teoria à Pratica, 2016.

In this way, combined with the IoT (Internet of Things) it is possible, for example, for a smart contract to be able to shut down or reduce the operation of vehicles from the moment the purchase and fiduciary alienation of the vehicle are programmed into the smart contract, therefore, the lack of payment of the installments will trigger the command provided in the contract code and automatically may, even before the creditor takes legal action, turn off the functions of the vehicle, subject to the technological conditions of the vehicle, obviously, which will reduce the cases of concealment of assets to avoid liability.

The significant economy of time and resources that would be spent by the creditor when he or she calls the Judiciary to declare the search and seizure of the vehicle will be remarkable, thus reducing the risk of it being stolen and transported to an uncertain place. Even if it is, current technology makes it almost common to locate vehicles in real time.

Another possibility of use of smart contracts applied in blockchain networks are the Decentralized Autonomous Organizations (DAO), which work from the interconnection of several smart contracts and according to Porto, Junior and Silva[36] these have the function of codifying the rules of operation and the structure of an organization.

The use of smart contracts can be of great value to the so-called cost sharing contracts, which according to Estrada and Bez-Batti[37] are contracts that aim to apportion the costs of research, development and services, since smart contracts have the ability to debit pre-determined accounts with previously defined values, thus facilitating the apportionment of expenses.

---

36   PORTO, JUNIOR e SILVA. Tecnologia Blockchain e o Direito Societário. Tecnologia Blockchain e Direito Societário: Aplicações Práticas e Desafios para a Regulação 2019, p. 11-30.

37   ESTRADA, BEZ-BATTI. Contratos de Cost Sharing e os Serviços de Computação em Nuvem. Discussões sobre Direito na Era Digital, cord. Ana C. Pinho. 1ª ed. Rio de Janeiro: GZ, 2021, p.687 – 701.

Furthermore, much has been discussed about Decentralized Finance (DeFi), which consists of decentralized finance protocols controlled by governance tokens that entitle their holders to vote on these finance protocols. This type of use allows overly bureaucratic and time-consuming practices to be carried out with extreme efficiency and time savings, however, like everything involving smart contracts, its use is still in the experimental phase.

Tokens, in turn, are digital certificates that represent some item, fungible or non-fungible (NFT) and that are commonly transacted on a blockchain, in the meantime, according to Mazzola and Lundgren "[...] on the blockchain network, virtually any item of any nature, whether physical or digital, can be represented by means of a token".

Tokens are very useful for smart contracts and represent in bits and bytes existing physical assets. Recently tokens representing a farm in Arapuanã[38] were issued to finance a mining project on its land. At the time, each token issued represented a portion of the land on this farm.

This "tokenization" economy has been growing a lot and, as a result, has drawn attention to a discussion about the need for registration of the public offering with the Securities and Exchange Commission (CVM), which, in turn, through the Administrative Sanctioning Procedure 19957.003406/2019-91 considered that a certain company offered tokens in an irregular manner.

In this procedure, it was discussed whether the crypto-asset offered should be considered a security in Brazilian law or not and, considering that the asset was publicly offered, purchased by people in a collective venture in expectation of profits, it was concluded that it was in fact a security, resulting in a fine to the issuer for offering securities irregularly.

Given these situations, there is still uncertainty regarding the development and spread of the use of smart contracts and blockchain, which can be

---

38   Available at https://cointelegraph.com.br/news/farm-in-amazonas-becomes-cryptau-the-first-fully-tokenized-property-in-brazil

justified due to the lack of regulation, a fact that causes uncertainty for people. However, the national regulatory bodies have been moving in this direction. The Brazilian Federal Revenue Service, for example, through Ordinance No. 1,074[39], published in June 2019, dispensed with formalities for the provision of information to the Individual Taxpayer Registry (CPF) and the Corporate Taxpayer Registry (CNPJ) if shared through blockchain. This is what can be inferred from the content of Article 1 of the aforementioned Ordinance, in verbis:

> Art. 1 The formalization of adjustments in existing agreements for the supply of information from the Individual Taxpayer Registry (CPF) and the Corporate Taxpayer Registry (CNPJ) to agencies, autarchies and public foundations of the Union, the States, the Federal District and the Municipalities, in the event of adoption of data sharing through:
>
> I - blockchain permissioned network;
>
> II - web services or application programming interface (API).

Furthermore, Normative Instruction 1.888/2019[40], also issued by the RFB, presented a legal definition of crypto active, in verbis:

---

39   BRAZIL. Federal Revenue of Brazil. Ordinance RFB n° 1074, june, 18th, de 2019. Waives the formalization of adjustments to agreements in effect for the supply of registration information to organs and entities of the public administration, in the cases mentioned. Available at: http://normas.receita.fazenda.gov.br/sijut2consulta/link. action?visao=anotado&idAto=101770. Access in: october, 26th, 2021.

40   BRAZIL. Federal Revenue of Brazil. Normative Instruction RFB n° 1888, may, 3rd, 2019. Establishes and regulates the obligation to provide information regarding the operations performed with crypto active products to the Special Secretary of the Federal Revenue of Brazil (RFB). Available at: http://normas.receita.fazenda.gov.br/

Art. 5 For the purposes of the provisions of this Normative Instruction, the following are considered

I - crypto-asset: the digital representation of value denominated in its own unit of account, whose price can be expressed in local or foreign sovereign currency, transacted electronically with the use of cryptography and distributed record technologies, which can be used as a form of investment, instrument for transfer of values or access to services, and which does not constitute legal tender;

Certainly, the subject under discussion still lacks legal regulation for the use of these technologies to be better used by society. However, in the wake of Sanas the interdisciplinary approach bringing together lawyers, developers and economists could contribute to the agility of this process and the issue of rules and regulations capable of enabling the development of these applications.

It is obvious that, nowadays, a revolution in contracting instruments in general cannot be delayed, since their widespread use, whether as a complete replacement for simple instruments such as instantaneous purchase and sale agreements or as tools to facilitate the formation of more complex instruments, would represent an important advance in the globalized and negotiating world.

Nevertheless, this storyline has also shown that although smart contracts are revolutionary they are not capable of replacing more complex instruments loaded with subjectivity, as may happen in corporate transactions such as mergers and acquisitions, which are integrated of several documents, such as memorandums and letters of intent, however, in contracts for the acquisition of products, goods, raw materials and other instruments or goods for the operation of the company's activities, the smart contract may certainly speed up

---

sijut2consulta/link.action?visao=anotado&idAto=100592. Access in October, 26th, 2021.

the process, besides being less expensive because it would put the businessmen in contact independently of the collaborators.

It is undeniable that the tools studied here will remain permanently in the legal universe and, in the words of Pereira and Nascimento[41] "[...] it is essential that lawyers, servers and judges use ICTs in their favor, since these exist to help these professionals in their work", in this sense, even if blockchain technology and smart contracts are removed from the category of Information and Communication Technology for technical or conceptual reasons, professionals should look at them with the same care.

CONCLUSION

Despite the doctrinal divergence about the degree of innovation that smart contracts along with blockchain technology can provide in the contractual practice, it is common ground that these technologies have conquered a definitive space in humanity and, consequently, in legal practice, so much so that the theme has been growing along with the use of these tools in Brazil.

Proof of this is the emergence of the Notarchain in the Brazilian notarial system, thus indicating that the notaries were the first to advance in this direction, even if with a certain timidity.

The tokenization of assets has also shown itself to be quite advanced, but, despite the level of technological security being quite satisfactory to users, the lack of regulation is still an obstacle to the propagation of the crypto economy, as well as to its reaching various layers of the Brazilian population.

---

41   PEREIRA, Pedro Paulo Prudente e NASCIMENTO. Luane Silva. As Tecnologias da Informação e Comunicação (tic's), o Direito Digital e a Transformação Digital em Razão da COVID-19. Discussões sobre Direito na Era Digital, cord. Ana C. Pinho. 1ª ed. Rio de Janeiro: GZ, 2021, p. 617 – 636.

Furthermore, the research found that the use of smart contracts in business activity is too attractive, due to its almost infinite potential combined with blockchain and IoT, however, further development of the crypto economy will be necessary to understand the limits of smart contracts.

It is not to be forgotten that traditional contracts are likely to be radically replaced by smart contracts, given their ineffectiveness in the formation of documents of complex matters, namely, corporate transactions and contracts with great subjectivity.

Therefore, we conclude that the development of the crypto-economy and the effective regulation of crypto-activities are essential to ensure legal certainty and financial security and, consequently, enable the widespread use of this technology in business activities.

BIBLIOGRAPHIC REFERENCES

BANDEIRA. Paula Greco. Os Smart Contracts no Direito Contratual Contemporâneo. Discussões sobre Direito na Era Digital, cord. Ana C. Pinho. 1ª ed. Rio de Janeiro: GZ, 2021, p. 557-576.

BRANDÃO. Pedro Ramos Brandão. Criptomoeda: o Bitcoin. 2020. Artigo.

CONCEIÇÃO. Tomás Morgado de Carvalho Conceição. Validation of Smart Contracts Through Automated Tooling. 2019.

DINIZ. Maria Helena Diniz. Curso de Direito Civil Brasileiro. São Paulo-SP. Saraiva Jur, 2020.

DIVINO, Sthéfano Bruno Santos. Smart Contracts: Conceitos, Limitações, Aplicabilidade e Desafios, 2018. Artigo

EFING, A. C., SANTOS, A. P. Análise dos Smart Contracts à luz do Princípio da Função Social dos Contratos no Direito Brasileiro. REVISTA DO PROGRAMA DE PÓS-GRADUAÇÃO EM DIREITO (Mestrado em Direito e Desenvolvimento Sustentável) Direito e Desenvolvimento, ISSN 2236-0859, João Pessoa, v. 9, n. 2, p. 49-64, ago./dez. 2018.

ESTRADA, BEZ-BATTI. Contratos de Cost Sharing e os Serviços de Computação em Nuvem. Discussões sobre Direito na Era Digital, coord. Ana C. Pinho. 1ª ed. Rio de Janeiro: GZ, 2021, p.687 – 701.

FIARRESGA, Victor Manuel Calhabrês. Criptografia e Matemática. 2010. Dissertação (Mestrado em Matemática para Professores) – Faculdade de Ciências, Universidade de Lisboa, Belas, 2010.

GONÇALVES, CAMARGOS. Blockchain, Smart Contracts e 'Judge As a Service' no Direito Brasileiro. Anais do II Seminário Governança das Redes e o Marco Civil da Internet, org. Fabrício B. P. Polido, Lucas C. dos Anjos & Luíza C. C. Brandão, Belo Horizonte: Instituto de Referência em Internet e Sociedade, 2017, p. 207-211.

JIMENE, Camilla do Vale. O valor probatório do documento eletrônico, São Paulo: Sicurezza, 2010.

MAZZOLA, LUNDGREN. Blockchain e Propriedade Intelectual: Impactos Práticos da Tecnologia. Discussões sobre Direito na Era Digital, cord. Ana C. Pinho. 1ª ed. Rio de Janeiro: GZ, 2021, p. 529 – 546.

NAKAMOTO, Satoshi. Bitcoin: A Peer-to-Peer Eletronic Cash System, 2008. Disponível em <https://bitcoin.org/pt_BR/bitcoin-paper>.

PEREIRA, Pedro Paulo Prudente e NASCIMENTO. Luane Silva. Inovações, Instrumentos e Ferramentas Tecnológicas no Direito. Discussões sobre Direito na Era Digital, cord. Ana C. Pinho. 1ª ed. Rio de Janeiro: GZ, 2021, p. 593 – 616.

PEREIRA, Pedro Paulo Prudente e NASCIMENTO. Luane Silva. As Tecnologias da Informação e Comunicação (tic's), o Direito Digital e a Transformação Digital em Razão da COVID-19. Discussões sobre Direito na Era Digital, cord. Ana C. Pinho. 1ª ed. Rio de Janeiro: GZ, 2021, p. 617 – 636.

PINHEIRO, Luís de Lima. Smart Contracts e Direito Aplicável. Discussões sobre Direito na Era Digital, cord. Ana C. Pinho. 1ª ed. Rio de Janeiro: GZ, 2021, p. 503 – 527.

PORTO, JUNIOR e SILVA. Tecnologia Blockchain e o Direito Societário. Tecnologia Blockchain e Direito Societário: Aplicações Práticas e Desafios para a Regulação 2019, p. 11-30.

SCHREIBER, Anderson. Contratos Eletrônicos e Consumo, REVISTA BRASILEIRA DE DIREITO CIVIL. ISSN 2358-6974. Volume 1, p. 88-110, Jul./Set. 2014.

SANAS, Caio Fernando. O Futuro dos Contratos: Pontencialidade e Desafios dos Smart Contracts no Brasil. Volta Redonda-RJ, Editora Jurismestre, 2021.

SANTOS et. al. Internet das Coisas: da Teoria à Pratica, 2016.

SZABO, Nick. Formalizing and Securing Relationships on Public Networks, 1997. First Monday, Disponível em <https://firstmonday.org/ojs/index.php/fm/article/view/548/469>. Artigo.

SZABO, Nick. Smart Contracts: Building Blocks for Digital Markets, 1996. Disponível em <https://www.fon.hum.uva.nl/rob/Courses/InformationInSpeech/CDROM/Literature/LOTwinterschool2006/szabo.best.vwh.net/smart_contracts_2.html/>. Artigo.

STARK, Josh. Making Sense of Blockchain Smart Contracts. Coindesk, 2016. Disponível em < https://www.coindesk.com/making-sense-smart-contracts/>. Artigo.

ULRICH, Fernando Ulrich. Bitcoin - A moeda na era digital. São Paulo-SP, Instituto Ludwig Von Mises Brasil, 2014.

WRIGHT, Aaron; DE FILIPPI, Primavera. Decentralized Blockchain Technology and the Rise of Lex Cryptographia, 2015. Artigo.

WOOD, Gavin, ethereum: A secure decentralised generalised transaction ledger, 2017. Artigo.

BRASIL. Lei n° 10.406, de 10 de janeiro de 2002. Institui o Código Civil. Diário Oficial da União: seção 1, Brasília, DF, ano 139, n. 8, p. 1-74, 11 jan. 2002. PL 634/1975.

BRASIL. Lei 9.307 de 1996. Brasília, DF: Presidência da República. Disponível em: http://www.planalto.gov.br/ccivil_03/leis/l9307.htm. Acesso em: 26 out. 2021.

BRASIL. Lei 13.874 de 2019, Institui a Declaração de Direitos de Liberdade Econômica. Brasília, DF: Presidência da República. Disponível em: http://www.planalto.gov.br/ccivil_03/_ato2019-2022/2019/lei/L13874.htm. Acesso em: 26 out. 2021.

BRASIL.CNJ. Provimento n° 100, de 26 de maio de 2020. Dispõe sobre a prática de atos notariais eletrônicos utilizando o sistema e-Notariado, cria a Matrícula Notarial Eletrônica-MNE e dá outras providências. Disponível em: https://atos.cnj.jus.br/atos/detalhar/3334. Acesso em: 18 out. 2021.

BRASIL. Receita Federal do Brasil. Instrução Normativa RFB n° 1888, de 03 de maio de 2019. Institui e disciplina a obrigatoriedade de prestação de informações relativas às operações realizadas com criptoativos à Secretaria Especial da Receita Federal do Brasil (RFB). Disponível em: http://normas.receita.fazenda.gov.br/sijut2consulta/link.action?visao=anotado&idAto=100592. Acesso em 26 out. 2021.

BRASIL. Receita Federal do Brasil. Portaria RFB n° 1074, de 18 de junho de 2019. Dispensa a formalização de ajustes em convênios vigentes para fornecimento de informações cadastrais a órgãos e entidades da administração pública, nas hipóteses que menciona. Disponível em: http://normas.receita.fazenda.gov.br/sijut2consulta/link.action?visao=anotado&idAto=101770. Acesso em: 26 out. 2021.

THE OTT VIDEO STREAMING SERVICES AND CONTENT REGULATION IN INDIA – A STEP TOWARDS ACCOUNTABILITY?

Authors:

Sunitha Abhay Jain

Chaitra V.

ABSTRACT

The Broadcasting and digital media play a very crucial role in forming public opinion and making the democratic system more accountable to its citizens. With the unanticipated developments in the new age technology, there is a mushroom growth of OTT platforms which has posed innumerable challenges in terms of content regulation. There are frequent instances wherein, the audiences are exposed to content which is violent, sexually explicit, and offensive. Likewise, the use of objectionable language, content depicting religious insensitivity and degrading moral, cultural values have fuelled the problem further. The Print and Broadcast Media are legally regulated in India.

However, the OTT Video streaming services /online curated content from various publishers across the globe were not in conformity with the domestic practice of content regulation and by and large remained unregulated until the recent passage of the Information Technology (Guidelines for Intermediaries and Digital Media Ethics Code) Rules, 2021. However, these Rules have invited criticisms from various factions alleging unconstitutionality and excessive governmental control. The present paper critically examines the new OTT rules in regard to content regulation. It also provides an understanding on the regulatory and censorship aspects of media regulation in India. The authors further examine the differences between regulatory models in the Broadcast Media and the OTT platforms. In conclusion, this would lead to some concrete suggestions for more deliberation.

Key words: OTT Platforms, Online Curated Content, Content Regulation, Information Technology (Guidelines for Intermediaries and Digital Media Ethics Code) Rules 2021, India.

OVER-THE-TOP PLATFORMS: AN INTRODUCTION

Media is regarded as the fourth pillar in a democratic system. It plays a very crucial role in providing information to its citizens by making them aware of the social, economic, political, legal issues and developments taking place across the globe. It also supports in building a strong and healthy democracy by acting as a watchdog of the government and brings to the fore the lapses on the part of the government. This in turn helps in making the democratic system more accountable, responsible and citizen friendly. A few years back, the primary forms of media were the print media and the broadcast media. However, the digital revolution has completely revamped the media and communication landscape. With the unprecedented growth in new age technology numerous platforms of media such as public forums, video streaming platforms etc., have emerged. In present times, these platforms are scaling new heights in the entertainment sector and diffusion of information. They are becoming increasingly popular amongst the public as they provide a vast and diverse range of creative content along with the ease of accessibility.

In recent times, the OTT's (Over-The-Top platforms) or the online curated content platforms have been increasingly attracting young crowd. International Telecommunication Union (ITU) defines OTT services as, "a service or application which is provided to the user over the internet."[1] The steady increase in the number of the OTTs has revolutionized the landscape of the media and entertainment business. According to a study conducted by Allied Market Research Company, the global OTT market is projected to reach $ 1039.03 billion by 2027 and is growing at a compound annual growth rate of 29.4% from 2020 to 2027.[2] According to Federation of Indian Chambers of Commerce & Industry and Ernst &Young, due to data availability and affordability there is an expansion in the OTT platforms in the Indian market and it is projected to reach $24 billion by 2021.[3] According to Boston Consulting group report the OTT content market in India is likely to reach $ 5 billion in size by 2023.[4] Further, there is a 49% growth in the digital

---

1   ITU Fact File: Over The Top Services (OTT), https://www.gp-digital.org/wp-content/uploads/2017/12/itu-ott-2.pdf (last visited Oct. 3, 2021)

2   Over-the-Top Market, Opportunities and Forecast, 2020-27, Allied Market Research, https://www.alliedmarketresearch.com/over-the-top-services-market (last visited Oct. 3, 2021)

3   Playing by New rules, India's Media & Entertainment sector reboots in 2020, FICCI & EY, March 2021, https://assets.ey.com/content/dam/ey-sites/ey-com/en_in/topics/media-and-entertainment/2021/ey-india-media-and-entertainment-sector-reboots.pdf?download (last visited Oct. 3, 2021)

4   Kanchan Samtani & Gaurav Jindal, Entertainment Goes Online, A $5 Billion Opportunity, Boston Consulting, November, 2018, https://image-src.bcg.com/Images/Entertainment-Goes-Online_tcm21-208006.pdf (last visited Oct. 3, 2021)

subscriptions revenues in India in 2020 as nearly 28 million Indians paid for 53 million OTT subscriptions.[5]

At the beginning, the OTT platforms were into content hosting and have recently ventured into the field of production and creation of their own content like movies, documentaries and web-shows catering to an audience of varied nature. OTTs have transformed the way in which content is created, conveyed and consumed on these platforms. In the year 2008, Reliance entertainment inaugurated Big Flix which was the first OTT video service in India. After eight years Netflix and Amazon entered the OTT market. In India there are many OTT Platforms such as Netflix, Amazon Prime video, Hotstar, Disney, Voot etc., offering various services like audio and video content, messaging, voice calling etc. There is a huge surge in the viewership, especially during the pandemic. These platforms are popular with the masses as they are easily accessible and also due to the fact that the programmes are streamed through the internet. Further, a person can view on one's own computers, tablets or smartphones and there is no requirement of cable or satellite television subscription. In addition, they are aided by Artificial Intelligence which makes suggestions and provides the users with content of their preferences. The players in the market have realised the potential of OTT's and the importance of creative curated content, thus offering a wide range of products which cater to the audiences of all age groups.

Though the rising popularity of the OTT's especially during the pandemic have been well received by the public, certain challenges are faced by the OTT platforms, content owners and the consumers and need to be addressed. There are numerous instances wherein the OTTs have streamed content which is fake, obscene and offensive. Further, original content creators are suffering huge loss as a result of digital piracy. Another area of serious concern is the infringement of the intellectual property rights. The economic impact of proliferation and consumption of the content over these platforms is yet another area of concern.

---

5   Supra note. 3

Recently the deliberation on regulation of digital content especially the OTTs in India intensified in the light of the incidents involving certain shows that hurt the sentiments of the public thus causing a threat to the harmony of the country. The Print and Broadcast Media are legally regulated in India. However, the OTT Video streaming services /online curated content from various publishers across the globe were not in conformity with the domestic practice of content regulation and by and large unregulated until the recent passage of the Information Technology (Guidelines for Intermediaries and Digital Media Ethics Code) Rules, 2021(hereinafter referred to as Rules, 2021). However, these Rules have invited criticisms from various factions alleging unconstitutionality and excessive governmental control. The present study critically examines the new OTT rules in regard to content regulation of the Video Streaming Services. It also provides an understanding on the regulatory and censorship aspects of OTT platform in India. Further the authors also examine the differences between the regulatory models of the Broadcast Media and OTT platforms. In conclusion concrete suggestions are given to address the issues relating to regulation of content over the OTT Platform for further deliberation.

GROWTH OF OTT PLATFORMS IN INDIA

Many factors have contributed to the growth and development of the OTT platforms in India. High speed internet connectivity and reasonably charged subscription-based services along with flexible tariff plans have acted as a catalyst for the growth of these platforms. The variety of creative content that is offered on the platforms has nudged the consumers to move over to these platforms from the traditional platforms like the television and cable connections. The geographical barriers have reduced with the onset of the OTTs as one can watch international shows or sports concurrently with the rest of the world. Another benefit of the OTT platforms is that they do not involve any supplementary devices like the set-up box or antennae. Ease of viewing the programs on smartphones, TV and laptops have made these platforms a pleasant experience amongst the masses. The use of Artificial Intelligence by these platforms has created a far more user-friendly interface experience as compared to the traditional mediums. The rapid growth and demand of the OTTs has resulted in the merging of different players both from the international and national levels. They are competing amongst each other to provide quality content in order to sustain in the market. The OTT industry in India has a promising future with numerous indigenous platforms like Voot, Hotstar, ALT Balaji, Jio-digital life etc., growing and strongly co-existing with foreign streaming platforms like Netflix, Amazon Prime video etc.

CONTENT REGULATION IN INDIA: ISSUES AND CHALLENGES

OTTs definitely offers a wide range of content options, including that of entertainment and rendering the audience with factual content, socio-economic position of countries, different lifestyles etc. Unfortunately, many times they do stream content that are offensive, violent and obscene which not only negatively affects the growth of the society but also has resulted in numerous FIR's filed against various shows across India threatening the harmony in the society. Tandav, a political drama series on Amazon prime was drawn into controversy for portraying Hindu Gods in an offensive manner and hurting the religious sentiments. Another show on Netflix received huge backlash as the actor put on Indian Air force uniform inaccurately and used objectionable language. Likewise, there are many other innumerable OTT shows which had caught the public attention due to objectionable content. They are also criticised for the display of inappropriate, indecent and unverified content which are held responsible for ascending crimes against women and children. It thus became imperative for the Government to devise measures when these concerns led to an increasing appeal for the regulation of content on OTT platforms.

The diversity and sensitivity of the Indian population in terms of religion, caste, languages, socio-economic status have always remained a challenge in regard to content regulation in the Broadcast media. The recent passage of the Rules, 2021 to regulate the OTT Video streaming services /online curated content has invited criticisms from various factions alleging unconstitutionality and excessive governmental control. In the light of these controversies the subject matter of this paper comes down to one evitable question: Whether the regulatory model enforced in India to regulate the content in the Broadcast Media is different from the OTT platforms??

CONTENT REGULATION OF OTT's – A JUDICIAL PERSPECTIVE

Before the passage of the OTT Rules 2021, in the absence of any specific law regulating the OTT platforms the alternative remedy that was available to the citizens, NGO's and civil society was to approach the court of law to seek relief. In the case of Justice for Rights Foundation v. Union of India[6] a petition was filed before the Delhi High court in the year 2018 requesting its directives for the formulation of guidelines in regard to regulating the content streamed across the OTT players like Netflix, Amazon Prime etc. The Delhi High court dismissed the petition and observed that there were enough procedural safeguards under the Information Technology Act.

Nikhil Bhalla v. Union of India[7] was a case filed against the Netflix series Sacred Games alleging derogatory language and defamatory remarks against the former Prime Minister of India. Concerns were raised regarding the setting up of a grievance redressal mechanism and framing guidelines for regulating the content on the OTT platforms. However, the court dismissed the case and upheld the stand taken in Justice for Rights foundation case.

---

6   W.P (C) No. 11164/2018

7   W.P. (C) No. 7123/2018

In Padmanabha Shankar v. Union of India,[8] a case filed before the Karnataka High court which emphasised on the need for setting up a regulatory authority to regulate the OTTs. It was argued that the Cinematograph Act should be applied to the OTT Platform. However, the court rejected these arguments and observed that content which is streamed on OTT platforms does not qualify as 'broadcast' and also observed that the Cinematograph Act, 1952 applies only to cinematograph films and not to transmission made via the internet.

CONTENT REGULATION IN INDIA: LEGISLATIVE & REGULATORY FRAMEWORK

Article 19(1) (a) of the Constitution of India guarantees freedom of speech and expression and also prescribes reasonable restrictions for the exercise of this right as laid down under Art. 19 (2) of the Constitution. Accordingly, the freedom of speech and expression could be restricted in the interest of sovereignty, integrity and security of India, friendly relations with foreign States, public order, decency or morality, or in relation to contempt of court, defamation or incitement to an offence.[9] Thus online content in India could be restricted if it falls within the purview of the restrictions as envisaged under Art. 19(2) of the Constitution. Further various laws such as Information Technology Act, 2000, Indian Penal Code,1860, Indecent Representation of Women (Prohibition) Act, 1986; Scheduled Castes and the Scheduled Tribes (Prevention of Atrocities) Act, 1989, Emblems and Names (Prevention of Improper Use) Act, 1950 etc., were resorted to in order to deal with issues relating to online content. Further, steps were taken towards self-regulation wherein several OTT platforms accepted to adhere to a self-regulatory code, the Code of Best Practices for Online Curated Content Providers under the

---

8   W.P.(C) No. 6050/2019

9   Article 19(2), The Constitution of India

aegis of Internet and Mobile Association of India (IAMAI). In response to various concerns being raised in regard to the regulation of OTT content the Government of India issued a notification in 2020 wherein it amended the Government of India (Allocation of Business) Rules, 1961 and has brought the OTT platforms which offer video streaming services under the purview of Ministry of Information and Broadcasting.[10] After consulting various stakeholders and the Ministry of Information and Broadcasting, the Central Government notified the Information Technology (guidelines for Intermediaries and Digital Media Ethics Code) Rules, 2021 under the Information Technology Act, 2000. These rules replaced the Information Technology (Intermediary Guidelines) Rules, 2011.

REGULATORY FRAMEWORK – THE DIFFERENCES OF REGULATORY MODELS IN THE BROADCAST MEDIA AND DIGITAL MEDIA

Content Regulation of Broadcast Media in India

The Cinematograph Act, 1952 regulates the exhibition of cinema films in India. The Central Board of Film Certification (hereinafter referred to as CBFC) constituted by the Central Government issues a certificate for the public exhibition of a film in India. It is empowered to sanction or refuse the film for public exhibition. Under the Act, a film shall be refused public exhibition if, in the opinion of the CBFC, the film or any part of it is against the interests of the sovereignty and integrity of India, the security of the State, friendly relations with foreign States, public order, decency or morality, or involves defamation or contempt of court or is likely to incite the commission of any offence.[11] Furthermore, the Central Government is empowered to issue such directions as it deems necessary by detailing the principles which shall

---

10   The notification is available at 223032.pdf (egazette.nic.in)

11   Section 5B (1), The Cinematograph Act, 1952 (India)

guide the CBFC under this Act.[12] Section 6 of the Act empowers the Central Government to call for the record of any proceedings of films which is pending for certification before the CBFC.[13] These provisions clearly indicate that the Central Government has more powers over cinemas in the country. The policymakers in the constitutional debates agreed and justified the active role of the central government in controlling cinema as the films were an important educational medium that has a major role in building the national character and that only the central government had the power to sanction films.[14]

The Information Technology (Intermediary Guidelines and Digital Media Ethics Code) Rules, 2021/ OTT Regulations 2021- A critical evaluation

The recent controversies in regard to content of the web series released on the OTT platforms stimulated the recent passage of the Rules, 2021/ OTT Regulations 2021. Setting out the general principles in the Code of ethics, the Rules prevents the publisher of the online curated content[15] from publishing or exhibiting any content which is prohibited under any law for the time being in force, exercise due caution and discretion to ensure that the content that

---

12   Section 5B (2), The Cinematograph Act, 1952 (India)

13   K.M. Shankarappa v. Union of India, ILR 1990 KAR 4082

14   Shubhangi Heda, how to regulate OTT streaming services in India, edited by Marius Dragomir available at Government of India, "Constituent Assembly Debates," 9. New Delhi: Government of India, 1949

15   According to the Rule 2 (q) of the Information Technology (Guidelines for Intermediaries and Digital Media Ethics Code) Rules, 2021, Online curated content means any curated catalogue of audio -visual content, other than news and current affairs content, which is owned by, licensed to or contracted to be transmitted by a publisher of online curated content, and made available on demand, including but not limited through subscription, over the internet or computer networks, and includes films, audio visual programmes, documentaries, television programmes, serials, podcasts and other such content;

does not affect the sovereignty and integrity of India, endanger or jeopardise the security of the State, detrimental to India's friendly relations with foreign countries or incite violence or disturb the maintenance of public order.[16] These restrictions come within the purview of the Constitution of India as the State can impose reasonable restrictions on the freedom of speech and expression as laid down under Article 19(2). Furthermore, the Cinematograph Act, 1952 has the same restrictions in granting/ refusing films for public exhibition in India.

However, restrictions laid down in clause II(A)(c) of the Code of Ethics of the OTT Rules has triggered debate among different groups alleging unconstitutionality/ threatening freedom of speech and expression. The clauses states as follows:

> *"A publisher shall take into consideration India's multi-racial and multi-religious context and exercise due caution and discretion when featuring the activities, beliefs, practices, or views of any racial or religious group."[17]*

However, it cannot be denied that in a diverse country like India, the OTT players should be equally conscious, responsible and sensitive to the socio-cultural climate and it is vitally important for the Government to ensure that the OTT players develop content that does not circulate prohibited content in the country, incite communal disharmony, violence etc. The regulatory approaches in few countries like Singapore provides that any content that is

---

16   Clause II (A)(a) and Clause II (A) (b) of the Code of Ethics, Information Technology (Guidelines for Intermediaries and Digital Media Ethics Code) Rules, 2021 (India)

17   Clause II(A)(c) of the Code of Ethics, Information Technology (Guidelines for Intermediaries and Digital Media Ethics Code) Rules, 2021(India)

prejudicial to the national interest or likely to denigrate any racial or religious group, or promote feelings of ill-will or hostility between different racial or religious groups etc can be refused classification.[18] Considering the diversity in India, it is highly likely there will be numerous grievances in regard to the content on different OTTs alleging the hurting the sentiments of different religious/racial groups thus threatening the creativity of the OTT players.

To enable the viewers to make an informed choice in regard to the content they want to watch, the OTT Rules mandate the publisher of the online curated content to classify the content based on age- U rating (suitable for all ages), U/A 7+ rating, U/A 13+ rating and U/A 16+ rating and A rating (restricted to adults).[19] It further requires the classification based on the nature of content- i) Themes and messages; ii) Violence; iii) Nudity; iv) Sex; v) Language; vi) Drug and substance abuse; and (vii) Horror as described in the Schedule, which may be modified from time to time by the Ministry of Information & Broadcasting.[20]

The OTT Rules have provided a three-tier system to address the grievances regarding content published by the publisher of online curated content. The first stage is the Self Regulating Mechanism wherein the grievance regarding content of aggrieved party shall be addressed by the Grievance Officer appointed by the publishers of the online curated content.[21] In stage two, if the decision of the publisher is not communicated to the complainant within the

---

18   CONTENT CODE FOR OVER-THE-TOP, VIDEO-ON-DEMAND AND NICHE SERVICES, Singapore

19   Clause II (B)(i) of the Code of Ethics, Information Technology (Guidelines for Intermediaries and Digital Media Ethics Code) Rules, 2021 (India)

20   Clause II (B) (ii) of the Code of Ethics, Information Technology (Guidelines for Intermediaries and Digital Media Ethics Code) Rules, 2021(India)

21   Rule 11(2), Information Technology (Guidelines for Intermediaries and Digital Media Ethics Code) Rules, 2021(India)

prescribed time limit of fifteen days or where the complainant is not satisfied with the decision of the publisher, the grievances shall be heard by the Self-regulating Body.[22] However the fifteen days' time limit on a Grievance Officer is impractical. The Self-regulating body shall be an independent body constituted by publishers or their associations which shall be headed by retired judge of the Supreme Court, a High Court, or an independent eminent person from the field of media, broadcasting, entertainment, child rights, human rights or such other relevant field, and have other members, not exceeding six, being experts from the field of media, broadcasting, entertainment, child rights, human rights and such other relevant fields. In stage three, the grievances appeal against the Self- Regulating Bodies shall be heard by the Inter-Departmental Committee[23] constituted by the Ministry of Information and Broadcasting.[24]

The Self- Regulating Body and Inter- Departmental Committee have the same powers in regard to the detrimental content i.e warning and censuring the publisher, requiring an apology, taking action to delete or modify the content for preventing incitement to the commission of a cognizable offence relating to public order, or in relation to the reasons enumerated in sub-section

---

22   Rule 10 (1) (b) and 10 (1)(c), Information Technology (Guidelines for Intermediaries and Digital Media Ethics Code) Rules, 2021(India)

23   Rule 14. Inter-Departmental Committee.— (1) The Ministry shall constitute an Interdepartmental Committee, called the Committee, consisting of representatives from the Ministry of Information and Broadcasting, Ministry of Women and Child Development, Ministry of Law and Justice, Ministry of Home Affairs, Ministry of Electronics and Information Technology, Ministry of External Affairs, Ministry of Defence, and such other Ministries and Organisations, including domain experts, that it may decide to include in the Committee

24   Rule 13 (1) (b), Information Technology (Guidelines for Intermediaries and Digital Media Ethics Code) Rules, 2021(India)

(1) of section 69A of the Information Technology Act, 2000.[25] It is pertinent to note that the self-regulating mechanism and self-regulating body under the Rules 2021 is a welcome step which is likely to reduce state censorship.

'In case of emergency nature' the Secretary, Ministry of Information and Broadcasting may, pass an interim order without an opportunity of being heard if he is satisfied that it is necessary or expedient and justifiable for blocking for public access of any information or part thereof.[26] However, such interim directions shall be placed before the Departmental Committee for consideration and recommendation and following the recommendations of the Secretary, Ministry of Information and Broadcasting shall pass a final order approving / revoking the interim order.[27] This legislative provision to regulate the content in the OTT platforms which prima facie gives excessive control to the Secretary, Ministry of Information and Broadcasting in emergency circumstances requires a relook. The provision in regard to interim measure to block the content in emergency circumstances is inevitable. However, placing such interim decision only before the Government constituted Committee for the final decision without giving an opportunity of being heard needs a re-examination to lower the danger of misuse of powers by the political party in power.

---

25   Rule 12(5) and 14 (5) Information Technology (Guidelines for Intermediaries and Digital Media Ethics Code) Rules, 2021, (India)

26   Rule 16 (2), Information Technology (Guidelines for Intermediaries and Digital Media Ethics Code) Rules, 2021(India)

27   Rule 16 (4), Information Technology (Guidelines for Intermediaries and Digital Media Ethics Code) Rules, 2021(India)

REGULATORY INTERVENTION FOR OTTS IN OTHER COUNTRIES – A TRANSNATIONAL PERSPECTIVE[28]

The regulatory approaches and restrictions adopted across the globe to regulate the content on the OTT platforms are not uniform due to the diverse languages, religions, varying moral and cultural values, legal and constitutional framework. Likewise, few countries have embraced stricter regulation to accommodate the prevailing cultural, moral and the beliefs in their respective jurisdictions. The authors have collated the current regulatory practices in countries like Singapore, UK, Australia etc., to explore better approaches in regard to content regulation on OTT's.

SINGAPORE[29]

Info- communications Media Development Authority (IMDA) is the regulatory body that monitors the OTT platforms in Singapore. Under the relevant code that regulates the OTT services in Singapore, it is mandatory for service providers to arrange their content on the basis of age-related classification- such as general category, parental guidance for below 13, restricted to 21 years and above etc. provided with parental locks. It also

---

28   Online content regulation: how is it done in other parts of the world? available at   https://www.ikigailaw.com/online-content-regulation-how-is-it-done-in-other-parts-of-the-world/#acceptLicense; THE CHALLENGE OF MANAGING DIGITAL CONTENT Paper for the 'ITU-TRAI Regulatory Roundtable', 21-22 August 2017, New Delhi, India available at ITU Report Regulating Digital Content 2017 Final.pdf (last visited Oct 3, 2021)

29   CONTENT CODE FOR OVER-THE-TOP, VIDEO-ON-DEMAND AND NICHE SERVICES (Singapore), Microsoft Word - OTT VOD Niche Services Content Code (updated 22 May 2019) (imda.gov.sg) (last visited Oct 3, 2021)

mandates the classification of content on the following themes- violence, sex, nudity, language etc which is to be displayed for all the viewers. The content published by the OTT service provides should comply with the domestic laws of Singapore and must not be prejudicial to the national interest and security or public order. Likewise, the content shall not offend the sentiments of any religious or racial groups or promote animosity amongst them. Such extreme content can be refused classification.

AUSTRALIA

The Broadcasting Services Act, 1992 is the statutory framework that regulates OTT services in Australia. Any complaint in regard to the program content can be made to the Australian Communications and Media Authority (ACMA) which shall investigate the same. There are various schedules under the Act - Schedule 5 & 7, dealing specifically with content which is hosted outside Australia and for content within the country to be streamed over these platforms. The Act mandates the classification of content on the basis of age-related categories and nature of content which is monitored by the Australian Classification Board. It also calls out for a code of practice that prevents the publication of any content which is violent, uses offensive language, depicts nudity or causes friction/disparages any section of the public on the basis of religion, nationality, race, age, gender etc.

THE UNITED KINGDOM

In the year, 2018 the government of UK released a white paper proposing new reforms to regulate social media including the OTTs in response to various concerns raised in regard to the content hosted on the online platforms. It had stipulated for the establishment of an independent regulatory body to monitor and enforce the regulatory framework, codes of practice etc. The white paper also suggests that Regulator to develop codes of practice cooperatively with the Home Office which shall empower the latter to issue directions to the

Regulator in regard to the content that threatens the national security and safety of children.[30]

TURKEY

The main body which regulates and supervises the OTTs in Turkey is the Radio and Television Supreme Council (RTUK). They follow a licensing system. The Broadcasting Code mandates on-demand broadcasting services to obtain a licence from the RTUK.[31] This license is valid for a period of 10 years. It further obligates the license holders to encrypt the audio and visual feeds and provide their access to the RTUK for remote monitoring and also share their IP licenses with the latter to enable the broadcast recording.[32] The information relating to the program catalogue, the structure of the company, the contact details of the representatives of the license holder are required to be shared with the RTUK.[33] These steps guarantee a strict monitoring and vigilance over the OTT platforms.

---

30   Katrina Baxter, UK Government releases new proposals to regulate internet safety in Online Harms White Paper, Media Writes (8 April 2019), https://mediawrites. law/uk-government-releases-new-proposals-to-regulate-internet-safety-in-online-harms-white-paper/ (last visited Oct 3, 2021)

31   Şahin Ardiyok and Sercan Sagmanligil, OTT regulation in Turkey Network Industries Quarterly | Vol. 21 | N°2 | June 2019, https://www.network-industries.org/wp-content/uploads/2019/07/OTT-regulation-in-Turkey.pdf (last visited Oct 3, 2021)

32   Supra note 28

33   Ibid

CONCLUSION AND SUGGESTIONS

In the light of growing concerns regarding the unregulated content on OTTs, a comprehensive regulation was imperative. The OTT Rules 2021 place more onus on the publisher to self-classify and display content based on the age rating and various themes thus making the OTTs accountable for content. It also mandates a publisher to take into consideration India's multi-racial and multi-religious context and exercise due caution and discretion when featuring the activities, beliefs, practices, or views of any racial or religious group has attracted criticism that it is likely to threaten free speech, expression and the creativity of the content. The diversity and sensitivity of the Indian population in terms of religion, caste, languages, socio-economic status have always remained a challenge in regard to content regulation. The OTT service providers are required to be mindful that the content does not in any way disparage or cast a section of the public in bad light. It is pertinent to note that in comparison to the regulatory approach adopted in regard to broadcast media, the OTT content regulation has embraced a model blending state censorship and self-regulation which is a welcome step to minimise state censorship. The constitution of self-regulating mechanism and self-regulating body under the OTT Rules 2021 assure the stakeholders exchanges and deliberation thus encouraging the settlement of grievances by the publishers of the OTTs without any intervention from the government. "Self-regulation preserves independence of the media and protects it from partisan government interference."[34] However, the Rules 2021 need a relook in cases of emergency circumstances as it gives excessive control to the Departmental Committee constituted by the Government. This may lead to misuse of the powers and may go contrary to the very objective of these rules.

Keeping in mind the unprecedented growth of OTTs in the past few years and its growing demand, the Government, publishers of online curated content

---

34   Indraprastha People v. Union of India, 2015(1) RCR(Civil)24

and the policy making bodies must strive towards creating an environment that balances the interests of all the stakeholders.

REFERENCES

ITU Fact File: Over The Top Services (OTT) available at

https://www.gp-digital.org/wp-content/uploads/2017/12/itu-ott-2.pdf accessed on 3rd October, 2021.

Over-the-Top Market, Opportunities and Forecast, 2020-27, Allied Market Research available at

https://www.alliedmarketresearch.com/over-the-top-services-market accessed on 3rd October, 2021.

Playing by New rules, India's Media & Entertainment sector reboots in 2020, FICCI & EY, March 2021 available at

https://assets.ey.com/content/dam/ey-sites/ey-com/en_in/topics/media-and- entertainment/2021/ey-india-media-and-entertainment-sector-reboots.pdf?download accessed on 3rd October, 2021.

Kanchan Samtani & Gaurav Jindal, Entertainment Goes Online, A $5 Billion Opportunity, Boston Consulting, November, 2018 available at https://imagesrc.bcg.com/Images/Entertainment-Goes-Online_tcm21-208006.pdf accessed on 3rd October, 2021.

Information Technology (Guidelines for Intermediaries and Digital Media Ethics Code) Rules, 2021

Katrina Baxter, UK Government releases new proposals to regulate internet safety in Online Harms White Paper, Media Writes (8 April 2019) available at https://mediawrites.law/uk-government-releases-new-proposals-to-regulate-internet-safety-in-online-harms-white-paper/

Telecom Regulatory Authority of India, Consultation (2015) Paper on Regulatory Framework for Over-the-top (OTT) services 27th March, 2015 available at

https://trai.gov.in/sites/default/files/OTT-CP-27032015.pdf

Scott Fitzgerald, Over-the-Top Video Services in India: Media Imperialism after Globalization Media Industries 6.2 (2019) available at https://espace. curtin.edu.au/bitstream/handle/20.500.11937/76812/77055.pdf?sequence=2

Rahul M, Dr.S.DineshBabu. (2021). A Comparative Study on Ott Platform Censorship and Policies in India. Annals of the Romanian Society for Cell Biology, 25(6), 11160–11167. Retrieved from https://www.annalsofrscb.ro/index.php/journal/article/view/7578

Sridhar V. (2019) Over-the-Top (OTT) Services—Should They Be Regulated Much like Telecom Services? In: Emerging ICT Policies and Regulations. Springer, Singapore. available at https://doi.org/10.1007/978-981-32-9022-8_11

Online content regulation: how is it done in other parts of the world? available at https://www.ikigailaw.com/online-content-regulation-how-is-it-done-in-other-parts-of-the-world/#acceptLicense

О НЕОДНОЗНАЧНОСТИ ПОНИМАНИЯ И ПРИМЕНЕНИЯ СМАРТ-КОНТРАКТОВ В РОССИИ И НЕКОТОРЫХ СТРАНАХ БРИКС

автор:

Савенко Наталья Евгеньевна

В статье проведен обзор законодательства, доктрины и иных информационных источников России и некоторых стран БРИКС (Китай, Индия) на предмет правового регулирования смарт-контрактов. Показано, что ни в одной из указанных стран не закреплено понятия смарт-контракта на уровне законодательства. В доктрине понимание смарт-контрактов различно: специальный договор (обязательство), электронный договор, электронный способ исполнения обязательства, компьютерная программа. В целом смарт-контракт рассматривается как институт, имеющий договорную природу. Сферы применения смарт-контрактов в основном сосредотачиваются на использовании его в системе блокчейн на рынке финансовых услуг (создание криптовалюты и проведение сделок с ней), а также в области электронной коммерции (торговли), страховании. В России имеются неоднозначные предложения по использованию смарт-контрактов вне договорной сферы: организация функционирования баз данных здравоохранения, избирательного процесса и др. В отдельных странах смарт-контракт находит применение в сфере энергетики, игрового бизнеса, торговли со странами ЕС. Делается вывод о том, что смарт-контракты, как продукты цифровизации, опосредованные системой блокчейн и тесно связанные с криптовалютой, в настоящее время широко распространены даже несмотря на отсутствие их законодательного закрепления. Обращается внимание на договорную природу смарт-контракта: суть смарт-контракта в том, что это, прежде всего, соглашение сторон.

Ключевые слова: понятие смарт-контракта, сферы применения смарт-контрактов; законодательство и законопроекты о смарт-контрактах; доктрина о смарт-контрактах, БРИКС, Российская Федерация, Китай, Индия.

Общеизвестно, что глобальные мировые процессы связаны с трендами цифровизации. Желание перевести различные правоотношения в цифровой формат присуще всем странам. Очевидно, что блокчейн, а вместе в ним смарт-контракты и криптовалюта, изначально являются продуктами технологий, а не права. Механизм правового регулирования вынужден подстраиваться под техническую индустрию. Практика порождает необходимость принятия правовых норм для регламентации цифровых продуктов в правовом поле. Классические институты права уже не способны в полной мере регулировать новые явления цифровизации.

Технология блокчейн, как цепочка блоков информации (платформа), призванная упростить и облегчить обработку различной информации, систематизировать и надежно ее сохранить, стала использоваться в различных сферах (банковской, торговой, страховой, медицинской и др.), чем неизбежно породила возникновения смарт-контрактов. Этому способствовало развитие экономических процессов, прежде всего, в инвестиционной сфере, а также электронной коммерции (торговли). Процессы цифровизации затронули классическую ситуацию, когда стороны – субъекты права, имеют синаллагматические обязательства по отношению друг к другу. Понимание договорных обязательств расширилось с применением смарт-контрактов.

В законодательстве Российской Федерации отсутствует понятие смарт-контракта. Для более полного понимания сущности смарт-контракта, необходимо пояснить, что мы исходим из того, что «контракт» – это юридически производное понятие договора. Согласно ст. 420 Гражданского кодекса РФ[1] (далее – ГК РФ) договор – это соглашение сторон о возникновении, изменении и прекращении гражданских прав и обязанностей. Соответственно, «smart» («смарт») в переводе с английского – сообразительный, умный[2]. В российском обиходе «смарт» принято понимать как умный, цифровой. Исходя из этого, смарт-контракт видится как умный, цифровой договор. В отсутствии понятия смарт-контракта в российском гражданском праве существуют положения в п. 1 ст. 160 ГК РФ о форме письменной сделки с использованием электронных либо иных технических средств, позволяющих воспроизвести на материальном носителе содержание сделки (то есть условия сделки, права и обязанности сторон). Коррелирующее положение содержится в и ст. 434 ГК РФ о письменной форме договора, которая также допускает его заключение путем составления электронного документа в соответствии с п. 1 ст. 160 ГК РФ. У российского законодателя были попытки ввести понятие смарт-контракта в правовое поле путём внесения отдельного законопроекта, регулирующего цифровые права, однако в финальную редакцию законопроекта это положение не было включено. Так, согласно первой редакции указанного законопроекта, под смарт-контрактом понимался

---

1   Гражданский кодекс Российской Федерации (часть 1) от 30.11.1994 г. № 51-ФЗ // КонсультантПлюс http://www.consultant.ru/document/cons_doc_LAW_5142/ (дата обращения: 16.10.2021 г.)

2   Словари и энциклопедии https://dic.academic.ru/dic.nsf/ruwiki/7397 (дата обращения: 16.10.2021 г.).

«договор в электронной форме, исполнение прав и обязательств по которому осуществляется путем совершения в автоматическом порядке цифровых транзакций в распределенном реестре цифровых транзакций в строго определенной таким договором последовательности и при наступлении определенных им обстоятельств». У тут же для полной картины приводилось понятие цифрового кошелька как «программно-технического средства, хранящего информацию о цифровых записях»[3].

Несмотря на отсутствие сформулированного на законодательном уровне в России понятия смарт-контракта, мы можем найти различные трактовки его понимания, даваемые как компетентными органами, так представителями науки. В 2018 г. Центральным Банком РФ опубликован Аналитический обзор по теме «смарт-контракты», в котором сказано, что смарт-контракт может быть определен как договор с особыми признаками (самоисполняемость, автоматизация, прозрачность и т.д.)[4]. Относительно мнения российских ученых, то данная тема находится в постоянной дискуссии. Поэтому обратимся к рассмотрению сформировавшихся позиций за последнее время.

Во-первых, смарт-контракт понимается как способ исполнения обязательств. Например, А.В. Захаркина в результате своего исследования формулирует предложения о внесении дополнений в ГК РФ путем включения в него новой статьи 327.2 ГК РФ «Об исполнении обязательств

---

3   Подробнее см. Законопроект № 419059-7 «О цифровых финансовых активах, цифровой валюте и о внесении изменений в отдельные законодательные акты Российской Федерации» // https://sozd.duma.gov.ru/bill/419059-7 (дата обращения: 16.10.2021 г.).

4   Аналитический обзор по теме «Смарт-контракты» // https://www.cbr.ru/Content/Document/File/47862/SmartKontrakt_18-10.pdf (дата обращения: 08.10.2021 г.)

с помощью информационных технологий (смарт-контракта)»[5]. В данном подходе видится рациональное зерно ввиду того, что автор предлагает внедрить правовую категорию смарт-контракта именно в общую часть кодекса, которая является отправной базовой точкой для регулирования уже специальных правоотношений (отдельных видов обязательств, договоров и др.).

Во-вторых, смарт-контракт понимается как договор. Подтверждением данного подхода является позиция таких авторов, как Л.Г. Ефимова, И.Е. Михеева, Д.В. Чуб, которые делают вывод о том, что смарт-контракт – это «особая разновидность электронного гражданско-правового договора любого типа»[6]. Авторы доказывают, что смарт-контракт – это несамостоятельная договорная конструкция. Действительно, отдельным видом договора смарт-контракт вряд ли когда-либо станет.

В-третьих, распространена позиция о понимании смарта-контракта в качестве компьютерной программы. По мнению Ю.В. Трунцевского, В.В. Севальнева, смарт-контракт – это компьютерная программа, автоматически выполняющая условия соглашения, которое является самоподдерживающимся[7]. Полагаем, что из приведенной позиции, смарт-контракт следует считать разновидностью письменной формы договора

---

5   Захаркина А.В. Смарт-контракт в условиях формирования нормативной платформы экосистемы цифровой экономики Российской Федерации // Вестник Пермского университета. Юридические науки. 2020. Вып. 47. С. 79.

6   Ефимова Л.Г., Михеева И.Е., Чуб Д.В. сравнительный анализ доктринальных концепций правового регулирования смарт-контрактов в России и зарубежных странах // Право. Журнал Высшей школы экономики. 2020. - № 4. С.94.

7   Трунцевский Ю.В., Севальнев В.В. Смарт-контракт: от определения к определенности // Право. Журнал Высшей школы экономики. 2020.- № 1.- С. 131.

(сделки), а именно, письменная электронная (цифровая / компьютерная) форма. Однако в литературе имеется противоположный взгляд на электронную форму сделки. Например, Л.Г. Ефимова придерживается того, что электронная форма сделки «представляет собой качественно новый способ волеизъявления субъекта права», в связи с чем автором предложено дополнить ГК РФ статьей 160.1[8]. Между тем, ученый также формулирует предложения по внесению дополнений в ГК РФ в виде включения ст. 313.1, в которой называет смарт-контракт компьютерной программой, создаваемой на базе цифровой платформы[9].

Также наряду с указанными позициями Е.А. Громова оценивает смарт-контракт как «нечто более масштабное и сложное, нежели просто классический договор в электронной форме. Дело в том, что в алгоритме смарт-контракта заложена возможность самостоятельного принятия решения об исполнении обязательств по договору при наступлении определенных условий. (…) отождествлять смарт-контракты и гражданско-правовые договоры не представляется возможным. Более того, сфера применения смарт-контрактов пока что ограничена реестром блокчейн, правовой статус которого также не определен»[10].

Все вышеприведенные взгляды, конечно, имеют право на существование. Относительно признаков смарт-контрактов, раскрываемых в литературе, стоит сказать, что характеристики и признаки смарт-контрактов (самоисполняемость, надежность,

---

8   Ефимова Л.Г. Альтернативный взгляд на правовое регулирование гражданско-правовых отношений в условиях цифровой экономики // Актуальные проблемы российского права. 2021. Т. 16. - № 8 (129). С.58.

9   Ефимова Л.Г. Указ. соч. С. 60.

10   Громова Е.А. Смарт-контракты в России: попытка определения правовой сущности // Право и цифровая экономика. 2018. - № 2. - С. 34 – 37 // СПС «КонсультатнтПлюс».

автоматизм) излагаются в большинстве случаев без учета специфики отношений субъектов и их статусов, сфер и видов их деятельности, то есть в широком смысле. Либо же совсем в узком значении – к отдельной узкой сфере правоотношений (инвестирование, например). Традиционным считается применение смарт-контрактов, прежде всего, в сфере финансовых услуг по распоряжению криптовалютой; инвестирование. На втором месте отмечается использование смарт-контрактов в сфере различного рода автоматических платежей в сфере торговли, страховании и т.д.

Вместе с тем, исходя из договорной природы смарт-контракта, нельзя не отметить появившуюся в доктрине тенденцию «фантазийного» понимании сфер применения смарт-контрактов, выходящих за область договорного регулирования. Собственно, возвращаясь к истокам появления смарт-контракта, нельзя забывать, что смарт-контракт – это, прежде всего, договор или обязательство, а не какой-то иной институт права. В литературе стали широко примерять смарт-контракт не только на договорную область как частную сферу гражданского либо предпринимательского права, но и на публичные отрасли. Предлагается, например, использовать смарт-контракты в медицине при хранении, использовании медицинских карт пациентов, систематизации медицинских исследований (анализов). Также предлагается использовать в экологической сфере при обращении с отходами (смарт-контракты как измерители объемов производства), в сфере организации избирательных процессов для подтверждения личности избирателя и записи его голоса; в сфере персональных данных личности при использовании биометрических данных[11]. Кроме того, наряду с договорной практикой, отмечается на перспективу возможность использования конструкции

---

11   Трунцевский Ю.В., Севальнев В.В. Смарт-контракт: от определения к определенности. С. 137-138.

смарт-контрактов и в правоприменительной практике[12]. Однако, при этом, авторы забывают об исходной правовой природе смарт-контракта – договорной. Кажется сомнительным применение смарт-контрактов в сфере публичной отрасли права – избирательного права. Избирательный процесс исключает договорные конструкции. Избиратель, реализуя свое пассивное избирательное право, ни с кем не договаривается: проголосовать ему или не проголосовать и за кого проголосовать. Это не поддаётся договоренности в силу установленной законом тайны голосования. А в приведенных примерах медицинской сферы по использованию медицинских карт и исследований также не наблюдается договоренностей между медицинским учреждением и пациентом, поскольку вышеперечисленные действия – это административные обязанности учреждения по соблюдению медицинской тайны историй болезни пациентов. По нашему мнению, все вышеуказанные конкретные случаи сфер применения смарт-контрактов, выходящих из договорной области, являются лишь частными примерами использования различных реестров системы блокчейн, как баз данных, выраженных в отдельных блоках. Предназначение таких реестров варьируется в зависимости от сферы и целей применения. В связи с чем, возводить смарт-контракт в ранг всемогущего инструмента цифровизации и придавать ему значение всеобщности и стандартизации во всех отраслях жизнедеятельности, права и законодательства, думается нецелесообразно.

Возвращаясь к идее нашего исследования относительно понимания и применения смарт-контрактов в некоторых странах БРИКС, обратимся к их законодательному и доктринальному опыту.

Что касается законодательства Китая в отношении смарт-контрактов, то как и в России, конкретных норм, содержащих понятие и признаки смарт-контракта в КНР, не принято. В ст. 2 Закона КНР «О договорах» (Принят 2-й сессией ВСНП девятого созыва 15 марта 1999 г.)

---

12   Ефимова Л.Г. Альтернативный взгляд на правовое регулирование гражданско-правовых отношений в условиях цифровой экономики. С. 58-59.

закреплено, что договоры – это соглашения между равными субъектами – физическими лицами, иными организациями – об установлении, изменении, прекращении гражданских прав и обязанностей. В ст. 11 указывается письменная форма договора – документ с использованием электронно-цифрового обмена. В силу ст. 39 при заключении договора с использованием стандартных условий сторона, предлагающая их, обязана руководствоваться принципом справедливости. Стандартными условиями признаются условия, которые заранее разрабатываются для неоднократного применения и которые не обсуждаются с другой стороной при заключении договора. Исходя из базовых норм китайского закона о договорах, очевидно, что место смарт-контрактам не нашлось. Однако в Китае они имеют широкое применение[13].

Напомним, смарт-контракты тесно связаны с криптовалютой (токены, биткоины) и блокчейном. Какой из этих феноменов цифровизации возник первым – определить сложно. Скорее всего, блокчейн как некий электронный продукт, изначально призванный стандартизировать и упростить процедуру обработки и хранения информации. Затем придумали криптовалюту, а чтобы ею распоряжаться появился смарт-контракт. В свете сказанного, по данным российского интернет-портала и аналитического агентства Tadviser.com, известно, что в 2019 г. Китай оценивался как государство, которое быстрее иных государств в мире развивает блокчейн-технологии. В 2020 г. в Китае технология блокчейн вышла но новый уровень: «пять крупнейших банков Китая создают блокчейн-платформу для межбанковских транзакций в области торгового финансирования. Для разработки продукта кредитные организации объединились с Китайской банковской ассоциацией

---

13   Закон КНР «О договорах» от 15.03.1999 г. / Интернет-справочник // https://chinahelp.me/information/zakon-knr-o-dogovorah (дата обращения: 16.10.2021 г.).

(CBA)»[14]. Это свидетельствует о том, что предпосылки для правового регулирования договорных отношений между участниками банковской сферы, осложненных цифровыми технологиями (смарт-контрактом), назрели. Тем более, что законодательство КНР до настоящего времени не содержит понятий блокчейн и вытекающих из него понятий криптовалюты и смарт-контракта. По данным того же информационного источника, блокчейн был упомянут впервые в Проекте национального пятилетнего политического плана КНР в окончательной редакции в марте 2021 г., в котором обозначены приоритеты страны до 2025 года: экологические мероприятия, развитие искусственного интеллекта и умных городов. И это при том, что примерно в то же время в Китае был введен общенациональный запрет на создание и использование криптовалюты[15].

Также по данным иного интернет-ресурса на 01.09.2021 г. «азиатский гигант проявил враждебность к криптоиндустрии, по сути запретив майнинг биткойнов и закрыв компании для транзакций. При этом у регулирующих органов есть другая история о блокчейне и его потенциале. Китай, похоже, намеревается применить технологии, лежащие в основе Биткойна, Эфириума и криптовалют, способом, противоположным принципам отрасли. Эта новая инфраструктура блокчейна будет централизованной, «унифицированной»[16], взаимосвязанной и будет направлена на создание «общего управления». Итак, с одной стороны, Китай продвигает развитие технологии блокчейн, с другой стороны,

---

14   Tadviser.com // https://www.tadviser.ru/index.php/ (дата обращения: 16.10.2021 г.)

15   Там же.

16   Blokchen.com // https://www.block-chain24.com/news/novosti-regulirovaniya/pochemu-sec-kitaya-issleduet-primenenie-smart-kontraktov-i-blokcheyna (дата обращения: 21.09.2021).

вводит запрет на криптовалюту, которая была опосредована указанной технологией и использованием смарт-контрактов для проведения сделок с ней. Таким образом, с недавнего времени смарт-контракты в Китае не будут использоваться в сфере инвестиций криптовалюты.

Еще одним нововведением Китая в сфере цифровых технологий, связанный со смарт-контрактами, является цифровой формат валюты (CBDC), так называемый «цифровой Юань», на который делает ставку Народный Банк Китая. По мнению Банка, владелец таких денежных средств может программировать их трату с помощью смарт-контрактов, используя шаблоны кода CBDC или самостоятельно написать приложение. «Умная валюта» создаст больше возможностей, чем просто оплата товаров и услуг[17].

Между тем, китайские ученые, например, Яо-Цзе Ху, Тинг-Тинг Ли, Димитрис Чацопулос, Пан Хуэй, анализируя действие смарт-контрактов, отмечают, что смарт-контракты – это программы, определяющие неизменяемые правила и хранящиеся в цепочке блоков. Смарт-контракты могут взаимодействовать не только с пользователями, но и друг с другом посредством обмена сообщениями. Кроме того, авторы анализируют применение смарт-контрактов в игровой среде[18]. Также китайские ученые Нин Лу, Бин Ван, Юнсинь Чжан и Венбо Ши совместно с итальянским ученым Кристианом Эспозито аналогичным образом оценивают смарт-контракт как компьютерную программу. Они рассматривают особенности использования, обеспечения

---

17   Criptor // https://cryptor.net/news/narodnyy-bank-kitaya-delaet-stavku-na-smart-kontrakty-v-rasprostranenii-cifrovogo-yuanya-7674 (дата обращения: 22.09.2021).

18   Yao-Chieh Hu,Ting-Ting Lee,Dimitris Chatzopoulos,Pan Hui. Analyzing smart contract interactions and contract level state consensus / Concurrence and Computation. Practice and Experiment. Volume 32. Issue 12 // https://onlinelibrary. wiley.com/doi/full/10.1002/cpe.5228 (дата обращения: 08.10.2021 г.).

безопасности смарт-контрактов на торговой платформе Ethereum, которая используется для купли-продажи и обмена криптовалюты. Смарт-контракт, по мнению ученых, может помочь Ethereum кодировать правила или сценарии для обработки транзакций[19].

Таким образом, почти все представители китайского научного сообщества считают смарт-контракты компьютерной программой, призванной исполнять договорные обязательства. Относительно сфер применения, как отмечено выше, в Китае смарт-контракты нашли широкое применение на рынке финансовых услуг. Помимо этого, особое внимание им уделено в сфере торговли. Так, в китайской литературе отмечается целесообразность использования смарт-контрактов в сфере электроэнергии для сетевых предприятий. Это поможет снизить затраты на доверие на рынке электроэнергии и повысить эффективность транзакций с электроэнергией и расчетов по оплате[20]. Также ввиду того, что Китай является крупным экспортером, отмечается актуальность использования смарт-контрактов и в сфере торговли пищевыми продуктами между ЕС и Китаем в контексте обеспечения безопасности пищевых продуктов. По мнению авторов, смарт-контракты в соответствии с особенностями трансграничной торговли пищевыми продуктами могут служить для внесения соответствующих записей

---

19   Ning Lu, Bin Wang, Yongxin Zhang, Wenbo Shi, Christian Esposito. NeuCheck: A more practical Ethereum smart contract security analysis tool // Softwart: Practice and Experiment. Volume 51. Issue 10 /https://onlinelibrary.wiley.com/doi/full/10.1002/spe.2745 (дата обращения: 16.10.2021 г.).

20   Jing Lu, Shihong Wu, Hanlei Cheng, Bin Song, Zhiyu Xiang. Smart contract for electricity transactions and charge settlements using blockchain / Applied Stochastic Models is Business and industry. Volume37, Issue3 Special Issue: Blockchain for Logistic Industry/ May/June 2021/ Pages 442-453 // https://onlinelibrary.wiley.com/doi/10.1002/asmb.2570 (дата обращения: 07.10.2021 г.).

в целях отслеживания данных об экспорте, проверке экспортера и импортера, отгрузке, импорте, так как развертываются в сети блокчейн[21].

Таким образом, относительно понимания смарт-контрактов и их применения в Китае, следует отметить, что они не закреплены в китайском гражданском законодательстве в виде понятия с их признаками; применение смарт-контрактов пока не носит повсеместный характер; одна из сфер применения смарт-контрактов – криптовалюта, с недавнего времени под запретом.

Относительно того, как развито регулирование смарт-контрактов в Индии, обратимся для начала к классическому законодательству этой страны. В Индии был принят Закон о договорах (контрактах) от 25.04.1872 г. № 9, действующий поныне. Впервые перевод на русский язык указанного индийского закона был сделан русским ученым А.В. Беловым, который отмечает, что «на сегодняшний день – это один из древнейших не только в Индии, но и на всем земном шаре (не исключая, между прочим, той же Англии) действующих законов. Индия – она хотя и британская, но все-таки Индия. Со своим собственным уровнем жизни, особенностями материального и духовного развития, обычаями и традициями, совсем не похожими на английские. Когда об этом вспомнишь, то не кажется удивительным следующий, например, факт: акта, хоть сколько-нибудь похожего по универсальности содержания на индийский Закон о договорах, никогда не существовало ни в Англии, ни в США[22]». «Норма ч. 1 ст. 10 устанавливает, что договорами

---

21   Jianping Qian,Wenbin Wu,Qiangyi Yu,Luis Ruiz-Garcia,Yang Xiang,Li Jiang,Yun Shi,Yulin Duan,Peng Yang. Filling the trust gap of food safety in food trade between the EU and China: An interconnected conceptual traceability framework based on blockchain / Food and energy security. Volume9, Issue4 November 2020 // https://onlinelibrary.wiley.com/doi/10.1002/fes3.249 (дата обращения: 07.10.2021 г.).

22   Белов А.В. Индийский Закон о договорах 1972 года (общие сведения, общий комментарий, оригинальный текст и русский перевод) // Правоведение.

(contracts) признаются всякие соглашения (agreements), совершенные свободно право- и дееспособными лицами, по поводу допустимого законом предмета и за действительное встречное удовлетворение при условии, что ничто в их содержании прямо не свидетельствует об их недействительности[23]». Итак, каким бы уникальным не был индийский закон о договорах (контрактах), но современных положений о смарт-контрактах, естественно, мы в нем не найдем так же, как и понятий блокчейн и криптовалюты. Впрочем, это не мешает применять в Индии указанные продукции цифровизации.

Вместе с тем, в Индии, одна из областей использования смарт-контрактов – это мир криптовалюты. Как и в Китае, в Индии к ней относятся неоднозначно. По данным различных информационных источников криптовалюта находится в Индии в настоящее время в подвешенном состоянии ввиду того, что в парламент этой страны неоднократно вносились законопроекты о запрете на частные криптовалюты, но они так и не были приняты. По мнению экспертов введение такого запрета «помешает наступлению цифровизации индийской экономики»[24]. В связи с чем, полагаем, что эта сфера может выпасть из сфер применения смарт-контрактов. При этом, индийские ученые Аджай Кумар, Кумар Абхишек, Пранав Нерургар, Мухаммад Рукунуддин Галиб, Ачют Шанкар совестно с ученым из Велокобритании

2014. - № 4 (315). С. 67.

23   Белов А.В. Указ. соч. С. 77.

24   Неопределенное будущее криптовалют в Индии // https://www.dandreapartners.com/%D0%BD%D0%BE%D0%BF%D1%80%D0%B5%D0%B4%D0%B5%D0%BB%D0%B5%D0%BD%D0%BD%D0%BE%D0%B5-%D0%B1%D1%83%D0%B4%D1%83%D1%89%D0%B5%D0%B5-%D0%BA%D1%80%D0%B8%D0%BF%D1%82%D0%BE%D0%B2%D0%B0%D0%BB%D1%8E%D1%82/?lang=ru (дата обращения: 17.10.2021 г.).

Сяочунь Чэн продолжают дискуссии на тему использования смарт-контрактов в блокчейне Etherium, особо поднимая аспекты обеспечения безопасности смарт-контрактов в данной финансовой сфере[25]. Также в индийской литературе обращается внимание на проблемы использования смарт-контрактов в энергетическом секторе, связанном с торговлей электромобилями посредством проведения аукционов. Отмечается, что в данных сделках не соблюдается конфиденциальность, не учитываются стратегические ограничения. В связи с чем, полагают, что смарт-контракты в данной области призваны служить для очистки рынка[26].

Проведенное исследование вопросов регулирования смарт-контрактов в России и некоторых странах БРИКС, позволяет сделать следующие выводы.

Во-первых, ни в одной из указанных стран не закреплено понятия смарт-контракта. В законах отдельных государств приняты лишь законы о договорах и их формах (письменные / устные), поэтому правоприменение ориентируется на классические нормы о договорах (контрактах).

Во-вторых, на доктринальном уровне смарт-контракт понимают различным образом: как специальный договор (обязательство),

---

25   Ajay Kumar,Kumar Abhishek,Pranav Nerurkar,Muhammad Rukunuddin Ghalib,Achyut Shankar,Xiaochun Cheng. Secure smart contracts for cloud-based manufacturing using Ethereum blockchain // Emerging Telecommunications Technologies // https://onlinelibrary.wiley.com/doi/10.1002/ett.4129 (дата обращения: 17.10.2021 г.).

26   Подробнее см.: Ritesh Mohan Acharya,Bokkisam Hanumantha Rao,Manickavasagam Parvathy Selvan. Aggregator free ancillary services e-market for electric vehicles using smart contracts // Electrical energy systems // https://onlinelibrary.wiley.com/doi/10.1002/2050-7038.13096 (дата обращения: 17.10.2021 г.).

электронный договор, электронный способ исполнения обязательства, компьютерная программа. В России в общей массе взглядов смарт-контракт трактуется как договор, а в зарубежной литературе превалирует понимание смарт-контракта как кода или компьютерной программы.

В-третьих, сферы применения смарт-контрактов в основном сосредотачиваются на использовании их в системе блокчейн на рынке финансовых услуг (создание криптовалюты и проведение сделок с ней), инвестирование, а также в области электронной коммерции (торговли), страховании. В настоящее время наблюдается тенденция о неоднозначном, скорее, негативном отношении к криптовалюте, например, в Китае введен запрет на ее использование. Были аналогичные попытки и в Индии. В России до настоящего времени нет запрета на использование криптовалюты, при этом, понятие криптовалюты отражается в понятии цифровых прав, которые и представляют собой сферу применения смарт-контрактов.

В-четвертых, в российской юридической литературе нами замечена тенденция, связанная с выдвижением неоднозначных предложений по использованию смарт-контрактов вне договорной сферы, что, по нашему мнению, является нецелесообразным.

В-пятых, в качестве итога, особо важно учесть, что попытки всех государств идти в ногу с мировыми трендами и вызовами цифровизации, глобализации, - понятны. Однако не стоит забывать о договорной природе смарт-контрактов. Кроме того, актуальным видятся замечания индийских ученых о необходимости исследования и налаживания технической стороны вопроса в использовании смарт-контрактов, которая напрямую затрагивает безопасность таких сделок. А безопасность технологии использования смарт-контрактов, в свою очередь, отражается на стабильности экономического оборота, участниками которой являются различные субъекты права.

СПИСОК ИСПОЛЬЗОВАННОЙ ЛИТЕРАТУРЫ

Ajay Kumar,Kumar Abhishek,Pranav Nerurkar,Muhammad Rukunuddin Ghalib,Achyut Shankar,Xiaochun Cheng. Secure smart contracts for cloud-based manufacturing using Ethereum blockchain // Emerging Telecommunications Technologies // https://onlinelibrary.wiley.com/doi/10.1002/ett.4129

Jianping Qian,Wenbin Wu,Qiangyi Yu,Luis Ruiz-Garcia,Yang Xiang,Li Jiang,Yun Shi,Yulin Duan,Peng Yang. Filling the trust gap of food safety in food trade between the EU and China: An interconnected conceptual traceability framework based on blockchain / Food and energy security. Volume9, Issue4 November 2020 // https://onlinelibrary.wiley.com/doi/10.1002/fes3.249

Jing Lu, Shihong Wu, Hanlei Cheng, Bin Song, Zhiyu Xiang. Smart contract for electricity transactions and charge settlements using blockchain / Applied Stochastic Models is Business and industry. Volume37, Issue3 Special Issue: Blockchain for Logistic Industry/ May/June 2021/ Pages 442-453 // https://onlinelibrary.wiley.com/doi/10.1002/asmb.2570

Ning Lu,Bin Wang,Yongxin Zhang,Wenbo Shi,Christian Esposito. NeuCheck: A more practical Ethereum smart contract security analysis tool // Softwart: Practice and Experiment. Volume 51. Issue 10 /https://onlinelibrary.wiley.com/doi/full/10.1002/spe.2745

Ritesh Mohan Acharya,Bokkisam Hanumantha Rao,Manickavasagam Parvathy Selvan. Aggregator free ancillary services e-market for electric vehicles using smart contracts // Electrical energy systems // https://onlinelibrary.wiley.com/doi/10.1002/2050-7038.13096

Yao-Chieh Hu,Ting-Ting Lee,Dimitris Chatzopoulos,Pan Hui. Analyzing smart contract interactions and contract level state consensus / Concurrence and Computation. Practice and Experiment. Volume 32. Issue 12 // https://onlinelibrary.wiley.com/doi/full/10.1002/cpe.5228

Аналитический обзор по теме «Смарт-контракты» // https://www.cbr.ru/Content/Document/File/47862/SmartKontrakt_18-10.pdf

Белов А.В. Индийский Закон о договорах 1972 года (общие сведения, общий комментарий, оригинальный текст и русский перевод) // Правоведение. 2014. - № 4 (315). С. 61-127.

Blokchen.com // https://www.block-chain24.com/news/novosti-regulirovaniya/pochemu-sec-kitaya-issleduet-primenenie-smart-kontraktov-i-blokcheyna

Гражданский кодекс Российской Федерации (часть 1) от 30.11.1994 г. № 51-ФЗ // КонсультантПлюс http://www.consultant.ru/document/cons_doc_LAW_5142/

Громова Е.А. Смарт-контракты в России: попытка определения правовой сущности // Право и цифровая экономика. 2018. - № 2. - С. 34 – 37.

Ефимова Л.Г. Альтернативный взгляд на правовое регулирование гражданско-правовых отношений в условиях цифровой экономики // Актуальные проблемы российского права. 2021. Т. 16. - № 8 (129). С. 52-62.

Ефимова Л.Г., Михеева И.Е., Чуб Д.В. сравнительный анализ доктринальных концепций правового регулирования смарт-контрактов в России и зарубежных странах // Право. Журнал Высшей школы экономики. 2020. - № 4. С.78-105.

Закон КНР «О договорах» от 15.03.1999 г. / Интернет-справочник // https://chinahelp.me/information/zakon-knr-o-dogovorah

Законопроект № 419059-7 «О цифровых финансовых активах, цифровой валюте и о внесении изменений в отдельные законодательные акты Российской Федерации» // https://sozd.duma.gov.ru/bill/419059-7.

Захаркина А.В. Смарт-контракт в условиях формирования нормативной платформы экосистемы цифровой экономики Российской

Федерации // Вестник Пермского университета. Юридические науки. 2020. Вып. 47. С. 66-82.

Неопределенное будущее криптовалют в Индии // https://www. dandreapartners.com/%D0%BD%D0%B5%D0%BE%D0%BF%D1%80%D0 %B5%D0%B4%D0%B5%D0%BB%D0%B5%D0%BD%D0%BD%D0%BE %D0%B5-%D0%B1%D1%83%D0%B4%D1%83%D1%89%D0%B5%D0%B5- %D0%BA%D1%80%D0%B8%D0%BF%D1%82%D0%BE%D0%B2%D0% B0%D0%BB%D1%8E%D1%82/?lang=ru

Criptor // https://cryptor.net/news/narodnyy-bank-kitaya-delaet-stavku-na-smart-kontrakty-v-rasprostranenii-cifrovogo-yuanya-7674

Словари и энциклопедии https://dic.academic.ru/dic.nsf/ruwiki/7397

Tadviser.com // https://www.tadviser.ru/index.php/

Трунцевский Ю.В., Севальнев В.В. Смарт-контракт: от определения к определенности // Право. Журнал Высшей школы экономики. 2020.- № 1. С. 118-147.

1%82%D0%BE%D0%B2%D0%B0%D0%BB%D1%8E%D1%82/?lang=ru

www.ingramcontent.com/pod-product-compliance
Lightning Source LLC
Chambersburg PA
CBHW071335210326
41597CB00015B/1457